Put the Money
in My Purse!

Put the Money in My Purse!

A History of Female Bank Robbers

Judith A. Yates

Jefferson, North Carolina

ISBN (print) 978-1-4766-8764-3
ISBN (ebook) 978-1-4766-4576-6

Library of Congress and British Library
Cataloguing Data are available

Library of Congress Control Number 2022000947

On the cover: Ethel "Etta" Place joined "The Sundance Kid," Butch Cassidy, and a third unidentified person to rob the National Bank in Villa Mercedes, Argentina, on December 19, 1805 (Library of Congress); Hannah Sabata robbed the Cornerstone Bank in Waco, Nebraska, of $6,256 on November 27, 2013. Hours later, she garnered millions of YouTube viewers as "Chick Bank Robber" by making a video boasting of the crimes and showing off the bounty (York County Sheriff's Office mug shot); Laura Bullion, mug shots, 1893; she assisted in bank robberies with "the Wild Bunch" who nicknamed her "Rose of the Wild Bunch." (Library of Congress); *background* © 2021 Photo-Art-Lortie/Shutterstock

Printed in the United States of America

Exposit is an imprint of McFarland & Company, Inc., Publishers

Exposit
Box 611, Jefferson, North Carolina 28640
www.expositbooks.com

For every woman who has ever worn a badge then and now
(bravery comes in many forms),
and for Mary,
who understood the times when I fell into the vault
and couldn't (wouldn't) find the combination

Table of Contents

Acknowledgments

Researching events that occurred as far back as the 1700s can be both frustrating and cumbersome to an author who is so dedicated to extracting the truth. Additionally, legal records are maintained for a certain time period. The Federal Bureau of Prisons' inmate records have a retention period of ten years. Some sheriff, police, and other local law enforcement departments have even shorter retention periods. Records may be filed in a huge warehouse with millions of other documents, or only the bare minimum of the records are kept filed while the details—arrest records, interview notes, etc.—are destroyed.

Many times I have had to rely on old newspapers, magazines, and journals for the sources, painstakingly cross-checking to ensure the information was as close to the truth as possible. While it is fascinating to read a newspaper printed in 1845, it is frustrating. Between the florid prose and the writer's imagination and opinion, it is difficult to discern the truth. And there is no way to fact-check: who will you interview? All of the witnesses are long gone.

As I was working on this project, many others became interested and jumped at the chance to help with their own digging. I am forever grateful to them for taking time to help me locate files, make copies, lead me in the right direction, suggest and explain, take the time to be interviewed, and assist in every way possible to help get this project completed. True crime authors are often asked if we are constantly saddened by the cases we write about; the truth is, the cases are horrific, but we meet the kindest people during our journey. Here are some of those people and organizations I had the pleasure to meet on this book's journey:

John Balance, Director of Photography, *The Advocate*, New Orleans, Louisiana.
Brown County Library, Green Bay, WI
Christina Bryant, MLIS, CA, Director, City Archives & Special Collections, New Orleans, LA Library
Buffalo State University Archives & Special Collections Department, Buffalo, NY
The Chicago Police Department & CPD Records & Archives
Chicago Sun-Times, Toby Roberts, Facilities Director, Editorial Department
City of Cleveland Police Public Records, Ohio
City of Terre Haute Office of the Clerk, Michelle Edwards, City Clerk
Cleveland Police Museum & Historical Society, 1300 Ontario St, Cleveland, OH 44113
Cleveland Public Library, Cleveland, Ohio
Terry Metter, Subject Department Librarian
Brian Meggitt, Photograph Collection Librarian
Cobb County Police Department, Georgia
Cumberland County Sheriff's Offices, Tennessee
Sheriff Casey Cox
Captain Jerry Jackson
Edward J. Curley, Esq., First Assistant Clerk-Magistrate for Criminal Business, Suffolk Superior Court, MASS
Cuyahoga County, Cleveland, Ohio
Daily News Journal, Murfreesboro, TN
Daniel DiLandro, MLS, CA (College Archivist and Special Collections Librarian), Buffalo State University Archives & Special Collections Department
Davidson County Sheriff's offices, Nashville, Tennessee
Ken Fujiuchi, Emerging Technology Librarian, Buffalo State University
Olivia Garrison, Reference Coordinator, Special Collections and University Archives at the Iowa State University Library
Green Bay Press Gazette, Milwaukee
Historic New Orleans Collection, New Orleans, LA
Dennis R Jacobs, Research, Local History and Genealogy, EH Butler Library at SUNY Buffalo State

The Lake County Courts Offices in Crown Point, IN
Library of Congress newspaper archives
Helen C. Logan, Sr. Administrator of Legal Services, Office of the General Counsel, The University of Pennsylvania, Philadelphia
Matthew Lutts, Associated Press
Gene Maddaus, for his excellent article in *LA Weekly* on the "Starlet Bandits"
Maricopa County Jail, Phoenix, Arizona
Marion County Clerk's office, Indianapolis, IN
Miami Dade PD Records Department, James, Miami, Florida
Kristin Morton, Document Clerk, Erie County Clerk's Office, Buffalo, NY
Sean Plaistowe, Archives Assistant, Framingham
Audrey Shulruff, FOIA Officer, Chicago Police Department
Sikeston Police Department, Sikeston, MO
The South Dakota Historical Society & Jeanne Kilen Ode, Managing Editor, *South Dakota History*
Suffolk Superior Court, Edward J. Curley, Esq., First Assistant Clerk-Magistrate for Criminal Business
Margaret Sullivan, Boston, MA. Police Department Archives Unit
The U.S. Department of Justice Federal Bureau of Investigations Department of Archives & Records
The U.S. Department of Justice Federal Bureau of Prisons Department of Records & Archives
The United States Marshals Services
The University of Chicago Library, Chicago, Ill.
Archives & Special Collections Department Staff
Brooke Williams, Liaison Librarian
Northeastern University Library, Boston, MA
Reference & Outreach Archives Staff
Destiny Williams, Historical Images www.ebay.com/str/historicimagesstore
Shawn A. Williams, Esq., Director of Public Records, Records Access Officer, City of Boston
Dexter S. Wright, Sr., Judiciary Clerk 2, Mercer County Criminal Case Management

I owe a huge "thank you" to Susan Kilby, Managing Editor—Development at McFarland & Company, for all the lifelines you tossed my way. A heartfelt thanks to Exposit Books for continuous professionalism and kindness in this project. Respect and gratitude to McFarland for their positive outlook and support.

Special thanks to Dr. Henry C. Lee, whom I value for his friendship and professional advice. His knowledge, experience, warmth, and laughter make him someone to admire and adore.

And, as always, thank you to Mary, who held down the fort while I disappeared into the vault.

Preface

In 1934 it became a federal crime to rob any national bank or state member bank of the Federal Reserve. Thus, bank robbery falls under the jurisdiction of the Federal Bureau of Investigation (FBI). The FBI releases an annual publication, "Bank Crime Statistics," separating this crime into robberies, burglaries, and larcenies. There is often confusion about these terms. "Robbery" is defined as "the taking of money or goods in the possession of another from his or her immediate presence, by force or intimidation." "Burglary" is trespassory breaking and entering with intent to commit a felony. "Larceny" is common theft.[1]

Bank robbery is often romanticized: the brazen walk into a stoic institution and take control, coolly scooping up untold amounts of cash and fleeing from justice. Or the cool, slick team bamboozles the corporation or bad people out of stacks of cash, with personality, wit, and cunning. Fiction is far from truth, but who doesn't dream of bags of free money made with little effort?

In the 1800s, trains and stagecoaches transported money and gold for banks. Often, robbing these stages and trains was considered "bank robbery." Even in these times, some female accomplices rode along in stages and train robberies, assisting by holding the male robber's horses while the men commandeered the train or stagecoach. Since the invention of the automobile, women usually acted as getaway drivers for male bank robbers. Their deeds as "brazen queens of the west" or "gun molls" made the pulp fiction and yellow journalism rags fly off the shelves. A female criminal made for exciting reading, particularly if the story was filled with half-truths and florid prose.

Bank robbery has remained a man's crime. From the first bank robbery to today, far more men have stepped up to a teller's window demanding cash at the end of a gun or demand letter.

I have lectured and written about female crime for more than 30 years. I have a keen interest in the correlation between history and criminal justice. I was intrigued by historical and social influences that would cause a woman to commit a predominantly male crime. I began research. In this book, with a few exceptions, I cover only female bank robbers who stepped onto the bank building premises to commit robbery. This book is not all-encompassing; not every female bank robber is listed, and only robberies in the United States are discussed. There is an overview of the times, of the situation each group of women found themselves in. Some things never change: a woman disguised as a man to rob a bank made headlines in the 1800s just as they did in the 1990s. The media always focuses on a woman's aesthetics more so than a man's. Surprisingly, today's bank-robbing female will probably purchase diapers with her ill-gotten gains.

Conversations, statements, and information cited are based on years of research to include media, legal records, interviews, and court transcripts. Although this is a work of nonfiction, some conversations are based upon multiple records, research, or interviews because no verbatim record exists. Alterations are as minuscule as possible in order to remain faithful to the story. Some people refused to be, or could not be, involved; therefore, their involvement is based on numerous sources, including cross-reference, media, and legal records. A few names were changed to protect the victim or because the person refused to be interviewed if their true name was given.

This project was fascinating. Reading through the pages of time and interviewing some of these women was an amazing journey. I do not condone their illegal activities. I do see them as people caught up in the times they lived in. I hope you do, too.

Introduction: "This will all blow up"

"I don't want to freak anybody out," said the pretty Hispanic woman as she set a straw purse on the bank teller's counter. "But my dad is waiting, and if we don't fill this up with all your money, then there are bombs, and this will all blow up."[1]

The bank robber's name was Starlene Casarez Delacruz; she was 31, and she stood at a teller's window in the Prosperity Bank located at 82nd Street and University Avenue in Lubbock, Texas. It was Friday, March 13, 2015. The time was 10:30 a.m.

Starlene Delacruz robbed the Prosperity Bank in Lubbock, Texas, on March 13, 2015. Her bank robbing career was short-lived (Lubbock County Detention Center mug shot).

A hidden camera whirled the entire time Starlene was in the bank, copying her image. Law enforcement would confiscate those images when they responded to the robbery call minutes later. Those images were sent immediately to a media that would air a female-robs-a-bank-and-caught-on-tape story.

Not too far from the bank, an employee named Liza[2] at the Damron Motorcycle Company car lot on South Loop 289 caught the news just before 5 p.m. and watched the bank robbery report. According to the newscaster, the Hispanic female robber was small in stature with shoulder-length dark hair. The robber was wearing a white knit blouse, blue jeans, and sunglasses. And not 30 minutes later, a customer matching the physical description of the bank robber came strolling through the doors of Damron's. She wanted to buy a car, the customer explained to Liza. So she was given an application. Under "employment," the customer wrote "unemployed." However, she said to Liza, she was paying in cash.

Furthermore, the last red flag: The customer was wearing a white knit shirt, blue jeans, and sunglasses—the exact outfit the bank robber reportedly wore when she held up the Prosperity Bank on University Avenue.

Liza excused herself and casually dialed the Lubbock Police Department. The operator kept her on hold while dispatching a squad car to Damron's. Upon arrival, the officers approached Liza's customer and arrested her. Starlene Delacruz, a female bank robber, had less than eight hours to enjoy her new career as a desperado.

Once in the Lubbock County Detention Center, Starlene immediately identified herself as the Prosperity Bank robber. A year later, Starlene would stand before a judge and receive 46 months in prison with restitution of $1,080.25. After her release, Starlene was on parole for three years.

The 2015 robbery of the Prosperity Bank in Lubbock, Texas, was one of 5,691 banks robbed in the United States that year.

Starlene Casarez Delacruz is one of the 359 females arrested for bank robbery in 2015.[3] She is typical of the female bank robbers of her time: She did not steal for riches, fame, or the sheer delight of "getting one over" on a corporation. Starlene Delacruz robbed because she had a basic need: she was homeless, unemployed, and needed a car to escape town. She is what has become a growing trend in American crime: the female bank robber.

Part I

It Begins

1

A Centralized Bank

The Eagle, Not the Turkey

The 13 colonies of what would later become the United States went to war with Great Britain, and the American Revolutionary War (also known as the War of Independence, 1775–1783) cost the American patriots an estimated 25,000 to 70,000 lives, with at least 17,000 dying from smallpox.[1] Smallpox would also play a role in the first bank robbery.

The 13 colonies had boasted of a thriving economy, but the end of the war left them floundering in debt. The circulation of now-worthless hard currency had declined, inflation was astronomical, and there were debts to France, the Netherlands, Spain, and even American merchants.

The crippling effect did not cease. Eventually, some states went bankrupt. And each state had a different form of currency. What is an independent nation to do?

Alexander Hamilton had served as senior aid to future President George Washington during the war. Hamilton was an elected New York representative; he would propose a standard form of currency and a centralized bank. It would also assist with this growing debt left over from the Revolutionary War.

Congress drafted this first bank's charter in 1791, and George Washington signed it with a flourish; $110,169.05 went into the creation of the building. Construction began with the ring of hammers and chisels sounding in Philadelphia, the nation's capital. The bank would move into Carpenter's Hall until 1795, the neoclassical design a nod to the ancient Greeks, the forefathers of democracy. It was christened "the First Bank of the United States."

When the eagle was selected as an official national symbol, Benjamin Franklin wrote, the "selected design looks more like a turkey." Franklin didn't want any birds—turkeys, eagles—on the Presidential Seal. To Ben's chagrin, an eagle crowned the Carpenter's Hall portico despite his rumblings.[2]

On the morning of September 1, 1798, this eagle would bear silent witness to another "first" in the history of the new United States of America: a bank robbery.

2

Setting the Precedent

Yellow Fever and the First U.S. Bank Robbery

Blacksmith Patrick Lyon probably considered himself lucky. It was late in the summer of 1798, and yellow fever was sweeping the streets of the nation's largest city: Philadelphia. At least 1,300 people had died. Lyon and his 19-year-old apprentice remained healthy.

The August 25, 1798, edition of the *Pittsburgh Weekly Gazette* printed "The Health Office of Philadelphia's August 9, 1798" report from the Academy of Medicine which noted, in part, that the yellow fever epidemic was the fault of "the timber of a ship after a sea voyage … from the foul air of several ships," and from "damaged coffee which arrived in a brig from Jamaica on the July 29." A "café of this fever exited in the city … appeared to originate from the putrid exhalations of alleys and gutters, and docks, and from the flagnating [*sic*] waters in the neighborhood of the city." The situation had grown so drastic that the Academy of Medicine suggested "the removal of all the families from those parts of the city where the difeate, from the contamination of the atmosphere, appears chiefly to exist, and the preventing thofe parts be vifited by the citizens [*sic*]."[1]

Some citizens were lucky to flee, to include Lyon and his apprentice. But first Lyon had to complete a rush job at the Bank of Pennsylvania before getting away from the "putrid exhalations." The blacksmith was assigned to make changes to fittings and locks on the vault doors. Finally, Patrick Lyon and his apprentice were off to sea. Just by boarding the small sailing vessel *Cape Henlopen*, they must have breathed sighs of relief—and clean air—escaping this horrible plague.

But by the time they stepped off the ship at Lewistown (Lewes),

Delaware, the apprentice wasn't breathing so well. He would die two days later. No record exists as to cause of death.

Lyon stayed in Delaware, listening to the talk of how the plague was emptying Philadelphia of its inhabitants. Now there was new gossip about someone emptying the safe at the Bank of Pennsylvania at Carpenter's Hall between the night of August 31 and the morning of September 1 to the tune of $162,821 (an estimated $3,200,000 today).

Patrick Lyon's interest was more than just listening to gossip. Before fleeing Philadelphia, he had that "rush job" for this same bank: He changed the fittings and locks on both iron vault doors. He had inside knowledge of the bank's operations, and he knew the locks on the vaults. It all made him a prime suspect! However, he was not the robber.

After realizing he was a suspect, Lyon began packing his bags to return to Philly and clear his name. He wound up a guest at the Walnut Street Prison for three miserable months instead.

Handcuffs would eventually click around the actual burglar's wrists. His name was Isaac Davis, a member of the Carpenter's Company, and he had an "inside man," a bank porter named Thomas Cunningham. A third team member had caught the plague infiltrating the city and died from yellow fever shortly after the heist. It had all gone as planned until the thieves did one stupid thing: they deposited the stolen money in the Bank of Pennsylvania—the same bank they robbed—besides other local banks.

The theft of the money from the Bank of Pennsylvania at Carpenter's Hall set a precedent: meticulous planning, well-done teamwork, and then a stupid mistake that would help catch the thieves.

The governor would grant Isaac Davis a full pardon because Davis returned the stolen money. Patrick Lyon sued the state; a jury awarded Lyon $12,000 ($250,000 in today's money). Lyon had a professional artist paint Lyon's portrait. (The Walnut Street Prison is in the background.) In 1799 the blacksmith turned author when he wrote a book titled "Narrative of Patrick Lyon Who Suffered Three Months Severe Imprisonment in Philadelphia Gaol on Merely a Vague Suspicion of Being Concerned in a Robbery of the Bank of Pennsylvania with his Remarks Thereon."[2]

The 1798 heist of $162,821 from the United States' first official bank, the Bank of Pennsylvania at Carpenter's Hall, is significant in the annals of crime. It was technically a burglary, not a robbery, but historically it is called the first major American bank robbery. It made Isaac Davis the first official bank robber in the United States. Many men would follow. It would take almost 100 years for a woman to officially join the list. Her name is Cora Hubbard.

3

Cora Hubbard

The First Lady of Bank Robbery

Typical of the pioneer era for a hardscrabble family of the plains, Cora Hubbard's birth date was either never officially recorded or is lost. She gave various dates, depending on who was asking. To one journalist, she said she was born on February 17, 1877. While imprisoned, around 1898, her age was given as either 20 or 25. She was probably born about 1877. She was born in Ohio as the sixth of seven children to Samuel, a Union Army veteran who was part Cherokee Indian, and Elizabeth (Garber). The family would eventually move to Missouri. Elizabeth died sometime between 1880 and 1885, and the family moved to Spring Hill, Kansas.

Drawing of Cora Hubbard from the *St. Louis Dispatch*, August 29, 1897, Sunday morning edition, p. 21. Journalists detailed her physical attributes and compared her personality to a man's (artist not credited, 1897).

Cora was not a big woman; she stood about 5'2", built sturdily at a bit over 100 pounds. But like many pioneer women, she had the muscles attributed to hard work and the toughness to survive the rigors of farm life.

Cora was 15 years old when she married her first husband, James (sometimes listed as Joseph) Russell. She would later give their wedding date as October 17, 1890. Russell was not a kind man. Cora left him to travel with her family; then she and Russell were divorced by 1897. It was not long before she said "I do" to a new husband, "Bud" Parker. They settled on a farm in what would become Oklahoma, about ten miles south of Coffeyville, Kansas.

A handyman named John Sheets began doing work on their farm. (Cora would later claim John was her husband, and she and John wed on June 6, 1897.) Al and William, Cora's brothers, lived nearby.

According to some accounts, Cora loved reading Wild West novels and stories of outlaws. She was acquainted with the notorious outlaw Dalton gang and was sweet on Bob Dalton. She carried a rusty .45 Colt six-shot pistol that bore his name scratched into the handle. Above the trigger guard, scratched into the gun were seven nicks, said to represent seven dead men in some distant Boot Hill, courtesy of Bob. Cora would later be relieved of this prize possession during her history-making bank robbery.

Newspapers of the day would have Cora a career criminal, but that may be the stuff of campfire legend or yellow journalism. Reportedly, Cora and a gang robbed a bank in Altamont, Kansas, relieving that bank of an undisclosed amount of cash. If this robbery was officially recorded, the records are long gone.

In June 1893, Henry Starr, Ned Christy, "Dynamite Dick," "Three-Fingered Jack," Belle Starr, and Cora Hubbard robbed the People's State Bank in Bentonville, Arkansas, of $11,300. The robbery was a messy one: Jack was killed and died in the middle of the street. Henry Starr was wounded. Bystanders were wounded. Cora's role is unknown, so this robbery is challenging to record as any woman's "first bank robbery."

What is recorded is how drifter Albert Whitfield "Whit" Tennyson came into Cora and Bud's lives one August, and that was when their bank robbery idea began to hatch. Whit boasted he had the skills, and William stated he was familiar with the McDonald County Bank in

Pineville, Missouri, because he once lived in that town and worked for a farmer nearby. William sketched out a bank map and the routes they would take to travel to and from Pineville's town. Bud, John, Whit, and Al chose to be the robbers. Initially, it sounded like a great plan.

But when it came time to saddle up and move out, Cora's husband, Bud Parker, and her brother Al Hubbard backed out. Suddenly, living on the right side of the law, albeit a poor one, sounded just fine to them.

Cora was furious. "I will not live," she snarled at Bud, "with a damn coward." She chopped her hair off short and donned men's clothing to disguise herself, slapping on a black slouch hat. Then Cora spurred her horse into action, and the future bank robbers headed out.[1]

They had a few stops to make before reaching Pineville. They pulled up in Coffeyville, Kansas, for John Sheets to buy a Winchester rifle and ammunition. The group unsaddled for an overnighter at Cora's father's farm in Neosho. Her father, Samuel, was taken aback to see his little girl dressed in men's clothing, her hair shorn down.

On August 16, 1897, they made it to Pineville, arriving just before daylight to set up camp outside the city. John Sheets and Whit Tennyson went into town to scout over the McDonald County Bank, returning to make a report to William and Cora: Everything looked fine; the bank was ripe for the pickin'.

On August 17, the Hubbard siblings came riding into Pineville with John Sheets and Whit Tennyson, William still clutching his map. Cora rode with them, still wearing her slouch hat, and now she had donned a coat and vest over her overalls. Multiple historians would record them as stopping right in front of the bank. John and Whit eased off their horses. They must not have trusted William's bravado because they handed their reins to Cora.

As part of her job was as lookout, Cora's dark eyes would have darted over the immediate landscape. The only building close to the bank was a house belonging to the Hooper family; it sat right next to the bank building.

As John and Whit started walking towards the bank, the landowner's son, Brit Hooper, appeared at the door of the house. Without flinching, Cora whipped out her pistol and leveled it at him. "Stand still." Seeing the young man's reaction, she advised him, "It's no use to get excited at a time like this."[2]

Witnesses would later say Cora sat easily in her saddle, holding the reins to the gang's horses. The heat must have made the animals snort and stamp a hoof, attempting to kick off the flies in the already hot air, as horses do.

Meanwhile, John and Whit were slipping around the edge of the bank building, silent as shadows, only the soft creak of gun leather giving them away. Because their prey never saw them coming, the victims would later tell the press.

Bank President A.V. Manning was sitting in front of the bank, enjoying the morning with Cashier John W. Shields and County Treasurer Marcus N. LaMance. Their enjoyment ended when they peered down the business end of guns to the sound of "we're here for the money, and we want it damn quick."[3]

John Sheets forced Bank President Manning and Cashier Shields into the bank while Whit Tennyson kept LaMance outside. Inside the bank, Cashier Shields attempted to resist the cursed demands to hurry it up. John Sheets slapped him to the ground with the rifle. As Shields picked himself up off the floor, nursing his jaw, the robber again ordered him to fill a sack with money. Sheets handed Manning the sacks with the order to hold them while Shields filled them. Coins clinked together and paper currency fluttered into the sacks until there was none left to fill the bags, a total of $589.23.

As the bank was being relieved of cash inside, outside Cora would later tell the press how she was getting fed up with one older man standing nearby. He stood looking her up and down, his hands in his pockets, squinting as if trying to figure out why a "little man" was sitting astride a horse, holding two others' reins. Cora was ready to level her gun's barrel at the nosy, old buzzard when the bank door swung open.

Now Sheets herded the men out of the bank to join LaMance, and the robbers hustled the men off the front porch, marching them into the street at gunpoint lest someone try to pop off a round towards the outlaws. As they stepped into the road towards Cora and William, Tennyson relieved Bank President Manning of a $15 silver watch. Like the nosy, old man, Cashier John W. Shields noted the "young man" on the porch guarding the outside of the bank; this little fellow was the bunch's calmest. Shields got a good look at his dark complexion, the shock of thick, black hair poking out from under his hat, and steady gaze. The

Artist's rendition of Cora Hubbard robbing the Pineville bank, with a sketch of Cora inset. Typical of the times, the artist played loosely with the truth (from *The Inquirer Sunday Magazine*, September 12, 1897, p. 1, artist not credited).

little robber wore a pair of overalls, a coat and vest, and a black slouch hat.

Still waving their guns at their captors, John and Whit saddled up, and then all four spurred their horses. With whoops and shots fired towards the sky, they galloped off and away in true Wild West fashion, heading northeast and away from Pineville, Missouri.

Just like too many future bank robbers, the gang departed, convinced the robbery had gone off without a hitch. And just like too many future bank robbers, one of them made a stupid, small mistake that would cost them all. In his haste to mount up, carry the money, and escape quick, William dropped his map.

John Sheets, William and Cora Hubbard, and Whit Tennyson made it safely away from the McDonald County Bank in Pineville, Missouri. It was August 17, 1897. All they knew was they had just robbed a bank of $589.23. They had no idea they had made history: Cora Hubbard was the first female bank robber on record. Nevertheless, it was no time to ponder anything else but getting away in one whole piece. An impromptu posse had formed and was heading out to the northeast. The posse did not know the gang had changed direction as soon as they were out of sight.

Once it was safe, the robbers were dividing up the cash. Then, as they were about to mount up again, one of their horses must have decided life was just too complicated, and the poor creature gave out. Lucky for the robbers and the old nag, along came a boy on a decent horse. The robbers forced the boy off his horse, initiating some horse-trading—albeit at gunpoint—and headed on their way.

While the robbers were practicing illegal horse switching, information about the bank robbery was crackling across the air to Noel, Missouri, via the Pineville telegraph. The message arrived in enough time for another posse to form, hoping to head off the gang.

The robbers unknowingly rode into an ambush. They were riding single file into Noel, with Tennyson in the lead. Their eyes were probably drooping with weariness, with the dust settling in between their teeth; no doubt, they were exhausted when the crack of gunfire snapped everyone to attention. A firefight began, the shots snapping, bullets cracking through the dusty air.

One version of the shoot-out has Cora's horse shot out from under her. Cora's beloved Colt .45 was shot out of her hand; it soon became the property of town marshal James Hatton. Several shots bore through her slouch hat. Whit's horse panicked and bolted, dumping Whit. Cora shouted to him and helped him swing up behind her saddle. They rode hell-bent until Cora located a wooded area. She let the horse go, and they hid out until she could dress Whit's wounds. Cora and Whit eventually parted ways.

Albert Whitfield "Whit" Tennyson may have had grand ideas about bank robbery, but he had no grand ideas when it came to criminal partnerships. A posse caught him as he was camping in the hills of Indian territory, just west of Pineville, on the following Thursday, August 22. He would snitch out his fellow robbers, Cora's lifesaving skills be damned. The posse also recovered some of the stolen loot. One posse member, a Mr. Yeargeain, noted to the rest of the self-appointed law dogs that, according to the map, Weir City was the robbers' rendezvous point.

Cora had indeed headed for her father, Samuel's, house in Weir City. Her brother and fellow bank robber, William, would later join her.

A posse was trailing them, and this posse included the McDonald County Bank's cashier John W. Shields. Shields knew that William Hubbard, an acquaintance, was part of the robbery gang. The posse, acting on Yeargeain's map and Tennyson's fat mouth, set up surveillance at Samuel Hubbard's home. Both Cora and William were arrested two days after the law was handcuffing Tennyson.

William had been in town, biding his time and waiting to see what his next move should be when he was arrested the following Sunday about 1 p.m. Then the posse, joined by the law officers of Weir City, Missouri, along with a few Weir City vigilantes, piled into three carriages and headed out towards Samuel's house. They were intent on catching the other bank robber. "It was a formidable-looking aggregation," the *Pittsburgh Daily Tribune* told its readers in the August 23, 1897, edition. "Officers with guns, features set, with Winchesters and shotguns, glistening in the sunlight. Upon their arrival, they scattered, surrounding the house and a small cornfield nearby."[4]

When Cashier Shields walked through the doorway into Samuel Hubbard's home, he observed a young girl there; she wore a calico "Mother Hubbard" dress, showing dimples with a shy, sweet smile. She was plain, dark complected, and her black hair shorn close. Her feet were bare, and she looked exhausted. Shields leaned close to peer into her face. He recognized her features then; this was the face of the "young man" guarding the bank during the robbery. That cool, calculating, young man was a calm, young woman.

Officers would later report that Cora showed absolutely no fear when arrested.

The officers demanded that Samuel Hubbard allow them to search his property, and he put up quite a stink. Cora was his little girl, after all! William was his son. Shouldn't a man protect his blood?

The officers pushed past the old man to search anyway, Samuel's muttered curses no doubt following them. Searchers found a box of money buried in the vegetable garden and located the clothes Cora had worn during the robbery. One of them held up Cora's black slouch hat with the bullet holes acquired during the shoot-out: more evidence.

Now everybody was rounded up, including Samuel, for his reluctance to assist in searching for the hidden money.

Cora and William were loaded up into a wagon and taken on a bumpy ride into Missouri, arriving about 7 p.m. and placed in a hotel. A newshound noted she was "slovenly" and "of lowly origin and not at all attractive in any way." This reporter from the *Daily Herald* interviewed Cora. "Were you scared during the robbery?" the reporter asked her.

"Not one damn bit," she snarled. "I wish we would've held up the whole damn town."[5]

Three days later, John Sheets ran out of luck when he drove up to Samuel Hubbard's house in a buggy. He hopped out of the buggy and into the arms of City Marshal James Hatton, McDonald County Bank Cashier John W. Shields, and Constable Ike Dennis stepping out of Hubbard's home. The posse had been inside, trying to find out the rest of the stolen money's whereabouts, when Mr. Sheets pulled up in his nice, new buggy. Shields recognized Sheets immediately as the fellow who had slapped him in the face with a Winchester.

Cora made the front page of the September 12 issue of *The Inquirer* Sunday Magazine. "Bravest and Wickedest Woman Ever Known in America at Last Behind Prison Bars," read the headline. The bylines accused her of murder, of train robbery, and other bank robberies. The author of the poetic and imaginative full-page article had Cora, not John Sheets or Whit Tennyson, walking into the bank; this Cora stood on the wooden porch and held the town at bay with her two pistols while the men rifled the tills. A large sketch of a faceless cowboy accompanied the story. *The Inquirer's* nameless journalist noted that Cora enjoyed hard liquor, could outshoot any man, and had a short temper and quick draw. Her language was peppered with an occasional "damn; she wrote and spoke clearly and it was obvious she had an education." Just like newspaper journalists wrote about outlaw Bonnie Parker some 35 years later, the author would accuse Cora Hubbard of the unpardonable sin of smoking cigars.[6]

Her bravado made for exciting reading, even if it was a large percent of poetic licensing, as Cora was called "the newest of new women, right up to date, fearless, dogged, and desperate." Her physical attributes were detailed in the description: "short, black hair … 5 feet 4 inches in height and rather stockily built. Her hair is course [*sic*] and black and

Cora Hubbard (with hand on lapel) holds the distinction of being the first recorded female bank robber. This photograph was taken after her arrest, showing her with accomplice Whit Tennyson and an unknown man. They robbed the McDonald County Bank in Pineville, Missouri, on August 17, 1897, escaping with $589.23 (photographer not credited, 1897).

her complexion swarthy, and she greatly resembles an Indian woman. Her features are course [*sic*] and masculine, as are her tastes."[7]

Cora Hubbard, John Sheets, and Whit Tennyson were bound over for trial and returned to the Newton County Jail in Neosho on August 28, on the same day her father, Samuel, and brother William walked out free from Pineville.

In 1897, every time Cora Hubbard's name appeared in a newspaper, it was followed by the fact she had dressed as a man during the robbery. Most of the accounts noted she was as tough as a man—and unattractive.

On January 12, 1898, Cora was arraigned in an Emporia, Kansas, courtroom and pled guilty. Cora, John, and Whit were all convicted of bank robbery. They were to serve their sentences in the state prison at Jefferson City. Whit received a ten-year sentence; Cora and John received 12 years each. So much for an "easy" bank robbery. This time, her name was relegated in the local paper to page six and overshadowed by a tornado in Ft. Smith that killed 41 people. It seems Mother Nature had ousted a cross-dressing bandit.

Still, Cora Hubbard's name was printed in newspapers from Kansas to Pennsylvania, from California to Connecticut. A female outlaw dressed like a man reportedly shot both six-shooters and shot glasses of whiskey with ease and robbed a bank; she was tantalizing news.

News of the "newest of new women" reached far beyond the borders of the United States. A small article in the February 14, 1898, issue of the *Fort Scott Daily Tribune* noted that Sheriff Wheeler in Fort Scott, Kansas, received a letter from a Samuel Davidson from Rathplani, County Down, Ireland. Mr. Davidson was inquiring about Cora Hubbard. Mr. Davidson was interested in corresponding with her.[8]

By now Cora was bedded down in her new home, the Missouri Penitentiary. Her need for excitement obviously still existed for she gave interviews from her cell to any journalist who asked. It was during one interview, in February 1898, that she claimed marriage to John Sheets. Cora also had no qualms about discussing vengeance. The law would not have caught her in this bank robbery, and she swore "had it not been for Tennyson and my folks giving John and me away. We will fix them when we get out. It don't take 12 years very long to roll around." The newspaper writer called her "an evolution of frontier lawlessness."

Her time behind bars sounds dull. She let her hair grow back and acted like a lady should act: she learned a trade as a seamstress, and she stayed out of trouble, obeying prison rules as a model prisoner. She dedicated her spare time to reading trash novels, her body growing softer and rounder from the starch-filled prison chow. She was no longer interested in newspapers or other reading unless her name was featured. Eventually, she took part in church services. As the years passed, it seemed the "Wickedest Woman Ever Known in America" was, at last, becoming a softie. "I am forever done with any such [illegal activity]," she told a reporter.[9]

On December 26, 1905, Missouri Governor Alexander Monroe Dockery commuted Cora's sentence with an official pardon. She walked out of prison on January 1, 1906. According to the news, Cora headed for Weir City. Time must have worn off her desire for revenge for she went home to her father and stepmother.

She clutched a letter of recommendation from the officials in the tailoring department where she had worked in the reformatory. "I learned the tailor business almost completely, and I hope to get sewing to do here [in Weir City]." She praised prison officials and gave advice on how to behave in prison: "All you have to do is to behave yourself, and they will take care of you." Before her release, she met with Marshal Jim Hatton, telling him she was glad to see him and promising she would never give him a reason to arrest her again. She blamed her downfall on the men she associated with, having no desire ever to see John Sheets or Whit Tennyson again.

The reporter who recorded these details of her release described her as: "short in stature dark and almost masculine featured, and possessed of a black, penetrating eye." However, the writer explained, "she does not look a day older than when she was imprisoned."[10]

This interview is the last time Cora Hubbard's name appears in newspaper print. Did she become a good, moral woman, staying at home and living life quietly? Or did she slip back into her old ways, the tug of excitement pulling at her soul?

The newspapers and dime-store novels often called Cora Hubbard "the Second Belle Starr" who "rivals the daring deeds of Kate Bender." This was not a fair comparison.

PART II

The "Wild Bunch" in Skirts

4

Queens of the Wild Frontier

The migration of Europeans from the eastern United States to the West did not happen in a vacuum. Even before Americans won their independence in the Revolutionary War, people were migrating West. The Louisiana Purchase in 1803, the Corps of Discovery Expedition (also called the Lewis and Clark Expedition), the War of 1812, and the Indian Removal Act of 1830 aided the United States citizens' migration towards the West. Then came journalist John O'Sullivan who, in 1845, told "Americans" they were morally superior, "destined by God to govern the U.S.," and it was their obligation to lift and assist less civilized societies (i.e., anyone not white and not considered "American," to include Indians). As crude as it sounds now, O'Sullivan's "Manifest Destiny" was a driving force for western expansion. It gave white people the right to move West, settle, and "own" land, a concept Indians initially thought ridiculous and impossible ... until forced to march off and away on the aptly named Trail of Tears.[1]

Today the term "cowboy" is used to describe the western lifestyle. But, any honest man from that period would be offended. In the 1800s, if one were to address a man as a "cowboy," it wasn't because the man was roping, riding, or herding. The title "cowboy" described a drunk or a cattle thief. A "legitimate rancher or landowner" was referred to as "rancher" or "cowman."[2]

Gold was discovered "in them thar hills"[3] in California in 1848; thousands of easterners headed towards the west coast to get rich. The "west"—the great frontier—had a wild, untamed reputation, and people in the east wanted to read all about it. Journalists and authors obliged them. And sometimes, if they could not tell the real story, a good yarn would suffice. Tales sold better than most truths. Thus legends were born: under a journalist's pen, sad alcoholics with a gun, like Calamity Jane (true name Martha Jane Canary), became wild, rootin' tootin' women who would rather shoot it out than act like a proper lady in bustle and parasol. Easterners ate it up that a solid citizen chose to become a Wild West outlaw, riding fast and shooting straight. It made for a good read, and if that citizen was female, all the better. And Myra Maybelle Shirley was the queen of them all.

Myra Belle Shirley, better known as Belle Starr, was born in 1848 in Missouri. As a teenager, she worked as a spy during the Civil War, reporting Union troops' movement to the confederacy. In actuality, Myra was a spoiled, rich kid who grew up to befriend and then ride with outlaws, known for her hard drinking and gambling in saloons. She would dress in buckskins or velvet but always with twin pistols stuffed in her belts. It is unknown if Myra directly involved herself in robberies or murder; what is known is she involved herself in planning cattle rustling, horse theft, and bootlegging. Myra also hid outlaws from the law. "I am a friend to any brave and gallant outlaw," she told a Dallas news reporter.[4] Myra Belle Shirley, aka Belle Starr, the "Queen of the Outlaws," was shot in the back and killed in 1889. Her murder remains unsolved. She was the female outlaw darling to anyone who picked up a dime novel or newspaper, craving excitement and intrigue.

Kate Bender's crimes were hardly "daring deeds." Between 1871 to 1873, Kate, her parents, and her brother committed a string of grisly murders. They were called "the Bloody Benders."

The Benders ran a store and an inn in Labette County, Kansas, where weary travelers could stop for a meal, seeking friendly company and a night's rest. The pretty proprietress, Miss Kate, might entertain them with her reported "gift of second sight," explaining she was a spiritualist. "Professor Miss Kate Bender" would show them one of the flyers she distributed throughout the country. The guest probably noted she had far better social skills than that of her rough parents and sibling.

The Benders made the visitor feel at home. It was small but cozy. There were two rooms divided by a canvas cloth. In the front room visitors took their meals at a table near a stove and grocery store. If they were the guest of honor, they sat in a chair sitting atop a hidden trap door with their back to the canvas, creating a perfect silhouette for whoever was in the second room. If the visitor was a good prospect, meaning they were traveling with a lot of money or valuables, they never saw the hammer coming down from the other side of the canvas. If they somehow lived through the blow, their throat was sliced open. A Bender would spring the trapdoor underneath the victim's feet, and down into the cellar they fell.

But the Benders' crimes eventually aroused suspicion, and they fled. Authorities investigated. Skeletons were found in the cellar and buried on the Bender property, all with demolished skulls. The Benders disappeared and were never apprehended.

The majority of female outlaws who picked up a gun did so to assist a criminal paramour, or in cases such as the Benders, to assist their family members. The family or friends of these women included the criminal element. And a few of them had their place in criminal history because they did ride with outlaw gangs, like the most infamous gang known throughout western history as "the Wild Bunch."

5

Etta/Ethel Place

The Sundance Kid's Second Partner in Crime

She went by the first name of Ethel. "A Pinkerton detective had copied 'Etta' erroneously off a hotel register, and that's how her name appeared in their files. Their Wanted posters referred to her as 'Etta' and the name stuck."[1] She may have been born in Texas around 1878. Because she was so vague about her life before crime, today she remains an enigma.

Anyone meeting her called her "refined," recalling she spoke with a cultured voice, possibly indicative of an East Coast upbringing. While she was well-read and educated, she was also a crack shot with a rifle. She revealed little about herself to the public, and what she did reveal was questionable.

Ethel Place is one of the West's figures whose life's details are lost to history. But it was about 1901 when she began to make history for she became the companion of Harry Alonzo Longabaugh, commonly known as "the Sundance Kid," a member of "the Wild Bunch" that included "Butch" Cassidy (aka Robert L. Parker). Cassidy is one of the most famous outlaws to come riding out of western history.

"The Sundance Kid" had many an alias, including "Harry Place."[2] This is where Ethel probably obtained her last name. Ethel possibly met Sundance while the gang was lying low in New York City, hiding from the Pinkerton Agency, the United States' premier detective agency. It is also possible Ethel met Sundance while she was working as a prostitute in a San Antonio brothel. Some stories have her employed as a school teacher, while others have her dumping a respectable family to run off with an outlaw. Anyone who knows the real story is long gone, and no one recorded the truth.

Ethel "Etta" Place joined "the Sundance Kid," Butch Cassidy, and a third unidentified person to rob the National Bank in Villa Mercedes, Argentina, on December 19, 1805. She was a skilled horsewoman and a crack shot with a mysterious past (Joseph B. De Young's Photographic Gallery, New York, 1901).

Ethel was one of only a handful of women to visit the Wild Bunch's hideout, "Robber's Roost." The Pinkertons stayed hot on the trail, but no lawman ever discovered the location of the Roost.

The Sundance Kid and Butch Cassidy were high on the "Most Wanted" by the Pinkertons. The outlaws had to continually sneak and hide, dodging the "Pinks," and that was getting old quick.

In the late 1800s, there was no one place they could settle without those Pinkertons hunting them down, no quiet life to live without having to sleep with one eye open. The United States had gotten too hot for Butch and Sundance. Canadian Mounties had a stellar reputation for catching the bad guys. Mexico did not sound any better. Somehow they started discussing Patagonia, in Argentina, South America, and all it promised. A man could make a decent, honest living there, away from peering American eyes, doing what the Kid and Cassidy knew best (legally): ranching.

An outbreak of the hoof-and-mouth disease had forced Europe to import mutton and beef. That meat was now being imported from

Patagonia, an ideal place for livestock located between the Andes Mountains and the Atlantic Ocean. Sundance and Butch discussed the situation and came to an agreement. In Patagonia, they could make some money away from law enforcement who knew their faces, obtain new identities, and sleep all night without jumping at every noise. Argentina, here we come!

But first, Sundance was to collect Ethel. She was going to join him in Argentina. Ethel's name was already accompanying Sundance and Butch's name on Wanted posters. On the 1906 poster, she was described as "classic good looks, 27 or 28 years old, 5'4" to 5'5" (163–165 cm) in height, weighing between 110 and 115 lb. (50 and 52 kg), with a medium build and brown hair." The Pinkertons began a file on "Etta," and documents in the file from July 29, 1902, list her as being "from Texas."[3]

Prior to their departure, Sundance and Ethel went to New Orleans to enjoy the finest hotels and gourmet cuisine. They traveled to meet his family. He introduced her as his wife. From there, Harry and Ethel traveled east by train to New York, arriving on February 1, 1901. "Mr. and Mrs. Harry Place" again stayed in a luxury suite and dined on fine food.

Only a few known photographs exist of Ethel. Her best photo was taken that visit in New York City. On February 3, Sundance and Ethel had visited the renowned Tiffany's jewelry store, where they purchased a $150 gold lapel watch and a diamond stickpin. They walked Times Square to 826 Broadway and 12th Street to step through the door of Joseph B. De Young's Photographic Gallery. The "Largest Photographic Gallery in the City" snapped one of the most famous photographs of that era. The couple looks dashing, wealthy—not at all like a thief and a prostitute who had left the dusty plains to hide from detectives.

Sundance sent a copy of the photo to a David Gillespie in Snake River Valley, writing on the back, "I married a Texas lady I have known previously."[4] His note may indicate Ethel's being a prostitute at the San Antonio brothel visited by the gang. Sundance also mailed a copy to another friend or family member; Pinkerton detectives paid off a postal employee, intercepted one of the photos, and used it for a Wanted poster. It never made its way to the addressee.

Soon, Ethel's "brother," a "Mr. James Ryan," arrived. He spent all his time with the Places. Ryan was a dead ringer for Butch Cassidy if anyone cared to look close enough.

The next step was to book a passage on a ship bound for Argentina. With Cassidy still posing as Ethel's brother, they sailed south on February 20, 1901.

They purchased a ranch in the Chubut Providence with ill-gotten gains, settling in for a peaceful life. Located near Cholila in west-central Argentina, it was nothing extravagant, just a four-room log cabin close to the Blanco River. They owned 15,000 acres thanks to a new 1884 law, and Ethel owned 2,500 acres of this land they were to develop. She was the first woman in Argentina to acquire land under this new law.

Eventually, Sundance and Ethel would make several trips to the States, traveling undetected back and forth to old stomping grounds from their new abode.

In February of 1904, two men robbed the *Banco do Londres y Tarapaca* in Rio Gallegos, located in the southern part of Argentina, riding off with $100,000. Although it smacked of the type of robbery the Wild Bunch would have pulled, it made no sense that Sundance and Butch would have committed the crime. For once, they were living a good life. They were making grand money by ranching. They lived unmolested and free of problems. Why screw it up with a dumb robbery? Besides, the boys had an ironclad alibi and did not resemble the thieves.

Still, the Buenos Aires police chief had a "Reward" poster of Sundance, Butch, and Ethel, courtesy of the Pinkertons. He had a high-profile case to close, and that reward money was not chump change. So the chief sent word to Sheriff Eduardo Humphries to come to Argentina to fetch those three *Americanos. Vámonos*!

Sheriff Humphries had taken a liking to Sundance and Butch and a shining to Ethel. And he chanced his job—and lost it—when he warned them about the Buenos Aires police chief rather than having cuffed them and brought them in.

Sundance, Ethel, and Butch packed up, sent notes to friends about their assets, and would eventually split the proceeds. They could not sell their homesteaded ranch. It would later play a part in the mystery of Ethel's story.

On May 9, Sundance, Ethel, and Butch would sail for Chile.

The *Banco do Londres y Tarapaca* robbery remains unsolved.

December 1905 found Sundance, Ethel, and Butch back together, meeting up in Villa Mercedes in San Luis, Argentina, several hundred miles away from Buenos Aires. Life took a change for Ethel.

Ethel had lived among outlaws and was common-law married to one. On December 19, 1905, she officially became an outlaw herself by joining in on a bank robbery.

The Sundance Kid, Butch, a male person never identified, and Ethel teamed up to rob the National Bank (*Banco de la Nacion*) in Villa Mercedes on Riobamba's corner and Belgrano Street.

Witnesses gawked as four horsemen rode up to the bank to tether their steeds to the hitching post. While one of the men held the horses, three people busted in, six-shooters drawn and ready for business. "Hand over all the money in the safe!"

The bank manager, a Señor Harleb, did something wrong and *whack*! One of the robbers made contact with the manager's head via the butt of a pistol. It took them four minutes to grab all the money, stuff it into sacks, and get out the door, past Señor Harleb nursing his bleeding scalp.

Those in the bank heard the thunder of four sets of hooves grow distant, but the bank treasurer, Señor Garcia, pushed past them all, pistol in hand, squeezing off a volley of shots at the parting thieves. Several armed men pulled their weapons and shot at the four riders as they rode off down the street. Still, the robbers and their mounts continued unscathed.

Ethel had the reputation of an expert marksman and was utterly fearless. She rode a horse with finesse. They had carefully planned, stashing supplies and fresh horses along the escape route. The robbers managed to make their way through a snowy pass at a 13,000-foot altitude to the Chilean border. They escaped with an estimated $130,000 (in today's U.S. dollars). Or perhaps it was $90,000. (It seems historians spend more time investigating Ethel's mysterious past and identity than into the actual amount stolen in this robbery.)

A posse followed the robbers to no avail. At one point, everyone exchanged gunfire. A posse member winged a robber. Then it started to rain. The robbers got away, crossing the Pampas lowlands, along the Andes Mountain ranges, into Chile.

The Pinkerton Detective Agency sent information to the Buenos Aires newspapers about their suspicions of who robbed *Banco de la Nacion* in Villa Mercedes. Their accusation included Ethel, as "Miss A.H. Place," as part of the gang. This time, the Pinkertons described Ethel as "an interesting woman, very masculine, who wears male clothing with total correctness, and who is dedicated more to the occupations of men than those of women … [a] fine rider, handles with precision all classes of firearms, and has an admirable male temperament."[5]

Ethel Place's whereabouts after this robbery become the debate of historians and western outlaw history lovers. Most agree that on June 30, 1906, she had Sundance take her to San Francisco. He left her there, with her cut of the robbery and money from the ranch. "[W]hen the Pinkertons last checked on her whereabouts about 1925; she was living in Oregon."[6]

By July 31, 1909, both Butch and Sundance were dead (unless one believes in conspiracy theories). A woman who closely resembled Ethel Place showed up in Bolivia on this date. She sought a death certificate to settle the estate of Harry Alonzo Longabaugh, aka "the Sundance Kid," aka Harry Place, her husband. "The estate" included the ranch in Cholila, where they had lived happily in Argentina. The officials denied the woman's request. Was it the real Ethel Place?

Ethel, aka Etta Place, is one of the few women recorded to rob a bank during the era known as "the Wild West." This is one of the facts known about this mystery woman. The other is that Ethel was the gang's confidante, and one detail proves it.

Ethel Place was one of only a handful of women to know the location of the Wild Bunch's hideout, "Robber's Roost." While there, she just missed out on meeting Laura "Thorny Rose" Bullion, the rare proven female gang member. The women never met because, when Ethel visited Robber's Roost, Laura was watching the world go by from behind jail bars.

6

Laura Bullion

The Thorny Rose

While there is no record of Laura physically walking into a bank to rob, there is a record of her committing forgery, having possession of stolen banknotes, and assisting known bank robbers. She probably had a hand in train robbery. Her name is historically linked to bank robbery in the 1800s just enough to mention here.

Laura's father was Native American, and her mother was German. Her heritage shines in her almond-shaped eyes and strong cheekbones in a face that stares bluntly into a camera for her mug shot. She is suspected of working in the same Texas brothel as Ethel. The brothel is probably where she met the Wild Bunch. During this time in history, if a woman was not a wife, a daughter, or of a wealthy family, there were few ways of persevering. Prostitution was one of those ways.

Laura was born on October 4, 1873, or 1876, possibly in Knickerbocker, Texas. In a time and place where records didn't follow an individual, especially one who followed few laws, a person could be anyone and any age they aspired to be. Her death certificate lists her parents' names as Henry Bullion and Fereby (Byler) Bullion.

Her father was a bank robber who was chummy with other criminals to include William "News" Carver, a well-known robber of trains and banks. Laura first laid eyes on William when she was 13. Laura grew up around various scalawags, thieves, and ne'er-do-wells.

When she was five years old, her parents separated, and Fereby took Laura and her sister to go live near their maternal grandparents, Mr. and Mrs. E.R. and Serena Byler, in Knickerbocker, Texas. In 1888, Henry died, and Fereby married again, leaving the kids to fend for

***Left and right:* Laura Bullion, mug shots, 1893. She assisted in bank robberies with "the Wild Bunch" who nicknamed her "Rose of the Wild Bunch" (origin unknown, possibly Pinkerton Detective Agency).**

themselves. Some written history has Laura living with her grandparents before setting off on her own. The 1900 Federal Census of Population lists a 23-year-old Laura Bullion (b. October 1876) in Arkansas, with an occupation as "housekeeper."[1]

Her grandparents would later move to a ranch in Douglas, Arizona. Laura eventually became estranged from her sister; there is no record as to why.

Taking up with outlaws ran in the family. Laura's aunt met William Carver, married him in 1891, then died of the fever soon after. Two years later, Laura headed for San Antonio, Texas, to work as a prostitute; she was 15 years old. She returned in a few years to take up with William.

William was riding with the "Black Jack [Tom] Ketchum Gang," and Laura begged to join them. William refused her. They would meet in between robberies, and Laura would ask again to join the outlaws.

William was on the run from the law when he took up with "the

Wild Bunch," Butch and Sundance included. Wild Bunch members nicknamed Laura "Della Rose" and "Rose of the Wild Bunch."

In the early 1890s, Laura became the mistress of the 6'1" Ben "the Tall Texan" Kirkpatrick after William's dalliance with a San Antonio prostitute from the famous Fannie Portal's Brothel. Laura would later claim the 6' 1" Kirkpatrick was the best man she had ever known, a kind, intelligent gentleman who took the best care of her.

She became part of the gang by working behind the scenes: selling the stolen goods, passing stolen banknotes, and replenishing the supplies. From time to time, Wild West novelettes and some newspaper writers had her dressing as a man to assist with robberies, but it is difficult to confirm if she actually walked into a bank to rob.

By 1901, Laura was involved with William Carver again, until his death in November, and she bounced back to Ben Kirkpatrick. She also had "relationships" with other gang members. In between romances, she continued to run errands and fence stolen goods for her gang. Some historical accounts have her taking part in train robberies. Laura possibly rode as a lookout and took part in the robberies by holding the gang's horses as they boarded the train to blow the safes with dynamite. She certainly helped plan Montana's 1901 Great Northern Railway train heist on July 3 of 1901; $65,000 in unsigned bills disappeared. The known robbers were O.C. Hanks, Ben Kirkpatrick, and Harvey Logan.

Thanks to a tip, handcuffs clicked around Ben Kirkpatrick's wrists in the fall of 1901. Officers found a Laclede Hotel key in Ben's pocket. The little piece of brass led them to Laura and an accomplice.

Laura's wicked ways came to a halt on November 6, 1901, when a pair of handcuffs snapped over her wrists at the Laclede Hotel in St. Louis, Missouri.

As is the norm with female criminals, newspapers of the day detailed her dress, how the well-dressed woman wore a tan dress and jacket with a man's white fedora hat. She carried a satchel and had a trunk of personal items with her. A well-dressed white man accompanied her. They were calling themselves Mr. and Mrs. J.W. Rose. Officers now joined the well-heeled couple in the hotel lobby.

An anonymous reporter for the *St. Louis Republic* wrote how the woman calling herself "Mrs. Nellie Rose" was aghast, sputtering angrily at the law's officers surrounding her and pulling her trunk and her satchel. Then her shoulders slumped, and she gave up when the law dogs recovered the $8,500 of banknotes in her possession, banknotes stolen from the Great Northern train robbery. Her name is listed as "Della Rose" in the arrest report, and her profession is listed as "prostitute." The official charge of record is "forgery of signatures to banknotes" (p. 2).

The officers also arrested Mrs. Rose's companion Mr. J.W. Rose, who claimed they were a quiet, law-abiding couple from Vicksburg, Mississippi. He was not as ready to give up any information, but the law suspected him to be the great thief Henry Longabaugh.

Officers brought Laura to be questioned by a Chief of Detectives Desmond for her role in the Great Northern train heist.

"I'm not feeling well," she told Detective Desmond. "And may I change my dress?" He allowed her to do so—she was, after all, a tiny, frail-looking thing. She removed a muslin dress from her trunk, left the room, and returned wearing the new dress, keeping the hat, the brim down over her eyes.

She gave her age as 25 years old and admitted she could be

Artist's rendering of Laura Bullion during interrogation. Laura possibly rode as a lookout on train robberies by holding the gang's horses as the men boarded the train (*The St. Louis Republic*, St. Louis, Missouri, November 8, 1901, p. 1, artist not credited).

quite the liar, but now she would be truthful. She claimed she was innocent; it was Bill Carver with a penchant for stopping trains and relieving them from their cash at gunpoint.[2]

The detective would later tell reporters he had no doubt the tiny woman with the leaden expression had it in her to plan and rob trains and banks, but she wasn't about to admit it. No problem. They had the men for the robberies, and they had her on the banknotes.

The *St. Louis Republic* reporter wrote, "Laura Bullion, who, like the majority of her sex, easily succumbed to the persuasive influence of the 'sweat box' after an all-day sledge, now plays only a minor part in the case" (p. 2). Like the female criminals before her, the media focus was first on perceptions of sex and then on her deeds.

Laura also freely admitted the man she was with, this Mr. J.W. Rose, was indeed Henry Longabaugh. He had lots of money when she met him last April in Ft. Worth, Texas, and even better, he was living and breathing. Her previous man, Bill Carver, was killed in Sonora last April. A girl has to survive, ya know.

Laura knew nothing about the train robbery, she told Detective Desmond. Why would she? When it comes to her men, she asks no questions. All she cares about is having money to survive. All she did was forge banknotes.

They suspected her of much more, but there was no proof. Chief of Detectives Desmond told the *New York Times*, "I would 'nt [*sic*] think helping to hold up a train was too much for her. She is cool, shows absolutely no fear, and in male attire would readily pass for a boy. She has a masculine face, and that would give her assurance in her disguise."[3] Another woman dressing and passing for a man was huge news decades before transgenderism became part of our everyday vernacular.

Laura received a sentence of up to five years in the Missouri State Penitentiary at Jefferson City. She served almost four, released in 1905. Laura and Ben Kirkpatrick kept in touch via letters. After her release, she told newspaper reporters that she was moving to Atlanta to be near him; Ben had been serving time in the Georgia city's federal prison. However, she had at least four other lovers while Ben continued to serve out his sentence; he was released in 1911—and shot dead during a botched robbery in 1912.

Laura Bullion moved to Memphis, Tennessee, in 1918. She left the

Laura Bullion after release from prison. She became a law-abiding citizen, dying in 1961 in Memphis, Tennessee. She was the last surviving member of "the Wild Bunch" (*The St. Louis Republic*, St. Louis, Missouri, September 21, 1905, p. 17, photographer not credited).

outlaw life for good, taking in work as a seamstress, a skill she most likely learned behind bars, for the Jennings Furniture Company. She changed her name to Freda Bullion Lincoln, aka "Mrs. Maurice Lincoln." This time, it was not to escape the law, only the lawless life. She told anyone who asked that she was a war widow. Her skillset improved to a dressmaker, interior designer, and drapery maker. Laura Bullion, who had one hell of a ride with "the Wild Bunch," died of heart disease on December 2, 1961, in Memphis, Tennessee. She was the last surviving member of the most famous gang of old west outlaws ever to rob banks and trains. Part of the epitaph on her grave marker reads, "The Thorny Rose." And that she was.

Part III

The Legends

7

J. Edgar Creates Monsters

Why the 20s Roared

Among the milestones in law enforcement's history, the decade of the 1920s is significant; it was the birth of organized crime in the United States and the era of "Public Enemy Number One."

There were several contributions to "the gangster era," or the period of organized crime in the United States.

First was prohibition. It began with the temperance movement, a religious-based idea that alcoholic beverages were the root cause of illegal and immoral behavior. After two failed attempts, Congress ratified the 18th Amendment on January 16, 1919, prohibiting "the manufacture, sale, or transportation of intoxicating liquors within, the importation thereof into, or the exportation thereof from the United States and all territory subject to the jurisdiction thereof for beverage purposes." The idea was to stop crime, or at least slow it down. The opposite came into effect: enter organized crime.

Criminals like gangster "Scarface" Al Capone made part of their mass fortunes in illegal booze. Prohibition gave us a whole new vocabulary: speakeasy, bootleg liquor, moonshine. The rumrunners souped up their jalopies to see who could race their jars of illegal alcohol to towns the fastest, giving birth to NASCAR. Everyone who manufactured it, carried and sold it could make a killing off liquor. Sometimes literally. A lot of spilled blood mixed with the booze.

Too many cops and politicians were on the take. Law enforcement has always been several steps behind society because humankind created a formal society before official law enforcement formed. Thus, the mobsters of the 1920s–1930s had faster cars and stolen guns that came from the armories, stored from battlefields of World War I, while cops drove mediocre cars and carried simple hardware. The 21st Amendment repealed the 18th Amendment on December 5, 1933. The 18th Amendment has been, at this writing, the only Amendment ever to have been abolished. So much for the government saving your soul by keeping you sober.

Better guns and faster cars meant bolder crimes, including kidnapping, professional albeit illegal gambling houses, drug trafficking, and bank robberies. The restricted jurisdictions of police departments, including the state lines, meant law enforcement had limited powers. Too many law enforcement officials, particularly in rural areas, were farmers and townspeople who were handed a badge and paid a small stipend. Enter a reformed Federal Bureau of Investigations—the FBI.

J. Edgar Hoover became director of the FBI in 1924, and he gave the federal law enforcement agency a complete overhaul. It included a strict hiring system, codes of conduct, formal training, and a national fingerprint database became part of the future crime lab. Hoover was also a master at public relations for his firm. If they couldn't catch the "famous" bad guys, they would settle for the petty criminals, using the press to create monsters from the mundane. In Hoover's press releases, frumpy, old women who helped hide their criminal adult children became vicious gang leaders. Scared teenaged girls were turned into gun molls. So when the "G-men" did capture these lesser-known crooks, it made for a splashy story and a coup for the new federal law enforcement agency.

Al Capone was the original "Public Enemy #1," a term used extensively during the 1930s. The "Public Enemy Era" is generally considered to be June 1934 to May 1936. Clyde Barrow and Bonnie Parker were on the list, as was "Ma" Barker. The Chairman of the Chicago Crime Commission, F.J. Loesch, coined the term "Public Enemy" in 1930: "I had the operating director of the Chicago Crime Commission bring before me a list of the outstanding hoodlums, known murderers, murderers which you and I know but can't prove, and there were about one hundred of them, and out of this list I selected twenty-eight men. I called them 'Public Enemies.'"[1]

To add to Americans' problems, the Great Depression began in 1929, and a worldwide economic downturn seemed to happen almost overnight. People who once strutted the best streets in the nicest clothes were selling their vehicles just to get cash for a meal. Folks from all walks of life stood in lines that trailed down city blocks for a chance of a menial day job. It was "the harshest adversity faced by Americans since the Civil War."

Industrial production fell close to 50 percent. Output and prices began to plummet. As a result, unemployment was close to 20 percent nationwide.

And it was international, creating a domino effect. "Virtually every industrialized country endured declines in wholesale prices of thirty percent or more between 1929 and 1933." Shantytowns grew up overnight, shacks tossed together with spare parts of wood and metal for the homeless. Hobos (an acronym for "homeless boy") caught rides on trains to travel cross-country to seek work or relief or anything to fill their stomach or fill their hope.

The stock market crashed in 1929. Next came the banks. There was a "banking panic": two in 1931 and one in 1932. The winter of 1933 saw the final wave of bank panics. One-fifth of the banks that were open in 1930 had closed by 1933.[2]

Some people turned to crime to just get the hell out of the dirty lives they were swirling in like a hopeless whirlpool. It was so difficult to look into the store window at fancy clothes or watch people who were unscathed by the harshness of hunger, eating in a restaurant, and not consider breaking the law. And big money, everyone knew, was in the banks—at least, the banks that hadn't closed down.

And to so many, the banks represented the government, the all-powerful being that had sucked the life out of Everyman and had taken his job, his house, and sometimes his very life. The banks represented big business, those corporations where the fat cats worked, living a lifestyle that 90 percent of the people who put their pennies and dollars in the accounts would never even see. The banks were nameless, faceless entities with stone and brick arms around big, metal boxes of unending bags of untraceable cash. That cash could buy a good time, a meal; that cash could make you a big shot, even if only for a little while.

Anyone robbing the bank could develop a Robin Hood persona: take from the rich; give to the poor. Give it to the big guys while helping yourself and your fellow man, too. (Clyde Barrow, one of the most famous outlaws of the era, developed such a persona despite most of his victims being law enforcement or small business owners just like his own family.)

Very few women made the lurid headlines during the gangster era as gangland leaders or hardnosed criminals. Instead, they were gun molls, hangers-on, or just women who loved their man and stood by him. And there were the women who claimed to love their man, but, when offered a good deal by the cops, snitched in a heartbeat, such as the infamous "lady in red" who helped catch John Dillinger in exchange for promises by the cops (promises not kept).

And there were families: the mothers and sisters, the womenfolk who refused to give up their boys and men living on the wrong end of the law. They knew it was only a matter of time before these guys would meet their destiny at the bullet's exit end of a gun, so better to get as much visiting time in while they could.

Too many times, the women were the recipients of the stolen wares. They dressed lavishly and ate fine food. Or of the illegal money paid for food on the family table and rent for one more month. Why turn in a cash cow for a paltry reward that, in reality, would probably not be paid out? With many law enforcement and the government officers making far less than gangsters, they could be easily bought off. (It is common knowledge Al Capone "owned" Chicago, even from jail.) Promise of a reward was suspicious, too; how was a bankrupt, corrupt city going to pay a big reward?

So, most of the hoodlums and gangsters continued to live the thug's life, and most of their women stood by them as companions and supporters, never actually taking part in the illegalities of robbing banks.

A few of these women would become legends thanks to the press and the media and an action-hungry public who needed escapism. Although they never actually committed the dangerous crimes of walking into the robberies or joining in the shoot-outs, their mythology remains. J. Edgar made sure the public was aware of what dangerous people they were, even when they weren't. Once again, a good yarn made for better entertainment than the truth: it sold more movie tickets, moved more papers, dime novelettes and magazines flew off the shelves. A woman stepping out of her role into a role totally unfamiliar, that of violence, made for a great, titillating read.

Two women's names stand out during this era of robbing banks. Bonnie Parker and "Ma" Barker are gangster era's crime legends. But, the truth is, neither ever robbed a bank, despite what legend tells.

8

Bonnie Parker

The Bank Robber's Darling

If there is a "Bank Robber's Darling," it has to be Bonnie Elizabeth Parker (October 1, 1910–May 23, 1934), the female half of the duo "Bonnie and Clyde [Barrow]." Sometimes they were labeled The "Barrow Gang," usually including Clyde and one or two male accomplices, either a relative or a friend.

Yet, she never robbed a bank. That is the stuff of legends and Hollywood.

Bonnie was born one of three children in Rowena, Texas, to Charles and Emma Parker. They had a good, steady income, were regular churchgoers, and the family was close knit. Charles's sudden death forced a move to a suburb of Dallas called Cement City to live with relatives. Reportedly this did not sit well with Emma, now forced to live and work in a lower socioeconomic lifestyle. But she had her three children to support, and Bonnie was the cutest. Bonnie was a curly-haired cotton top with big blue eyes, a sweet girl who could be mischievous, who loved to make others laugh. She was a favorite of many, and family members and grade school teachers loved to hug her and admire the adorable doll-like little girl.

But she could also be a scrapper. When some older girls stole pencils from her and her sister, Bonnie lay in wait after school and gave the girls what is called in Texas a "good whuppin.'"

She was a smart kid, a quick study who made good grades and won prizes for her writing, speaking presentations, and spelling. Bonnie walked away with the championship ribbon at a school spelling bee, proudly showing off her certificate.

Bonnie Parker was Clyde Barrow's true love, true crime's darling, but nobody's bank robber. She would wait in the getaway car or away from the robbery. This is the photograph she despised: "I don't smoke cigars!" (photograph seized in a police raid on April 13, 1933, in Joplin, Missouri).

Little boys were smitten with her dimples and charm, bringing apples and candy, little trinkets to woo this skinny tow-headed girl. According to a story told by her cousin and best friend, Bess, a little boy named Noel was Bonnie's favorite little "feller" until he crossed her. She followed him home from school, jumped him, and was beating on him mightily until adults intervened. "Bonnie had a piece of razor blade in her hand threatening to cut Noel's throat for him if he ever made her mad again, and he was fairly blubbering he was so scared."[1]

Her family recalls how Bonnie dreamed of being famous: an opera singer, perhaps. A movie star, like the ones in the picture shows that she loved to watch. She considered being a dancer, or a singer, a poet, a writer. Anything exciting to get her out of Cement City, Dallas, where, she penned in her diary, there was nothing to do, no one special to meet, and no promising jobs.

Bonnie grew to stand barely over five feet tall and never weighed more than 100 pounds. With her blonde curls, pretty eyes, and a sweet, natural charm, she was popular and fun to be around. Boys drew to her. One of those boys was Roy Thornton. Bonnie drew to Roy. In 1926, at 16, she dropped out of school to say "I do" and become his wife, much to her mother's chagrin. Bonnie even had his name tattooed on the inside of one thigh, which was so taboo for nice girls that it practically screamed, "Tramp!" They set up housekeeping a few blocks from Emma's home, but Bonnie's bouts of longing for her mother finally forced Roy to move them both in with Emma.[2]

Roy was in a tough crowd that Bonnie would eventually come to know well. It would include one Raymond Hamilton and a family with the last name of Barrow. It turned out that Roy was a professional thief, and he would disappear for weeks at a time. Then he would come waltzing in, and Bonnie would fall into his arms with kisses and hugs. But in January of 1929, after much sad diary entries and tears, Bonnie told Roy the marriage was over. It was the right timing because not much later cops nabbed Roy and sent him to Huntsville prison for a five-year stretch. Then Bonnie couldn't bear to file for a legal divorce, so she kept the marriage certificate and the ring.

While Bonnie worked as a waitress in a downtown Dallas café, she was the favorite of many a local, to include a few law enforcement officers who were later sworn to hunt her down, dead or alive. The café was near the courthouse, and law dogs with pistols on their hips frequented the café, eating stock southern favorites like eggs with white gravy and slurping down coffee while flirting with the cute blonde who could dish it out as much as she could take a good ribbing. "Pickin" they call it in Texas jargon.

Bonnie met Clyde Barrow (March 24, 1909–May 23, 1934) when introduced in 1930. She was out of work and helping a girl with a broken arm do household chores at the time. Her family described Bonnie as being "a nice girl" despite the fact their cotton-haired doll sported that tattoo, stayed married to a career criminal, and was familiar with some of Dallas' rowdy characters. She seemed to slip easily into a life of crime, as Clyde was already a seasoned petty criminal when they met. Within a month's time, she helped him escape from jail. That's when it really started, this criminal life she led.

Most of their robberies were from small grocery stores and gas stations, with Clyde pointing guns at the type of people that could have been their own families: salt-of-the-earth people who were trying to make a hardscrabble living during tough times. During most robberies, Bonnie was in the car, either behind the driver's seat ready for the getaway or in the passenger seat, for it was Clyde who was the master behind the wheel.

Despite the legends and claims from pulp dime novels, Bonnie never took part in any robberies except to sit and wait. She never stepped inside the bank to "case" the place; she never pointed a gun at anyone with the intent to rob them. Her name is forever attached to the name of Clyde Barrow, who was indeed a robber and a killer, but Bonnie never took a life. She was there because she loved Clyde. Perhaps it makes for a more romantic or thrilling story to place Bonnie Parker next to Clyde Barrow, shooting it out or pointing guns to demand money; it just did not happen.

Between 1932 to 1934, ten banks were known or suspected of being robbed by Clyde Barrow or "the Barrow Gang." Of those banks, they procured a little more than $46,000 in total.[3] Clyde, always the boss, ensured the money be split evenly between himself and Bonnie and whoever else was in on the job, usually at least two other men. The "gang" usually involved boyhood pal Raymond Hamilton, family friend teenager W.D. Jones, or friends Clyde met during his stint in the Texas prison system. Friends like Henry Methvin, who would turn rat and help lawmen catch Bonnie and Clyde, leading to their being drilled to pieces on a dusty Louisiana road.

From 1932 to 1934, Bonnie Parker and Clyde Barrow kept law enforcement on the run in the depression-era United States. The press and pulp magazines painted them as notorious and daring. In reality, they were petty, common criminals who killed police officers and innocent people, with Clyde behind the gun. Clyde was cruel; he shot first with his weapon, usually aimed at unarmed or unaware people. They lived in squalor continually on the road. In just a few months' time, stress and a 1933 car crash left Bonnie Parker spent and crippled. As evident of photographs, Bonnie lost her good looks; she had turned into a ragged woman looking far older than her years. Many witnesses reported her as a drunk. But she remained a spitfire.

She raised hell about one photo of her published in all the newspapers. It was one photo of many seized when police raided their rented apartment in Joplin, Missouri, in April 1933. During one playful picture-taking session with Clyde, Bonnie, and a few of the "gang," she improvised. Bonnie playfully posed with a gun and one of Clyde's cigars, foot on the front bumper of a stolen car, eyes squinting into the camera. Now it was all over the United States, and she officially became "the cigar-smoking gun moll." Never you mind about the dead and dying her lover and his cronies left in the dirt or the money they took from innocent people. Bonnie was pissed about the publication of that photo because she didn't smoke cigars.

Some historians see Bonnie Parker as a girl hopelessly in love with a man who adored her. Others pen her as a drunken sociopath who enjoyed the notoriety. Regardless, the two outlaws led a hardscrabble life until a hailstorm of bullets from a roadside posse cut them both down on May 23, 1934.

Their crime spree was short-lived compared to other infamous criminals, including the Barker gang, allegedly led by the notorious "Ma" Barker.

9

"Ma" Barker

J. Edgar's Gal

Then–FBI Director J. Edgar Hoover would call the dowdy, old woman "a veritable beast of prey." Barker gang member Harvey Bailey staunchly disagreed: "That old woman couldn't plan breakfast." Perhaps she was part of the inner circle of the bank-robbing gang, maybe not. Her last day on earth made FBI history, a shoot-out that left her dead. The law or the press never interviewed her.

She is usually listed as a bank robber in history books or part of a bank-robbing gang. Yet she never walked into a bank to rob anyone. Again the stuff of legends and Hollywood, fluffed up by J. Edgar himself.

Arizona Donnie Clark (October 8, 1873–January 16, 1935) was born into poverty in Ash Grove, Missouri. She left school at age ten. She loved to sing, and she could play the fiddle, but she also boasted an ill temper. "Arrie" was not a girl to be crossed.

A turning point in her young life was watching the outlaw Jesse James and his gang ride through her hometown. She watched how they sat tall astride their horses, their haughty expressions, how the townspeople seemed to shirk in fear but nod in respect. Immediately, Arrie decided she needed both an exit from the dirt-poor existence destined to drag her down and the adventures life could offer. There *had* to be a way out.[1]

Marriage to George Barker in 1892 and even changing her name to "Kate" soon revealed marriage was not the exit Arrie was seeking. George was quiet, soft-spoken, and not wealthy. Four sons named Herman, Lloyd, Arthur, and Fred quickly followed, and, as they grew, she refused to discipline them, raising a bunch of wild March hares and hooligans. George was a believer in hard work, discipline, and following the law. Too many times, he found himself alone in the age-old parental battle of "how to raise the children." And there was the question of his wife's loyalty: it seemed she was loyal to her children and not so devoted to her marriage.

Kate "Ma" Barker. She took part in bank robberies only by hiding the culprits and living off the spoils. FBI Director J. Edgar Hoover created a monster of the dowdy old woman (FBI Wanted poster, circa 1933).

The family moved to Tulsa, and George finally gave up the fight. Sleeping with one eye open can be exhausting. In 1928, he left the unruly bunch and their no-count, philandering mother. Good riddance to a bunch of ne'er-do-wells, he most likely muttered.[2]

The same year George Barker abandoned this wild bunch, his oldest son Herman was stopped by a police officer after Herman committed a robbery. Herman shot and killed the officer. A second officer shot Herman as he fled. Dying from the lethal shots, Herman put his gun to his temple and cried out, "Forgive me, Ma!" He squeezed the trigger and dropped dead.[3]

George Barker would eventually outlive his sons and even Ma. When the feds killed Ma and Fred in January 1935, their bodies were first displayed by the FBI as trophies and then lay unclaimed and stored until October. George, ever the nice guy, retrieved the bodies to have them laid to rest in Welch, Oklahoma, near Herman's grave.

Fred Barker would meet Alvin "Creepy" Karpis in prison, forming the Barker-Karpis Gang catalyst. Now here was the adventure Kate had been craving! Living vicariously through her boys and their criminal enterprise, Kate made excuses for her sons' criminal lifestyle and hid her precious boys as they wreaked havoc via robberies, kidnappings, theft, burglaries, and murders, leaving innocent people for dead across the country. Arizona Donnie blossomed into "Ma" Barker.

Ma became a wanted woman as she was aiding and abetting by hiding her boys and living off their ill-gotten gains. When the boys weren't in prison, she and her brood frequently moved under many aliases. She had a paramour for a short time until he had too much to drink and talked to strangers about the company he kept and their illegal enterprises. The poor man was found dead with several bullet holes in his torso. His murder was never solved, although it is generally believed one of her sons pulled the trigger. Some people think Ma assisted in disposing of the body. There is no doubt Ma Barker's sons were as loyal to her as she was to them.

But was she a thug? Alvin remembered she was "superstitious, gullible, simple, cantankerous, and … law-abiding." The Director of the FBI, J. Edgar Hoover, saw differently. "The most vicious, dangerous, and resourceful criminal brain of the last decade!"

Thanks to Hoover's descriptions, the public saw Ma Barker as a hellcat protecting her devilish kittens. Was it Hoover's excuse to kill a "notorious" gangster? A way to gain press for the new FBI? Whatever the reason, J. Edgar hated that old bat with her squinty eyes and big nose. And he swore he'd have her head as a trophy.

Some of the gang, when later apprehended, swore they'd press coins into Ma's rough palm and send her off to see a picture show while the robberies went down so she would have no hand in them. Perhaps they were protecting the woman who protected them. Loyalty ran thick in Ma Barker's house.

Alvin "Creepy" Karpis would later share his impression of Ma Barker: "[She was] an old-fashioned homebody from the Ozarks. The most ridiculous story in the annals of crime is that Ma Barker was the mastermind behind the Karpis-Barker gang.… She wasn't a leader of criminals or even a criminal herself. There is not one police photograph of her or set of fingerprints taken while she was alive … she knew we were criminals, but her participation in our careers was limited to one function: when we traveled together, we moved as a mother and her sons. What could look more innocent?"[4]

Harvey "Old Harv" Bailey, sometimes called "the Gentleman Bank Robber," was in on the Fort Scott, Kansas, bank robbery with the Barker gang in June 1932. He would later insist Ma had nothing to do with any of the bank robberies. "When we'd sit down to plan a bank job, she'd go into the other room and listen to 'Amos and Andy' or hillbilly music on the radio. She just went along with Freddie [Barker] because she had no choice. Freddie loved his mother and wouldn't leave her to fend for herself."[5]

Some historians argue Kate "Ma" Barker was part of the planning of the June 17, 1932, robbery of the Fort Scott, Kansas, bank. While other criminologists argue her only role was to hide her precious boys and the loot. What is a fact is the gang hid at her apartment at 4804 Jefferson Street, Kansas City, Missouri. Nonetheless, she stayed on the Most Wanted registry, and J. Edgar Hoover was slavering to cross her off the list.

On March 29, 1932, Fred, Alvin, and three male gang members robbed the bank, snagging over $250,000 in cash and bonds.

April 4, 1933, marked the next bank robbery; this time, it was the Fairbury National Bank in Fairbury, Nebraska. While Ma probably had no hand in this planning, again, she most certainly lived off the spoils of the robbery.

Arthur was paroled in September 1932 and quickly joined his brothers and mother. The boys plotted another bank robbery for December, but, drunk with the March 29 robbery's success, they were sloppy. This time they hit the Third Northwestern National Bank in Minneapolis. A violent and bloody shoot-out with the cops ensued, and J. Edgar labeled them the most vicious gang in America.

On January 8, 1935, agents raided two of the gang's hideouts in Chicago. In one of the hideouts, they found a Florida map with the Ocala area circled. Then one of the gang snitched: Ma and Fred were living in a lake house somewhere in Florida.

The line cast, it was time to reel it in.

It didn't take long to locate Ma and Fred in a house in Ocklawaha, Florida. The FBI surrounded the house on January 16, 1935.

An FBI agent put a bullhorn to his mouth. He called out for the Barkers, ordering them to surrender.

Silence.

What became the most prolonged gun battle in the FBI's history began as tear gas canisters smashed into the windows. A barrage of machine-gun fire from Fred's gun was the reply. In four hours hundreds of bullets were spent back and forth, with the FBI running out of ammunition after discharging 1,500 shots into the lake house.

And then, finally, silence again.

The house was quiet as a morgue. Agents dared to creep into the building, weapons at the ready, nervous fingers jiggling the triggers of their guns.

Fred was full of lead in an upstairs bedroom. Ma, a machine gun at her feet and a single bullet hole in her body, was gone. So was a gangster legend.

10

Estella Dickson

"(Not So) Sure Shot Stella"

If it wouldn't have been for that loudmouthed social worker, Estella Mae Redenbaugh was probably fuming to herself, *I wouldn't be in this damned predicament in the first place....*

But here she was, on a train to Los Angeles, California, through no fault of her own, saying goodbye to her hometown of Topeka, Kansas, and her childhood. In her purse, Estella had a $35 check stolen from her mother. The calendar read April 1938. She was 15 years old.

"Stella," as her friends knew her, was an average teen who loved to hang out with friends. She lived with her mother, whom she adored, and a distant stepfather. She was trying to get a sense of normalcy like her other pals: styling her pretty, thick, blonde hair, giggling about boys, like the nice fellow she met at the skating rink, a guy who introduced himself as Johnny O'Malley that June of 1937.

Stella was a petite, pretty girl at 5' 3" and just over 110 pounds. Her hair tumbled to her shoulders. Her high cheekbones shone when she smiled. Stella could tell Johnny liked her. He was handsome, with a triangular face, bright, blue eyes, and dark hair shaved short in the back and parted on the side, a popular style. Johnny had a delightful, goofy smile. He could match her quick wit, was a gentleman, and educated. He was 26 years old. Despite the decade between them, they dated for a time.

Stella loved the skating rink; it was one of the few places in town kids her age could hang out and talk and laugh. But it was after a night at the rink in October 1937 when Stella's life began to spin out of control.

She had been walking home with her friend Mary Robinson when

WATCH YOUR CREDIT LINE: PHOTO FROM WIDE WORLD:

901573-NAMED PUBLIC ENEMIES BY G-MEN.

WASHINGTON, D.C.-PHOTO SHOWS ESTELLE DICKSON, 17, AND HER HUSBAND, BENNY DICKSON, WHO WERE NAMED AS "PUBLIC ENEMIES" BY DETROIT FEDERAL AGENTS WHO ARE SEEKING BOTH OF THEM FOR BANK ROBBERIES AND A KIDNAPING.

D-11/30/38

A 1937 photograph of Estella Dickson, 17, along with her husband, Ben, in a flyer sent to banks from the FBI. The flyer was sent to warn banks that this robbing duo was on the loose (FBI files).

they were offered a ride from a guy the girls thought they knew. But once in the car, they realized he was a stranger. Well, he seemed safe, as he was kind and polite, dropping Mary off safely at the Robinson house. But he drove Stella out past city limits. He tried to get fresh with her, so Stella slapped him, and he beat her until she passed out, and then he raped her. Then he drove back to the city limits and dumped her off on the edge of town, dumped her out like an unwanted dog, and she was so humiliated and scared she told no one.

Eventually, she had to confide in her mother, who took her to a clinic. Stella had contacted a case of gonorrhea from her rapist. The current medical treatment for gonorrhea was so excruciating. The medical staff had not even told her why they inserted harsh chemicals via catheters and hot probes into her rectal and vaginal cavities for hours. She had always been a spunky girl, so when she told them she was no longer going to tolerate that painful, humiliating process, they labeled her "incorrigible," "resentful," and "sullen" and sent her off to the State Industrial School, Lansing, Kansas.[1]

The social worker who took Stella's case could not keep her mouth shut, so the news spread quickly through the town of Stella's predicament and the venereal disease. Everyone told one another that only sluts contracted VD. So there went her previously stellar reputation. The social workers didn't deny the rumors. Strange looks, snarky, whispered comments, and outright glares followed her wherever she went; rooms fell strangely silent whenever she entered. Soon it went around the school that she was a nasty slut. (What did she *do* to entice a stranger into the woods, exactly?) Stella decided if she didn't get out of there, she would kill herself or die. One night she stole a check from her mother, packed her bags, and headed for the land of promise. California, here I come!

Enter Johnny O'Malley back into her life. Enter a life of new problems.

It is unknown if they made plans to meet in California or if it was happenstance. When Stella arrived, she stayed with her old friend Mary Robinson. Johnny was with another woman, but it didn't last once Stella came to town.

"Johnny" would eventually come clean and spill his guts to Stella. Johnny, true name Ben Dickson, was also from Topeka, Kansas, and he, too, was fleeing. The son of a father who was a high school chemistry teacher, Ben was an amateur boxer and high school student when a teenaged prank had landed him in court with a judge who evidently decided teenage hanky-panky was the problem of the world today and ruled with an iron fist. He sentenced Ben to prison time. From there on, Ben had a granite chip on his shoulder and an attitude to match. When he left prison, he also had a pocketful of ideas on making money without a day's work. The tough criminals behind the walls had taught him well. Ben popped in and out of the prison's revolving door, each time promising his family he would make them proud *this* time. He would start college courses, try to get an honest job, and his father would send Ben books and assign him work. According to Ben, either the system or the cops would keep him down, so he finally lit out of town after punching a city employee in the nose over a stupid argument.

In Ben, Stella must have found a soul mate. She called him "Johnny" until the day she died. They tied the knot on August 3 and honeymooned at Ben's family cabin in Lake Preston, South Dakota. They had love, but they didn't have money. And you can't live on love.

Ben had already served time for bank robbery. That was where the money was—perhaps he decided he had learned from past mistakes that had landed him in the big house.

On Thursday, August 25, 1938, a dirty 1936 Ford pulled up in front of the Elkton Corn Exchange Bank in Elkton, South Dakota. It was 2 p.m. A pretty, young lady got out of the passenger seat. She wore a big, floppy hat, sunglasses, and men's coveralls. She looked like she had just hopped off a train outrunning the dust bowl. She carried a newspaper, wrapped loosely and tied with string. No one could see that inside the newspaper was a long-barreled .38 caliber revolver.

A handsome young man stepped out of the driver's seat. His clothing was shabby, but at around 2:15 p.m., he sauntered into the Elkton Corn Exchange Bank. Once inside, he pulled a gun on two employees. "This is a holdup. How much money is in the bank?"[2] Unfortunately for him, he was too early for a robbery: the bank's time lock safe was not yet open.

Well, when was it scheduled to open?

Around 3 p.m., employees advised.

Time lock safes were purposely invented to deter crime. Specifically, they were to prevent bank robberies. They also kept thieves from kidnapping or taking hostages, forcing the hostages to give up the combinations through threat or fear. Mounted on the inside of the safe door, the locks will not open until a time preset by the bank officials. Even if the bank employees use the exterior combination lock on the safe, the safe remains closed until the time lock opens on the set time.

Well, thanks to this ingenious measure of prevention, the robbery was delayed for 30 minutes or so. While he waited, Ben Dickson allowed about 20 people to come into the bank to do their day's business. He just did not let them leave. Ben forced male customers and staff to walk around behind the tellers' windows and then sit on the floor. Women were allowed to sit in the lobby. As the hostages walked to the teller's window, he demanded to see their account balances. If they had more money than Ben felt they needed, he helped himself to part of their account. If they did not, he left them alone. It was the Depression. Folks had to have a little money.

One person dropped a $20 bill. Ben scooped it up and handed it to the customer. Ben was not wholly dishonest.

One of the people who came in was a pretty, poorly dressed girl who carried a package wrapped in newspaper. Now Ben was pissed off. Stella's one job was to stand outside and be a lookout! She became worried about him, she would later explain, so she wandered into the bank to make sure he was okay.

But for now, he maintained their cover. Acting as if Stella were a stranger, he told her to stay in the lobby.

The bank president came strolling in, and he, too, was asked to step aside with the customers.

When the time lock finally clicked on to allow access, Ben cleaned out the vault and then forced the people into the vault, one by one. When a man tried to enter the vault before a female, Ben became irate and shoved him aside, telling the man to mind his manners. Ladies first!

The pretty girl in the big hat did not go into the vault. This was when one hostage realized the woman was part of the robbery.

Ben locked them all in, but he did not close the main door that rendered the vault airtight. He wanted them all to get out alive and breathing.

And then Ben and Stella fled. This time he didn't hand back any of the money. They were $2,187.64 richer.

Later, he bought Stella a 16th birthday gift, and they used some of the ill-gotten gains to get the hell out of South Dakota. They made sure they drove the speed limit on a route decided beforehand. They stayed at a Minnesota farm where Ben buried some of the money, then moved to Stella's mother's home to enjoy the Kansas state fair. Ben and Stella often mingled with law enforcement officers, who would report neither was nervous or acted suspiciously.

Later, in the local papers, they would be described as a "handsome young couple." But right now, it was 8:30 in the morning on Monday,

October 31, 1938. Ben and Stella were in Brookings, South Dakota. It was the Northwestern Security National Bank that was about to fund the young couple's lifestyle.

They parked the dark-color Buick near the bank entrance.

Witnesses would later remark on how well dressed the robbers were. Ben had donned a double-breasted gray Herringbone suit with a brown hat and glasses. He could have been mistaken for a lawyer or a banker. Stella wore an aqua dress; over that, she had a salmon-colored coat. Initially, they were a fine sight to folks on a Monday morning.

At 9 a.m., the assistant manager was opening the Northwestern Security National Bank for the day when Ben came up behind him and forced him, at gunpoint, to continue with his task.

This time, Stella entered the bank shortly after Ben. Witnesses would later recall the pretty girl as nervous; she paced the room, biting her lower lip and glancing out of the front windows. She carried her newspaper-wrapped package again, but this time her hand was in the package; her finger was on the trigger.

Ben motioned to the employees and told Stella to keep an eye on them.

Ben must have been surprised when—again—he was told the bank's time lock safe was not yet open. It would be almost three hours' wait this time.

So the "handsome young couple" worked to blend in amongst the 100 plus customers who walked in and out of the bank, making sure the bank employees didn't try any funny business.

Stella paced the lobby, her fingers working the wrapped newspaper. The package occasionally shifted from under one arm to the next; she would sit down in one of the lobby chairs, one slender leg crossed gracefully over another. Stella watched several people closely, and if she thought they bore close watching, she would get up to stand in line behind them to observe their transaction at the teller's window.

Ben, however, was in his element. He sat back in his chair, quietly observing the transactions over the bank manager's shoulder. No one suspected this handsome man in the lovely, double-breasted suit was waiting for the safe's time lock to click open so he and the nervous girl in the lobby could make a haul at the expense of Northwestern Security National.

The time lock finally opened at 11 a.m. Ben produced four pillowcases, which he doubled into two, and the duo forced two bank employees to scoop up $17,593 in cash to place in the pillowcases. The haul included many coins from the tellers' drawers, more than $16,000 in securities, including "stock certificates from Standard Oil, J.C. Penney, Sears Roebuck, and Chrysler."[3]

The pillowcases weighed at least 80 pounds each, and Ben made the bank employees carry them out to the robbers' waiting cars. Struggling bank employees managed to lift and shove the bags and get them into the robbers' dark-color Buick. After much exertion, the bags went into the car.

Ben made the bank employees stand on the getaway car's running boards to build a human shield. He drove for a few blocks then ordered the men to jump. As he and Stella took off, the employees began shouting for help. The last thing they saw was Stella's broad smile and her friendly goodbye wave. A few miles ahead, she would dump a box of nails out of the window into the road should they be followed.

Cross-country travels led the couple to both run from the law and visit tourist attractions, as evidenced by what they left behind in abandoned vehicles. Ben left some of his books. From what officers discovered, he also liked to write.

They took three men hostage to garner time during one escape, which resulted in kidnapping charges. They became Public Enemies on the FBI list. J. Edgar was shrieking. These were vicious, cunning, evil, and cruel people, he warned the public. Murderers. And Estella Mae Redenbaugh Dickson was just as wicked as her male counterpart. Hoover's G-men went to interview and harass Ben and Stella's family and friends so often that certain loved ones finally told the officers that even if they knew anything, the FBI would be the last ones they would tell. They were sick of the fake news stories that the FBI was releasing, via newspapers, radio, and even pulp dime-store comic books, that little Stella and sweet Ben were bloodthirsty killers.

Ben's history revealed he was not a killer. On November 24, 1938, Ben, Stella, and a family friend were surrounded by law enforcement at a tourist camp. One of the surrounding cops shouted at Ben to give up as the trio emerged from their room. Then 48 rounds were dispersed by the officers, placing Stella, the friend, and any innocent person within range in danger. Ben was armed, but instead of returning fire, he fled. Stella also outran the cops, hiding under a bridge for 24 hours.

Stella shot at a police car during another pursuit, but Ben had told her to shoot only at the engine lest she hurt someone. For this, she received a grazed forehead by a policeman's bullet and carried the scar until death. Still, the media dubbed her "Sure Shot Stella." They were not privy to the day when Stella, not checking the safety of a gun, accidentally shot a hole in the roof of their car and probably left the occupants' ears ringing.

Both families adored their in-laws. Ben did not drink, smoke, or swear; he was educated and treated Stella like a queen. Stella was a pretty "city girl" with shy, quiet ways. The FBI tapped the Redenbaugh and the Dickson family phones; the families' mail was intercepted (perfectly legal during this time). Because of Ben's mama's frail mental and physical health, the family never told her about Ben's predicament, believing it would kill her with worry. They all knew the end was coming soon. Look what happened to Bonnie Parker and Clyde Barrow.

In December 1939, Ben and Stella rented an apartment in New Orleans, Louisiana, but the FBI was breathing down their necks, so the Big Easy was not so easy. Still, Ben had penned Stella a poem:

> In the eyes of men I am not just
> But in your eyes, O life, I see justification
> You have taught me that my path is right
> if I am true to you[4]

But the path of this just man ended in April 1939 in the Forest Park section of St. Louis, Missouri.

Working with several informants, the FBI arranged an intricate setup meeting with a woman Ben knew and trusted. They prepared for the woman to have Ben meet her. The woman obeyed, and she set up the meeting for April 6, 1939, at a hamburger stand.

Ben and Stella arrived in the area at about 7 p.m., with Ben parking nearby and Stella waiting in the car. FBI agents were secreted and also sat overtly in plain clothes stationed around him and the informant. Finished with the meeting, Ben exited the hamburger stand to walk down the sidewalk. FBI agents surrounded him, ordering him to stop. Ben tried to get away via a door next to the shop, but one agent fired twice, plugging him in the back and side. Only then did the FBI agents have their snitch identify the body as that of Ben Dickson. The FBI's official report would have Ben drawing his pistols and pointing them at the agents, forcing them to shoot. The record did not note how there were no guns near Ben's body until the ambulance transported it to the morgue. Two pistols miraculously appeared on his still chest.

So no one noticed Stella as she drove past. And she kept driving.

Stella hired a professional driver to take her to Topeka, back to the safe arms of her dear mother. She almost made it. The driver snitched her out, and the FBI picked her up. In their report, the agents noted Stella's possessions: $70 in cash, three rings to include her wedding set with seven diamonds, a key to the couple's New Orleans' apartment, and Ben's poem. An exhausted, 90-pound Stella told them she just wanted to get home to her mama.

Stella was taken to South Dakota to stand trial. By her attorney's suggestion, she was clutching a doll through the proceedings. The 16-year-old widow must have tugged at the prosecution's heartstrings because there was a suggestion that coverture be applied to her case. This meant that Stella was directly under the influence and protection of her husband, thus had no power or control over the couple's activity, legal or otherwise. The man was the king of his castle—and apparently, of the banks they robbed.

Stella pled guilty to two counts of bank robbery in the federal district court in Deadwood, South Dakota, on August 21, 1939, before U.S. District Judge Lee A. Wyman.

But, like Ma Barker before her, Estella Dickson was not about to receive special treatment; she was a hellcat and criminal scum, according to J. Edgar Hoover, and he demanded she was to be sentenced as such, regardless if she held a doll or wore a brassiere. Under the watchful eyes and political pressure of Hoover, Judge Wyman stared at little Stella from his dais and sentenced her to two concurrent ten-year sentences, served in a West Virginia federal prison. Happy 17th birthday!

A battery of testing through the prison system included an I.Q. test, which revealed Stella's score of 121. She was bright, but she was keeping to herself. She trusted absolutely no one. She preferred her own company to anyone else's. She did not like groups, and she did not make friends. She seemed to light up only when discussing her short but dangerous days with Ben Dickson.

To prison staff, Estella was living on dreams. Estella and Ben Dickson were the last of the big-time 1930s outlaw gangsters to fill the lurid headlines. Estella would read about the outbreak of World War II in newspapers, about J. Edgar Hoover's FBI and how their focus had shifted from the 1930s' gangster era to a time of war spies and criminals: "G-men" were broadcast as professional, honest, out to make the United States a safe place for families. Thanks to excellent public relations, the FBI were trustworthy public service agents who could sniff out and take down crooks, commies, and thugs with their unique training and top-of-the-line equipment. *Yeah*, Estella probably thought bitterly from her prison cell, *I can tell you all about that.*

Estella Mae Redenbaugh Dickson walked out of prison at 24 years of age in 1946. She found work as a flight attendant, then took the helm of a register at America's discount store: Kmart. Stella was a union activist, proud she had worked to unionize grocery checkers at one of her jobs. She lived in Kansas, caring for her disabled brother. There were two more marriages, but they did not last because neither of them was Ben Dickson. No man could ever measure up.

A comic book appeared on news stands in November 1947. The title blazed

"Stella Mae Dickson: The Bobby Sox Bandit Queen."

There was a sketch of a curvaceous Stella, a pistol in each hand, threatening a "bullet between the eyes" of any bank employee or customer who dared try to stop the robbery.[5]

Stella now lived a quiet life, far from her past, except for receiving a presidential pardon from Nixon. Her biggest loves were her dogs and her family. But her story was still far from over.

Despite a life of working minimum wage jobs, she always had money. She took care of her family, bought and sold houses, and her mother and brother wanted for nothing. When she died on September 10, 1995, she left an estate of $77,000. She willed $5,000 to an animal charity and $5,000 to a neighbor.

Money, in Stella Dickson's later life, was not an issue. And she never explained how that came to be....

Part IV

Rosie the Riveter Robs a Bank

11

World War II, a Turning Point

Gun Girls, Child Brides, and Show Girls

She is not an actual person. In art, she appears as a white woman because, when she was invented, women of color did not star in such campaigns.

She is a cultural icon who began representing the new working force that sprang from the American households in World War II: the working woman. Her name is "Rosie the Riveter," and she is the subject of songs, advertising, government posters, and a movie. A 1942 poster featuring a woman in blue factory coveralls and red bandana flexing her arm to the slogan "We Can Do It!" was erroneously labeled a "Rosie" image. Norman Rockwell's "Rosie" graced a 1943 *Saturday Evening Post* cover. Whoever she was, wherever she appeared, she inspired women to untie the apron strings and don working coveralls, military uniforms, factory hardhats, and do their part to help win the war.

The Second World War's official start is September 1, 1939, when Germany invaded Poland. Japan was already at war with China to dominate the Pacific and Asia. World War II was a global war lasting from 1939 to 1945 and involved most of the world's countries, which meant more than 100,000,000 people in more than 30 countries would be affected. It cost 50,000,000 to 85,000,000 fatalities, including an estimated 20,000,000 military personnel, and was marked by mass genocide to include the Holocaust.

On December 8, 1941, an Army nurse was enjoying a leisurely walk near Hawaii's Tripler Hospital. She heard the hum of a low-flying plane and looked up to see the aircraft cruising towards her, and she tracked it as it flew overhead. The pilot waved at her, and she waved back. Then the pilot swooped around to drop bombs and obliterate U.S. battleships and aircraft nearby.

Unwittingly, the nurse had waved at one of 353 Japanese torpedo and dive-bomber planes seconds before they began bombing Pearl Harbor. An estimated 2,335 people lost their lives that day, including more than 2,000 navel men. Patients arrived at Tripler Hospital so quickly, nurses were marking the wounded's foreheads with lipstick to assist triage.[1]

Downtown Honolulu hosted a notorious area where "nice people" avoided the streets. One of those streets was Hotel; on Hotel, a person could find prostitutes of all shapes, sizes, and colors who would do anything for pay. After the attack, and without compensation, the ladies of the night became ladies of rescue. They lined up to donate blood. They assisted medical personnel with cleaning and washing. The prostitutes turned one brothel into a makeshift hospital. The prostitutes held hands and cried with the dying and whispered kind words to survivors. Even after the gallons of donated blood, the sleepless weeks of giving time and energy, and tears and prayers with the dead and wounded, the "Women of Hotel Street" were never formally recognized except for a mention, years later, by the Pearl Harbor Visitor's Bureau. A website recognition states, "When the attack was over, the prostitutes of Hotel Street organized themselves into an unexpected relief effort, becoming some of the first providers of assistance."[2] (Note they are labeled as prostitutes first, then as volunteers.)

With Pearl Harbor, America officially entered the war. More than 15,000 military personnel headed off to fight.

"Although women have served in military conflicts since the American Revolution, World War II was the first time women served in the United States military in an official capacity." Three hundred fifty thousand women proudly donned uniforms in three segregated branches of service: Women's Army Auxiliary Corps, Women's Air Force Service Pilots, and the Women Accepted for Volunteer Military Service. Seventy percent of women held "traditional" jobs, such as office positions and medical corps.[3]

There were strict rules. Enlisted women had to be single; the minute the ring slipped onto that left hand, they slipped off the armed force's payroll. That rule changed in 1943. Still, a woman could not be both a mother and in the military. On the home front, jobs were considered important, for besides maintaining critical communications and running offices, they freed positions so males could fight overseas.

Military operations included both the advancement of research on the home front and targeting enemy research. Besides ships, vehicles, and tanks, weapons would now incorporate chemical and biological warfare. Rocketry would advance with the discovery of new automatic aircraft and the atomic bomb. World War II was historically the only wartime use of nuclear weapons.

The way of life was changing globally, causing a trickle-down effect. The social structures and political alignments forever changed across continents. Economic systems rose and fell. Entire cities and villages either disappeared, were crippled in population, or populations soared due to women moving from rural areas to the cities for better-paying jobs. Technology took a giant leap forward, and wars advanced from this time forward.

By the end of the war, some 7,000,000 women had become "Rosie the Riveter" by entering the workforce to keep their homes running and keep the factories and businesses in business. Women quickly took over positions previously closed to the "fairer sex." At the same time, women organized home front initiatives such as drives, fundraising, and conservation efforts. Many women were learning the role of wife, mother, and homemaker was not the sole option in life. And the paycheck in the bank spoke volumes. A woman's salary was not the same wage as a man would have earned in the same position but was far better than "traditional" women's jobs.

Thus, "war work" not only helped the home front, but it paid well. Women built and tested planes, worked in munitions plants, spied on the enemy, inspected artillery, worked sheet metal, lathes, gears, and engines and were chemical analysts to keep their soldiers safe and strong overseas. Many had never stepped foot outside a home to earn a wage. Women of color, "older" women (in this case, over the age of 35), newlyweds who said "I do" and then said "goodbye" to their soldiers, all worked side by side.

On September 2, 1945, Japan was the last to surrender, and the deadliest conflict in human history came to an end. The American soldiers would be coming home. However, they were coming back to a whole new era. When many soldiers came home expecting the wife to cook the meals, clean the house, raise the kids, and wait on them, they found that their wives had discovered new roles. Surveys and polls proved that women wanted to stay in the workplace. Women had found independence and confidence through the crisis that forced them into a traditionally male role. "Their wartime experiences combined with collective memory not only affected their daughters, sisters, and friends directly but also reinforced the deep foundations of the equality crusades … that would take center stage in the postwar generations."[4]

For the women who stayed at home with their men, life often turned into a new war—at home. There were few social services for veterans, few mental health services. Men were expected to come home after experiencing battle, pick up their lives, and move on as if a war was only a short, painful experience. A study of the physical and mental health cost of traumatic war experiences found "strong relations between traumatic exposure (e.g., witnessing a larger percentage of company death), comorbid disease, mental health ailments, and early death."[5] More than 1,000,000 of the 8,000,000 American servicemen "were discharged for combat-related neuroses … in 1945, 10,000 returning veterans per month develop[ed] some kind of psychoneurotic disorder … [in 1944] there were more than 300,000 of them and with fewer than 3,000 American psychiatrists and only 30 V.A. neuropsychiatric hospitals" available. By 1946, America had its highest divorce rate in history (until 1972).[6] Post-traumatic stress disorder (PTSD) didn't have a formal name then. Men traditionally had to be tough and not cry or talk about being afraid. The bottle helped. Drugs did, too. And rages were prevalent with PTSD.

There were no escape paths for these women by way of battered women's shelters. "Domestic violence" was not spoken of in public, meaning outside the home. A man's home was his castle. To escape the walls, one had to have cash. That was hard to do when the king controlled the money chest.

Women were tentatively learning they could work the same jobs as men. They were also learning they could commit violent crimes. This included bank robbery. Banks remained the source of much cash made quickly now when a person wanted to escape a home of brutality or drudgery and needed the funds.

Still, these female bank robbers remained "girls." The media gave them these childish monikers. Much press ink was still dedicated to debating the female robber's hair color, detailing the clothing they wore, their physical attributes. These criminals had monikers like "gun girl," "child bride," "show girl" and "woman robber." Apparently, in too many opinions, even when waving a weapon or threatening to detonate an explosive, women remained those delicate, silly gals who did foolish things.

The tellers who faced these bank robbers probably disagreed.

12

Opal Dixon

The Brunette with a Syringe

The Des Moines campfire girls troop was about to get a treat as they settled in the district courtroom to observe the proceedings on Saturday, January 25, 1947. The girls squished into the wooden benches along with the rest of the crowd who came to watch this specific high-profile case. Not only had the robber struck twice, but she was a female. Her name was Opal Dixon, and she was here on an arraignment—for bank robbery.

Thirty-five-year-old Opal Dixon, dressed smartly in a long-sleeved white blouse, gray striped skirt, and gray fur coat, was accompanied by Deputy Sheriff Bess McIntyre. They sat at the defense table. The courtroom door opened, and heads turned to watch attorney Milton Strickler stride down the aisle and through the bar to speak with the defendant. He had a message from a man at the Hotel Cargill. They whispered back and forth.

Opal was more worried about her husband's release from jail than what the next hour held for her future. "I don't want him out and around the girl," she said, referring to her husband and teenage daughter. "I hope they keep him locked up for a while."[1]

She told her story to the *Des Moines Register*, speaking sotto voce. "If I had gotten by with that job," she said of the bank robbery, "my family would be eating nice juicy steaks today," she sighed. "I'm a nursemaid with a headache now. I'm sorry it all happened." Then she told the reporters that she was a nurse, and she had been working at a hospital. So why did she rob banks? "You won't believe this but, just before I robbed that bank in St. Louis, I had a dream. I dreamed I had a lot of money. Maybe that's what gave me the inspiration."

The *Des Moines Register*, referring to Opal as an "attractive, 35-year-old brunette ... small, raven-haired woman" also quoted her as saying, "I wouldn't advise any woman to take up bank robbing."[2] Opal's story made headlines on the front page, reducing the infamous mobster Al Capone's life-threatening stroke to two short paragraphs.

In 1947, Opal Dixon robbed two banks. She used a strange weapon, claiming it was an explosive. An all-female jury cried when they sentenced her (Des Moines Police Department mug shot, 1947).

The county attorney must have had an inspiration, too, because their office's information was filed against Opal. This served as a grand jury indictment, their purpose to speed up proceedings.

Court was called to order. District Judge Russell Jordan would be presiding over the hearing. Once he took his seat, the room was inevitably full of shifting bodies and feet sliding on the floor as everyone sat.

Judge Jordan reminded Opal Dixon why she was there: Dixon had walked into the Des Moines Bank & Trust Company on the prior Wednesday, January 22, and walked out with $2,950 of the bank's money. Despite her trying to dump the cash, cops apprehended Dixon less than an hour after leaving the bank. And when caught, she admitted to also robbing the United Bank and Trust Company in St. Louis of

$582. The Des Moines campfire girl troop, and the adults in attendance for this Saturday morning saga, listened as District Judge Russell Jordan charged Dixon with "Intent to Rob."

Judge Jordan told Dixon she had until Tuesday, January 28, to enter a plea. Her bond was not going to change, so she would be figuring out her future from behind bars.

The formalities over, Deputy Sheriff McIntyre prepared to escort Opal back to the Polk County Jail when two lovely young women rushed over to see her. "My oldest daughter, Mrs. Louise Asjuin," Opal pointed out one of the girls to McIntyre. "She's 18. Please, can we have just a minute?" McIntyre relented. Jewell, her youngest daughter at 16, joined in.

They took seats in the gallery now, as the crowd was filing out. The girls each had one of Opal's arms. "We have an attorney for you," her daughter told her. "His name is C.A. Lingenfelter!" They told her he was there with them, waiting outside.

"Do you need anything?" one of the girls asked.

Opal indicated her clothes. "I need a change. This is the outfit I was arrested in." The girls promised they would bring her clothes to the jail.

Deputy Sheriff McIntyre finally told Opal that she had to go. Opal hugged and kissed the girls, pulling them tight against her. Then she stood, adjusted her fur coat, and walked out with the deputy sheriff.

Opal Dixon did not consider her options for long. On the same day, and while behind bars, she decided she would go to trial.

Sitting behind bars gives a lady time to think. And Opal probably did a lot of thinking, to include just what brought her there.

The Dixons had been living at the Hotel Cargill. Opal would leave her husband for months at a time, he would later tell a detective.

Unhappy with married life, Opal knew she needed a good chunk of money to start over. Women just couldn't up and leave. How would she support herself? She had to have money—a nice nest egg to feather the future nest.

On January 22, Opal had her "inspiration," she would tell a newspaper reporter. She was strolling past a Kreage Five and Dime store in the busy downtown of Des Moines. "I went inside and purchased the syringe and some Listerine. And, I walked straight up to the bank and did it."[3]

"It" meant Opal Dixon walked "straight up" into the Des Moines

National Bank and Trust company. She stood in line, demure, like just another customer, a manila folder tucked under one arm. She wore a white blouse with a big, loopy bow at the throat, a gray striped skirt, and a gray fur coat. Then, at 1:20 p.m., when it was her turn to speak with the teller, the woman came alive. She stepped up to teller Rex C. Cisco.

Unbeknownst to Opal, as she stepped up to Rex Cisco's window, Deputy Sheriff Sid Craiger was stepping away. He was not in uniform. He would later tell the bank president that he could not take action during the robbery because "he was powerless without his gun."

When Rex Cisco looked up to greet the woman customer, smiling at her, she began yelling at the bank employees and the customers. "This is a stickup! Don't anybody move—this place is covered!" She pulled the syringe from the envelope and waved it over her head. "I have enough stuff in here to blow the place to pieces, and I'll go through with it! I mean business." She tossed the envelope, and it slid coolly across the marble counter at Rex Cisco as she told him to fill it up with cash, and dawdling was not in his best interest. He pulled the envelope through the slot under the security cage.

Petrified, Rex Cisco stuffed money into the envelope while Opal took a step away to glare at the customers. She was holding the syringe like a dart, and she was reminding everyone that she had no qualms about sending them all to meet their maker. "Capone is going to take care of us! You're all covered. So don't anyone make a move. I'll blow you all up in four minutes if I don't get the money!" A witness would later report he could see her hands were shaking, causing a silver bracelet to jingle, and the Listerine sloshed in the syringe.

A man named Hawkins had been standing behind Opal in line, and he would later report his first thought was that the woman with the syringe had gotten hold of a flask and imbibed a bit too much.

Cisco had put $500 in the envelope, and he pushed it through to Opal, who looked at him like he had lost his mind. "That's not enough!" She shoved it back at him. "Don't move!" she shouted at the customers and employees.

Rex Cisco was 28 years old. He ducked under the counter to grab packages of $1 and $5 bills, wrapped in $500 each, filling the envelope. As he squatted under the counter, he caught the eye of another teller,

Margaret Anderson. Meaning the burglar alarm that rang the police headquarters, he hissed at Margaret, "ring that thing!"

Margaret hesitated. The woman with the syringe had told them all not to move or there would be an explosion. Margaret did not want to die in tiny pieces on the floor of the Des Moines National Bank. The bank had had some false alarms, too, and she did not want the embarrassment of being the one who caused a huge brouhaha over a false alarm. After all, the bank's last robbery had occurred in May of 1942, and—

—Rex, again hissing at Margaret, "ring that thing!"

So Margaret's lips whispered a little prayer as her thumb mashed the silent alarm so hard that it jammed. Unknown to her, others had squashed down their alarm buttons, too.

Now Rex was standing upright, shoving the full envelope under the cage to the woman with the syringe full of sloshing liquid. Evidently, the amount of cash now passed the robber's approval. Opal snatched up the envelope, shoved past Hawkins and another male customer, her open-toed black shoes clicking on the stone floor, and out the door she went. A bank employee named F.L. Flene dared follow her after giving her a few seconds head start. But she had turned north on Sixth Avenue and simply vanished.

There were cries at the bank, and people started to shout at one another; adrenaline dumps let loose.

Opal Dixon had dressed sharply for this robbery, but she had forgotten a mandatory piece of clothing, a *de rigueur* of the 1940s that the average woman would not be seen without, and it got her busted. When two policemen arrived at the Des Moines National Bank, the employees described Opal: "a woman with black hair in a grey fur coat—she was *not wearing a hat*."

Opal had stopped at the Equitable building a half block from the bank. There she entered and rode the elevator to the 11th floor to the office of Dr. Donald Drake, DDS, to pay a $75 bill for a set of dentures, using $5 bills she had just taken from the bank. After paying the bill, she requested the key to the ladies' restroom.

She had to stash the cash just in case the cops busted her and to keep her husband's hands off it. She eyed the ventilator and experimented by sticking $14 into it, but when the money swooshed in and disappeared, so did that idea. So Opal removed two wall containers holding toilet paper, stashing $1,000 in one and $1,200 in the other. She replaced the toilet tissue and—*voilà*—hidden from sight.

There was still the syringe and the money left over in the envelope. Opal chucked both into a metal trash can. Then Opal Dixon returned the restroom key to the dentist's office with a sweet "thank you," took the elevator down, stopped to purchase a magazine at a newsstand, and exited Locust Street.

At the same time, Des Moines police officers Russell Lewis and Paul Nessen were about to have a story to tell their grandkids. They had been searching for at least 45 minutes, but every dark-haired woman in a gray coat was wearing a hat. Then—boom! Just like that, here comes this woman out of the Equitable building who matched the exact description: no hat.

They arrested Opal the minute she walked out of the building. Lewis and Nessen walked her into the bank, and it was like an explosion: "That's her!" "That's the woman!" "Had a syringe!" "—Said she was going to—"

Per protocol, the cops took Opal to an office in the bank, but it was glass partitioned, so everyone inside the bank could see the woman talking to the smartly dressed FBI agents. She sat in a chair holding her magazine, dry-eyed. Her interrogators realized they were getting nowhere, so she was hauled off to jail for one more interrogation.

Once in the police station, sitting with the Des Moines police and the FBI feds, Opal Dixon smiled sweetly and again denied any knowledge of any bank robberies. "Who, me? I'm just a part-time nurse and a waitress." She and her family lived at the Hotel Cargill, she explained. She and her husband, Jesse G. "Mack" Dixon, lived in one room. Her daughters were both married; they lived in adjoining rooms. Jesse worked for Watson Brothers Transportation. The girls were married, but the youngest was getting divorced. Both girls were struggling financially.

And then she said something so offhand that detectives raised their eyebrows at one another. "I suppose you are suspecting me of the St. Louis bank robbery, too."

FBI Agent Roy Meadows kept trying to pin her down, but Opal wasn't about to be had. He tried every interrogation trick the FBI had taught him, and then some. Opal Dixon just smiled at him. When he paused, waiting for her answer, she licked her lips, crossed and uncrossed her legs casually, and said, "I think you're cute."

Inspector Watson may have considered smacking her, right in front of his peers. The FBI did not have as many legal limitations during this time period.

"Keep on talking," Opal encouraged him. "I like to hear your voice. You look cute, too."[4]

Now the cops brought in her husband Jess and both daughters, Jewell, the youngest, and Louise. Jess was a heavily jowled man at 59, liver spots dotting his hands and eyes set deep in dark sockets. The girls were stunning. Privately, Jess told the cops, "I don't know why [Opal] would pull such a thing." Jess was escorted to the county jail and booked in; investigators were just not convinced he was so innocent. The daughters were free to go, but only after they quietly conferred with Opal.

The three women spoke privately for some time. And when her daughters were walking out of the police station, Opal was sitting down with detectives, fresh-lit cigarette in hand, ready to talk.

She told the roomful of male investigators about her life, adding, "I never was in any serious trouble before in my life. This thing just sort of grew onto me. That's the only way I can explain it."

That was lie number one because Opal Dixon's name appeared in the December 12, 1946, records for "Threatening to Commit a Public Offense." It was a charge filed by the Dixons' former landlady because Opal had gotten into a heated argument with someone at the apartment house and threw a table. That charge would eventually be dropped.

Like most serial bank robbers, she found the first bank robbery so easy that she decided to try it again. Now she told her interrogators about the January 22, 1947, robbery: the purchase of the syringe, waiting in line, and then springing it on the teller, Rex C. Cisco. That led to telling the cops where and how she hid the rest of the stolen money in the Equitable building's women's restroom. Officers were dispatched to search the bathroom and would return with the money.

"I simply was tired of living without having any money. That's why I did it," Opal said as she signed her name to the confession.

Opal was locked up in the Polk County Jail. She was placed in a cell by herself. She didn't want to be in a section with other women, she told the female jailers when asked. She wanted to be alone.

But cops still had some questions to ask. That next morning, they wanted to discuss the December 26 bank robbery of the United Bank and Trust Company in St. Louis. What the hell, Opal must have figured. They pinched her on this one. Cigarette lit, she settled in to tell the story.

Opal had taken the bus from Des Moines to St. Louis to fetch up Jewell, she explained to the cops, who had just stood before a judge and said "I do" to her new husband. On December 26, 1947, Opal was at the St. Louis bus station with Jewell when, she told the cops, "I decided to rob a bank." She said nothing of her plan to Jewell. She left the station and headed for the bank. Like every well-behaved customer, she stood in line, but she was not a friendly customer when she got to the teller's window.

Teller Robert S. Walden was working the window, and when he looked at his customer, he saw "a brunette with a wild look in her eyes."

"Hand it over," the wild-eyed woman growled at him. "The place is covered." She leaned in closer. "Or I'll blow this place up!"

Robert immediately snapped open the teller's window and shoved $582 into the woman's hands. He didn't question her. This woman looked like she meant business, he would later report.

Demure again, the smiling robber walked casually out of the bank and right back to the bus station. She joined her family in time to board the bus that would take them safely to Des Moines. Once home, she used the money to purchase things like steak dinners, an electric clock, and a radio.

She had told no one until now, in this room full of cops that smelled like cigarettes. She shrugged it off. "The $582 is all spent now."[5]

In the follow-up interview, Opal would say that her husband Jess knew all about the robbery but disapproved and would not accept one red cent of the stolen monies.

Detective Chief Tom Watson, detectives Robert O'Brien, and Harold Traffley interviewed 59-year-old Jess "Mack" Dixon on Thursday evening, the 23rd. He lamented, finally, he did know his wife had robbed the United Bank and Trust Company in St. Louis on December 26, but it was some time after she had pulled it off; she had shown him a bagful of $1 bills and loftily explained she had scored somewhere between $400 and $500 in St. Louis. And Jess remembered the dates of the St. Louis hit because she did not cook for him. His Christmas dinner that year was donuts and coffee.

But he had no idea she was planning to hit the Des Moines Bank until some newshound came to Jess's work, pounding on the dispatcher's door of Watson Freight Lines, asking for a comment.

Jess Dixon's statement gave an account of a marriage that read nothing like Opal Dixon's account. It was his fourth marriage; he had no idea how many times Opal had said "I do." She was in a St. Louis restaurant and, out of pity because she seemed so ill, Jess gave her money. Finally, he married her. They did indeed live a flotsam existence. Opal worked as a nurse at times. "She worked for the Carnegie Steel Company in South Chicago for a while ... she laid off for a few days ... telling [the boss] that I was dead."[6]

Jess signed off on his statement and was escorted back to the city jail. His wife still languished in the Polk County Jail on a $50,000 bond. Jess wanted to know if the court was going to charge him with anything. No one was sure at this point, so he was just to cool his heels. The next day, the district attorney determined there was not enough evidence to prove Jess had anything to do with either robbery, and Jess was free.

Opal Dixon made instant headlines, and for each photo, she smiled broadly for the press. Every mention in the newspaper noted she was attractive, and her hair was brunette. The reporters always seemed to note Opal's hair color, like journalist Lillian McLaughlin in the *Des Moines Tribune*, who, when listing Opal's esthetically pleasing attributes, called Opal "the black-haired woman."[7] Opal herself assured one female reporter that her hair was the natural, luxurious brunette color. This was lie number two because the Dixons' landlady, who had filed the December 12, 1946, charge, was too happy to tell the press that Opal had used the landlady's teapot to boil dark tea to dye her hair that shade of brunette.

That made the news—Opal Dixon was a *gray-haired* woman!

Finally, Opal willingly signed a confession about the robbery.

The court offered Opal Dixon a plea bargain. Plead guilty to aggravated robbery and receive 25 years max, or go to trial and risk life. Opal chose to gamble. She was going to put her future in the hands of a jury.

"I don't expect a thing," Opal said of the courts in one interview.

"It's done now, and I'll leave it up to the court to do what it wants. If I'd expect anything, I wouldn't have talked—" She hesitated. "And I can be pretty stubborn when I want to." This time, Opal told the reporter she filled the syringe at her Des Moines hotel room, a syringe she had purchased long before the robbery. She described her childhood financial situation as "moderately poor." She added how she "didn't see how anyone could get along with Mack."[8]

Opal Dixon was formally charged with robbery of the United Bank and Trust Company in St. Louis, Missouri, on December 26, 1946. The trial began the following February 6. Both Opal's prosecution and the hunt for Elizabeth Short's killer shared the local front page; the woman dubbed "the Black Dahlia" found sliced in pieces and lying in a Los Angeles park would keep the public guessing about her murderer for decades afterward. Opal Dixon probably read this article, along with thousands of others who came to realize the devil had arrived to live amongst them. Did the innocent Elizabeth Short's plight have any influence on Opal's decision to take her case to trial? Opal said that once people heard Opal's own story, they would see just what an innocent she was.

The trial lasted 14 days. Defense Attorney Ray Hanke was her counsel. The jury box was inhabited solely by women.

On February 17, 1947, Opal took the stand to tell her life story. And the spectators got quite a show. It made the front page, and two ladies in the gallery fainted.

Opal was born in 1911 in Kennett, Missouri, she explained quietly. For her, "Missouri" was more like "misery," because her family lived in extreme poverty. She did not complete school. She had been married five times. Her first husband, Lyman Allen, lasted two months; she quit school at 15 to wed. She then married her two daughters' father, but he never had money, and they fought constantly. Despite taking a nine-month business course, she toiled away at a $5 a week restaurant job for two years. Her work history included one of Illinois' brothels.

The packed courtroom, the all-woman jury, and the judge had to lean forward to hear her; Opal spoke so softly. People who stood in the aisles shoved one another to peer at the woman in the striped suit and light-colored bow. That was when two elderly spectators fainted and had to be carried into the hallway for fresh air. The judge then announced only spectators with seats would be allowed in the courtroom.

The judge also had to tell the spectators there would be no reactions tolerated—not shouting, no clapping of hands. Business over, Opal continued her story.

Opal explained she had married a man who was, by trade, a tap dancer and a clown, but he wasn't much fun; he was so abusive that she once pulled a gun and took a shot at him. She had to clock her fourth husband—literally—when he was punching on her daughters; she grabbed an alarm clock to whack him over the cranium to stop him. The next and current husband, Jess G. Dixon, started pimping her out with a few other women shortly after they wed in 1938.

Next, Opal detailed she had been arrested for kidnapping when she removed her daughters from relatives' homes, a charge that would be dropped. Hospitalization followed, and she blamed her illnesses on her forced illegal activities. Her husband was currently threatening her daughters' safety if she didn't return to prostitution for him.

Going to the police never helped her plight. She had been born and raised in poverty, had no education or resources. Opal needed a man for financial stability. Not that there was stability in the Dixon house. Actually, it was "houses." The family moved constantly.

And it all came down to January 22 when Opal Dixon walked into the bank intending to scare the hell out of people to make easy money.

She "wanted to scare everyone real bad, the way I've been scared for the past eight years," she explained.[9] She didn't want to return to the streets, and she was afraid Jess would kill her or her daughters. In desperation, she robbed the bank.

And now came the juicy story the court watchers were waiting for: the day Opal robbed the banks.

Opal told the court that she walked into the United Bank and Trust Company in St. Louis on December 26, intending to apply for a loan. She observed a teller named Robert S. Walton counting money. According to Opal, she just asked him, "You've got a lot of money there; why don't you just give me some?" He handed her $582. "I never dreamed I'd get out of there," she explained. "I wanted to attract attention, but nobody seemed to do anything, so I just had to walk out, shoving some people to get out of my way." Poor Opal. No one ever paid her the right kind of attention. Except teller Robert S. Walton was paying plenty of attention, and when the initial shock wore off, and he called the cops, here's what he later testified: "A brunet in a silver-colored fur coat went to [my] window on December 26, I thought she drew a revolver and said, 'hand it over, buddy, the place is covered.' A total of $582 was taken."[10] Opal also explained to the court that she offered Walton an IOU, but he refused it.

Of robbing the United Bank and Trust Company, Opal told the jury, "I knew I had to do something big enough to get to the FBI so they could help me." She was hoping to bring attention to her husband's brutal ways: his pimping, his threats, and his sloth. But then she told them she did not plan the robbery. "Something just came over me."

She had dressed nicely for this robbery, wearing the same silver-colored fur coat that she would wear later for the December 26 robbery in Des Moines.

Opal Dixon wanted money to provide for her daughters, Louise and Jewell, who lived with her. Some of the money she used for bus fare, and the remainder was taken away by Jess.

When Jewell Collins and Louise Asplin testified on behalf of their mother, it was difficult not to show emotion. They echoed their sentiments of a hardscrabble life, abusive men, and living in fear: of moving place to place, being beaten by both stepfathers and their biological father.

When the prosecution and defense rested, the jury departed to determine if Opal Dixon was guilty of "entering a bank with intent to rob." While they were in the jury room, the United States' District Attorney's Office issued a warrant charging Opal with the December 26 Union Savings Bank robbery in Des Moines.

The jury spent a day debating the verdict. When they notified the bailiff that they had reached a verdict, 150 people scrambled for seats in the gallery. But Defense Attorney Ray Hanke called: he could not come in. Opal's daughters were not in the room this time. So Opal stood between two deputies, without personal support, as the jury filed in.

A juror named Mabel Jones was the only one who could look at the defendant. When she looked Opal in the eyes, Opal stared back as if she already knew. Everyone else suddenly became very interested in the floor, the ceiling, their chair.

Regardless of Opal's sad stories, the jury had to follow the law. Jane Huthchens was the jury's foreperson, and it was difficult, but the final decision was "guilty" on the bank robbery charge. Opal Dixon was just given a mandatory life sentence in Iowa's state prison.

Formalities over, the all-female jury departed one by one, single file, out of the courtroom. Only then did Mabel Jones let her feelings rush forward; she burst into tears. Juror Ora Warren, stepping close behind, also cried.

The jury waited in the court lounge. Opal Dixon's law enforcement escort walked her past them. Surprised to see her, five of the women glanced away, tears coursing down their cheeks. Two others dabbed at reddened eyes.

Opal just smiled at them.

On February 28, 1947, Opal sat before Judge Russell Jordan as he refused her attorney's motion for a new trial. Then Judge Jordan sentenced her to spend the rest of her life in the Rockwell City Women's Reformatory in Iowa. Yet there was to be another surprise.

As Opal sat and talked with her daughters, one of them stood to open the courtroom doors. In walked Jess G. Dixon.

Jess attempted conversation.

Opal snarled at him to get out and stay out. Perhaps she meant the courtroom. Or maybe she was talking about her life. He made another snarky comment, and Opal was on her feet and after him in a rage when a deputy sheriff and the two young women got between them. The deputy advised Mr. Dixon to leave.

A camera snapped Opal's picture as she waved a cheery goodbye, her deputy sheriff driver, hands thrust deep into his pockets, grinning next to her. Opal Dixon had gathered her personal belongings at the Polk County Jail, where she took up residence during the trial. She was wearing the silver-colored fur coat and fur-lined boots she had worn in both bank robberies.

Once at the reformatory, Opal became inmate number 1627 and was given the job of making buttonholes. The prison assigned her to house and farmwork, including gardening. She would eventually divorce Jess, husband number five. She kept in touch with her daughters.

As spring turned into summer, Opal developed a strange affliction. She began walking on her toes on her right foot, and while standing, she kept her foot in that position. When asked, she told the staff that she couldn't straighten out her leg no matter how hard she tried. The doctors at Rockwell City could find nothing physically wrong with Opal. In late July, Opal transferred out of Rockwell City to the Cherokee State Hospital for the Insane "for observation following attacks of hysterical frenzy" as a "guest patient." It was customary for female inmates to have "nervous disorders," a Cherokee State Hospital representative told reporters.[11] In September of 1948, Opal came through the same doors again for the same diagnosis. After being tested, she returned to prison.

It was December 6, 1949, a Tuesday, and the dinner bell was ringing at 6 p.m. at the Rockwell City Women's Reformatory. There were about six "lifers" serving their time there; they resided in one cottage. The women headed for the dining hall. Five made it.

After some confusion, officers determined that inmate Opal Dixon, the famous "Syringe Bandit," had escaped by just walking out the cottage's front door. Alarms began ringing.

Opal was hiding out in a nearby cornfield, crouching down among the rows of dry stalks, listening to them scratching above her head. The prison dresses were of cheap, blue broadcloth, and search parties guessed she was most likely freezing in the December wind. After almost seven hours of this misery, she stood up to limp back towards the lights of the Rockwell City Women's Reformatory. A few hours of freedom and doing what she wanted must have seemed, initially, to be worth it.

The November 29, 1953, edition of the *Des Moines Register* continued to report on the woman who made so many headlines in 1947, noting an unnamed prison magazine called Opal a "model inmate" who always had a "cheery greeting" with "infectious laughter"; a "'good listener' who was also an interesting conversationist … gracious … [and] ladylike" (p. 25).[12]

Opal Dixon was paroled in 1957. It didn't last long. She immediately began frequenting bars, chugging booze and causing a ruckus wherever she went. She married, but husband number six began working almost immediately to have an annulment; he was unaware of her criminal career until after saying "I do." She refrained from severe criminal behavior, but multiple establishments had to toss her out for disturbing the peace. In November 1957, the Rockwell City Women's

Reformatory welcomed her back. Both her parole and the revocation made the front page, along with the fact there was a new white streak in her glossy black hair.

And then, after that—nothing. Opal Dixon dropped from the headlines and the media. The *Des Moines Tribune*, who for years reported on her hair color and her clothing, reported in the June 16, 1958, edition in a column called "What Has Happened to Them?" that Opal, at 56, remained in the Rockwell City Women's Reformatory "and is reported to be cheerful" (p. 6). And that is the last that readers and followers read of Opal Dixon, "the Syringe Bandit."

13

Esther and Patsy Whiting

The Family That Robs Together

Esther Amelia Whiting was no doubt feeling life weighing her down with every order she took, every table she wiped clean at the all-night restaurant where she hustled blue plate specials and smiled at customers whether they deserved it or not. She was 41 years old. It was 1951. It just seemed like everything and everyone was moving faster.

Mass production of vehicles and the new idea of subdivisions created a mass exodus into what became known as "the suburbs." Home ownership, along with the numbers of marriages, was skyrocketing. The woman's role was to be a savvy shopper, great parent and wife and homemaker. And here was Esther, twice divorced, with kids living at home, working as a part-time waitress.

So it most likely seemed like everyone—sans the Whiting house—was in the money. The country was feeling prosperous and safe. There was talk of some scientific weapons called "nuclear" being tested in the Nevada deserts; politicians told constituents these weapons would keep the United States safe from foreign invasion. The term "nuclear family" was born, thanks to the Cold War. And talking on the telephone was about to go direct-dial, coast to coast! Politicians promised that this type of first telephone call would be made in November, from Englewood, New Jersey, to Alameda, California. It would be more difficult, as it required a ten-digit phone number, but now everyone could talk to anyone in the country. Esther wondered who she would speak to and about what. Fashion? There were those cute fur collar coats and dresses, and now there were suits for ladies with skirts in place of trousers.

But who had the money for a new suit? And where would Esther wear it?

Esther was living at 1360 Velp Avenue in Green Bay, Wisconsin, with her 25-year-old son from her first marriage, Charles French, Jr. Charles had returned from the war with a disinterest in an honest day's work. Esther's daughter Patsy, who was 14 and in junior high school, was one of her children who lived with them. They also had a boarder, a Mr. Edward Strnad, 52.

In profile, Patsy looked like her mother. They both had the same large nose and small chin, the same dark eyes. Esther wore her dark hair short and neat; Patsy's hair hung to her shoulders. Esther looked older than her 41 years; she wore eyeglasses with the heavy black frames that were fashionable for the day. Charles had Patsy's same facial features, and he sported a thin, pencil mustache.

Charles had an affinity for taking other people's things and making them his own. And it would later prove his family didn't mind sharing the wares.

Charles made friends with a tall 20 year old named Albert Curtis Small, a World War II veteran who worked at the Appleton Post Office. "Worked" in Albert's case was questionable, as he was evidently allergic to doing anything productive. Both of them would meet a man named Wilford (sometimes appearing as "Wilfred" in the news) Joseph Smith, who lived in Brussels Smith. Wilford, who wore his hair shaved close on the sides, with a pointy nose and heavy chin, did not appear smart or successful. The three became pals and spent their time trying to make the most money with the least amount of work.

Perhaps Charles had decided to go straight and get a good job; maybe he was fishing for something he could exploit. Nonetheless, he approached a man named William Walters and asked about employment. Walters was supervisor of Walters, Inc. Armored Car Service. Charles asked about job openings for guards. William turned him down.

The year 1951 was a busy time for the Whitings when it came to theft.

On September 19, Edward Strnad joined Charles Jr., Patsy, and Esther on a nighttime drive to the farm of Tony Diedrich in West DePere. Under the cover of night, Charles shot one of the farmer's

400-pound bulls with a .22 rifle. Somehow they hauled the carcass into the car and took it back to the Velp home where it was chopped up with a machete. Wilford Smith received a portion of the beef. Esther canned the rest. The viscera was tossed into nearby Duck Creek.

Also in September, there was a series of burglaries on Green Bay's Preble Street. On September 20, thieves broke into the home of L.E. Liehmann and carried away almost everything the family owned.

On September 22, the suspected same group broke into Mr. Lynn Lucia's home not far from Liehmann's. And the burglars must not have been happy with those hauls because there was another burglary of a house near the Brown-Oconto county line soon afterward.

It fell under the jurisdiction of Sheriff Gordon Zuidmufider to investigate the burglaries. The items taken were of both monetary and esthetic value: coins, furniture, decorative items, expensive clothing. Then something happened that was considered much more important than a string of home burglaries.

Charles French was hating being poor, and he loved to remind others that he was poor. So people around him wondered how, after so much bellyaching about being low on funds, he was suddenly purchasing a vehicle.

On Tuesday, October 16, Albert Small picked up his paycheck from the Appleton Post Office. He did not return, and no one missed him. The next time they saw his face, it would be on the front page of the newspaper.

Early on Friday morning of October 19, 1951, Wilford Smith was driving to meet his pals Charles and Albert when his car broke down. And later that Friday, a gang robbed the Laona State Bank in Laona, Wisconsin. Both of these incidents were related.

It was business as usual that October 19 in the Laona State Bank when two men and a young boy came striding in. The tallest of the men stood to watch at the entrance. The boy was holding a .38 revolver on the employees. The other man went from till to till, scooping up cash and shouting at the bank employees to shut up, do as they were told, and not try anything stupid. The boy eventually joined in on scooping up cash. They were not well prepared for they hadn't brought bags to carry cash in, so the boy and one man stuffed money in their pockets until coins fell jingling to the floor and bills drifted down. The three then ran out the front door, $11,534.93 in their pockets, leaped into an awaiting car, and off they went. There was a woman at the wheel. She would later be identified as Esther Whiting.

As the getaway car roared off, the "young boy" removed his cap to shake out a thick mane of dark hair that tumbled to the shoulders: Patsy Whiting. She was excited—she had gotten away with her disguise!

The men would give Wilford Smith $200 to keep his mouth shut. He didn't get to be in on the robbery as planned due to his car trouble, but he still got a cut of the money. Wilford had no issue with complying and lit out of town.

One of the biggest mistakes a bank robber can make is to cry poor one day and become King Midas the next. Charles's purchase of the vehicle only a few days ago aroused suspicion, but the fact that his new car matched the getaway car driven by the robbers determined something was amiss. The robbers' car description was given out to the public by Chief H.J. Bero of the Green Bay Police, Sheriff Kline of Forrest County, and Sheriff Gordon Zuidmufider's office. Soon, all three offices became inundated with tips. Someone had just purchased a car matching that description, and they lived at 1360 Velp Avenue in Green Bay, tipsters were reporting; Charles French told everyone who would listen how hard-pressed for cash he was, and now he had money. And Charles had a kid sister; the cops hastily scribbled down the tipster's information. Could that be the "young boy" who had helped rob the bank? Then there was the call from the witness who had observed Charles and an unidentified man (later identified as Smith) walking to the back of the family garage holding something; upon their return, they were empty-handed. And then William Walters came forward with the information of Charles's interest in being a guard for Walters, Inc. Armored Car Service.

The FBI had at least ten agents on the case, and Green Bay Police and Sheriff Zuidmufider contacted the feds with their intel. The FBI made a trip to 1360 Velp Avenue.

That Tuesday, October 23, Commissioner John D. Kehoe was rousted out of bed to appear at his office. Kehoe signed arrest warrants for Esther Amelia Whiting, Charles French, Jr., Wilford Joseph Smith, and the "young boy"—who officers believed to be the cleverly disguised Patsy.

Meanwhile, Esther, Patsy, and Charles must have been celebrating their good fortune. It had been four days, and no one seemed the wiser. The women may have been planning what to buy and where to go. Feelings of elation probably deflated when the feds came knocking at the door that morning.

The cops quizzed each of the family members. Charles finally admitted he buried the bank loot in a tin box and a jar behind their home's garage. Charles quickly gave up his accomplices; Charles would tell the investigators he had only just met Albert Curtis Small, the third robber, although officials would wonder if the two had been buddies in the war.

Esther admitted her role as the driver, and Patty was, yes, disguised. After questioning, one of the agents asked Esther if she wanted a lawyer.

"What good would that do?" Esther asked. "I gave a statement this morning."[1]

A search warrant for the residence of Esther Amelia Whiting was drawn and served. Now armed with their search warrant, shovels hit the dirt behind the garage, and when the metal of the shovel hit the metal of a box, it gave a new meaning to the words "pay dirt."

But when the officers opened the box to seize the money, a diamond-studded watch tumbled out into the investigators' hands. Later, Mr. L.E. Liehmann would identify the timepiece as one of the items pilfered from his home during the September 20 burglary.

Albert Curtis Small's arrest came soon in Hammond, Indiana. Bank employees identified him as the tall fellow who guarded the door while Patsy and her brother scooped up the cash. Wilfred Joseph Smith's arrest occurred on October 23 at Sturgeon Bay.

Allowing crime victims to identify their stolen property in the 1950s worked a bit differently; one of the burglary victims, Mr. Lynn Lucia, was notified, and when he arrived at Esther's home on Velp Avenue, he was allowed to walk through the residence to see if he recognized anything stolen from his home. Mr. Lucia began to identify items stolen from his residence during the September 22 burglary. "That's our vacuum cleaner," he began. "That's our floor lamp." Glancing out the window, he did a double take. "Those are our curtains!" When the walk-through of the Whiting home was completed, Lucia would tell the press he had recovered almost everything stolen from his home.[2]

Eventually, burglary victims would recover other items. L.E. Liehmann and residents from the Brown-Oconto county line house found their belongings in the Whiting residence.

Esther, Charles, and Patsy, along with Wilford, made the local news front pages, and the photographers were there during the October 24 morning arraignment. Lynn Lucia was reading about the bank robbery in the local paper, and it was her turn to make an identification. "That's my coat!" She pointed at the photo of the nice coat that Patsy had worn for the court appearance.

Esther, Charles, and Wilford were each held on a $25,000 bond.

Represented by defense attorney Robert Parins, Esther and Patsy Whiting appeared before the United States Commissioner John D. Kehoe on the following Wednesday morning, October 24. They were photographed sitting parallel to Commissioner Kehoe's desk, their backs against the wall, heads down, studying the floor. Because of their likeness, it was easy to see they were mother and daughter. Patsy was dressed nicely, again wearing the stolen red coat with leopard collar. (Eventually, the rightful owner would recover her coat.)

Kehoe would confer with defense attorney Parins that, per the United States Attorney in Milwaukee, Patsy's case would most likely be disposed by federal court due to her being a juvenile. The United States Marshals would be transferring Patsy to Milwaukee on Monday, and the court would determine her fate. Until then, it was the juvenile detention home. She would not be wearing the red coat with fur trim.

Charles had already waived his hearing, ready to just take his punishment.

Parins asked the judge for a reduction in bond for Esther. He asked for a $10,000 bond. It was more affordable, and he did not believe Esther would be running off anytime soon.

Kehoe declined. This was a serious case. But, he explained, he would approve a $15,000 bond, only if it were furnished by sureties who could qualify for $20,000. That did not look even remotely possible for Esther. So until her transfer to Milwaukee, she would cool her heels in the county jail.

On Thursday, October 25, Edward Strnad was questioned by two officers from the Outagamie County Sheriff's offices regarding possible thefts. "I might as well tell you, I'm in on this stuff," Strnad reportedly admitted. He told them about the September 19 shooting of Tony Diedrich's 400-pound bull. The investigators indeed located the canned beef in the Velp Avenue home's basement. Strnad told the investigators how French Jr. had been busy in Door County, stealing other people's things. Strnad then agreed to make a formal statement that next morning on October 26.

The same time investigators were quizzing the boarder for intel on the Whiting family, Esther and Patsy, along with Wilford (listed as "Wilfred") Smith, were standing outside of the courthouse, waiting for the U.S. Marshals to give them a ride to Milwaukee for trial. One photographer was there to capture the story in pictures. "How about a nice smile?" he called out to the threesome.

Esther was pissed. "What do you want me to do? Wink?" she shouted. "Go to hell!" A click of a shutter and their likeness was captured for the front page: Wilford in profile, Patsy in her saddle shoes, and Esther grinning, looking like someone's grandma waiting for the church bus.

And then an even stranger thing happened in this case.

Edward Strnad spent the night of October 25–26 chain-smoking and pacing the floor of the Whitings' home on Velp Avenue. He gulped coffee like a madman. Finally, at 7:30 a.m., as two of the Whiting children stood on the front porch preparing for school, Strnad burst out of the front door as a gravel truck rounded the corner. Strnad crouched on the road's edge until the truck roared past the house. The Whiting children watched as Strnad dove under the rear wheels. The driver heard and felt the crunch of what the coroner called Edward Strnad's "instantaneous death" with a "broken neck, crushed chest, and internal injuries." The driver was not held at fault.[3]

Esther would receive four years for her part in the bank robbery. Patsy was placed in the custody of the attorney general for three years. After they stopped making headlines, the public lost interest in the mother-daughter-son bank-robbing family. It was a new decade, and there were more important things to worry about: there were rumblings about black Americans who were becoming disgruntled with their station in life. There was the threat of Russia and spies and right now,

Congress was having hearings designed to stop "un–American activities" that were going on in schools, the government, in Hollywood. It did not matter if the hearings would never expose Communists or acts of treason; many people would lose their jobs, friends, families, and livelihoods. A bank-robbing "gang" made up of a pasty woman, her silly daughter, her slimy-looking son, and his goofy friends were small headlines compared to America being threatened. And so it was; bank robbery slowly began taking a back seat to the headlines of what was perceived to be more significant threats to the nation. And women, now considered by many to be silly and inept, but perfect to be mommies and housewives, were not a threat at all.

14

Dorothy Mary Platt

Despondent Gun-Girl

The Buffalo, New York, photographer caught the bank robber in an unflattering pose. Newspapers wrote of the bank robber as if it was all about the robber's appearance, not about her bravado. Probably because it was 1953, and a young female was not supposed to be committing dangerous crimes, let alone bank robbery. But 24-year-old Dorothy Mary Platt had robbed a bank. And she had gotten caught. But the story of her capture was the most thrilling saga.

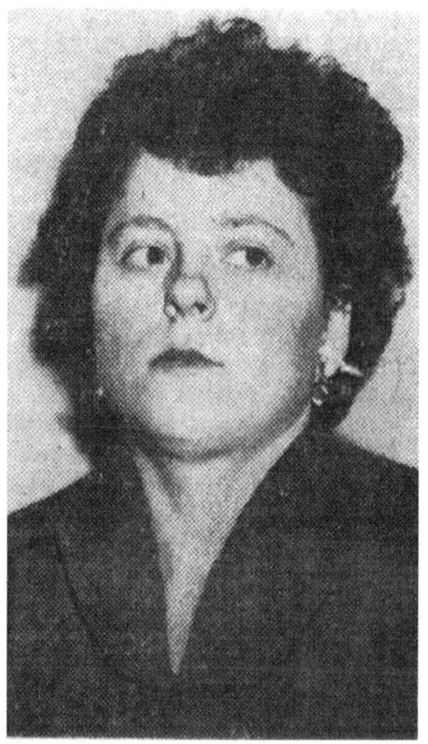

She made the front page only once. On the day of her capture, a photograph was printed on page one of the January 27, 1953, evening issue of the *Windsor Daily Star* with a headline "'Despondent' Gun-Girl Held for Bank Robbery." The story is five short paragraphs.[1]

At 24, Dorothy Mary Platt robbed the Elmwood-Auburn branch of the Manufacturers Traders Trust Company bank in Buffalo, New York. It was her capture that made the big headlines (photograph dated January 29, 1953, courtesy Archives & Special Collections, SUNY Buffalo State College).

Little is known about her case; legal records have long since been destroyed. On January 27, 1953, Dorothy pointed a gun at two tellers working at the Elmwood-Auburn branch of the Manufacturers Traders Trust Company bank in Buffalo, New York.

One report called her a "pretty brunette" and an "attractive young woman." Dorothy walked in that Monday and sat down with the assistant manager. She wanted to join the Christmas club, she told him. The $1 club to be exact. But as he prepared to begin the formal paperwork, she rifled through her purse, then said, "I'm sorry; I don't have a dollar."

Thinking business was over, the assistant manager dismissed her as he left the office and walked to a teller's cage. Dorothy followed him. *Perhaps she found the money*, he thought. When he asked, the answer was evidently a "no" because the girl pulled a gun from her coat and said, "this is a holdup. Give me the money."[2]

The assistant manager, looking down the business end of Dorothy's gun, was Leroy R. Rupp, who was about ten years Dorothy's senior, and the teller was Rose Vera, a woman not much older than the robber. Leroy and Rose began shoving the cash towards the robber while trying not to freeze, staring down the barrel of the .25 caliber automatic pistol that was aiming for their noses.

Dorothy Mary Platt left that bank $8,000 richer.

As Dorothy ran out the door, she must not have noticed the bank employees, including the two she had just robbed, following her a short distance behind.

At the same time, Lorraine Fisher was driving past the bank, her neighbor's children in her car. They were returning from a routine visit to a doctor. Their day was about to get more exciting.

Fisher heard someone, either Leroy Rupp or Rose Vera, shout, "She's got a gun!" That's when Fisher observed a tiny, dark-haired woman running down the street, away from the bank.

Fisher slowed her car to follow the dark-haired bandit for three blocks. There was a fire station up ahead, and Fisher swung her car into the drive, slammed it into reverse, and alerted the firefighters as to what was going on, pointing out the path of her prey. Then she followed on foot, leaving the neighbor's kids with some of the fire station crew. Fisher saw the bandit dash inside a house, and more firefighters surrounded the house.

The wailing sirens in the background told everyone the cops were on their way.

It was only about 15 minutes after the bank heist when police broke down Dorothy Mary Platt's door. She didn't fight or struggle. "I just got mad," she told them. "I was going to get a plane and go to Miami." She still carried all of the $3,000 and her loaded .25 automatic pistol.[3]

Dorothy also told police, "I picked the bank because I wanted to get a lot of money."[4]

Searching her things, officers determined it was "boy trouble" that made Dorothy focus on Miami as the best place to start anew.

Police charged her with first-degree robbery and carrying a loaded firearm. "I needed money to get out of town," the tiny, dark-haired girl told the cops. An article in the *Panama City News* (Florida) referred to her as "a young brunette." An unaccredited United Press photograph shows Buffalo Chief of Police William T. Fitzgibbons as he fingerprints the fugitive, his back turned to the camera, his fedora hiding his face. Dorothy's eyes are upturned, but her face lowered, giving the impression she is either exhausted or stoned. "This pistol-packing woman is shown ... after her capture," reads the typed caption.

The pistol owner turned out to be a William Bennett, who was also missing $60. Dorothy's mother was horrified; she worked as a maid for Mr. Bennett, and now her daughter jeopardized her job. Strike two against Dorothy.

Meanwhile, the newspaper writers would later praise Lorraine Fisher's grit in her role of fugitive–nabber, in part because of Lorraine's size, sex, and occupation. "Sunday School teacher foils girl bank bandit" a byline read. "Mrs. Fisher, 4 feet 11, is superintendent of the Sunday school at the First Unitarian Church."[5]

"Sunday School Teacher Nabs Bank Robber, Both Women," reads another headline.[6] Readers as far away as Amarillo, Texas, knew where Lorraine Fisher was employed, what church she attended, and how tall she stood.

Once the madness of the capture and her booking were over, the reality of what she had done came crashing down on Dorothy's small shoulders. Sometimes, she told the arresting officers, she felt so sad and desperate that thoughts of suicide crept into her mind. Thus, she was now under observation at the Meyer Memorial Hospital with a 24-hour police guard.

She thought she would get a little money, move away from everyone she knew, and start over with her life—the same dream of too many people in so many places. She wasn't yet 25, but she felt far older, she told reporter Margaret Wynn in an "exclusive interview." She told the reporter that she called two different orphanages "home" since she was 12, and her formal education had stopped when she was in the sixth grade. "I worked for a laundry for five years," she told the sympathetic Wynn; it was "dull" work. She quit to find something better but ended up at another laundry, a place called "Cadet Cleaners."

If a woman didn't have a husband to support her, she might be able to exist on a paltry salary. If she had a no-count husband that was utterly unreliable, a lady was on her own. If she didn't have a family to support her, and there were no prospects for a husband, she would have to hunt for a job. But then she would be competing with all the other women out there, and a slew of men too, and the men were far more likely to get the job. A woman may have earned a good salary during the war, only to have it taken away. And men would draw a better paycheck than a woman, even at the exact same job. Having never gotten her high school diploma also counted against her, Dorothy said.

Dorothy would toil all day at Cadet's, then walk home alone, exhaustion riding her backbone. She would stop at shop windows to envy the pretty dresses in the display windows, the perky shoes, and fashionable jewelry. Prettier girls would swish past on the arms of young men, and they always looked so light and happy. Dorothy speculated what her reflection would be like, to be one of those girls. To always have pretty dresses with shoes to match and someone to dress up for. But a paycheck of $35 a week did not stretch far enough for basic survival and many nice things. She would buy dresses, wear them a few times, then lose interest.[7]

Perhaps Dorothy felt she didn't fit in. About the only equal rights women enjoyed during this time was the right to vote. "Rosie the Riveter" was seen by too many people as a necessity during wartime; returning soldiers took Rosie's job. The war was over, the allies won, and it was time to return to conformity. Between 1950 and 1959, only 5.7 percent of American women completed a four-year college degree compared to 8.8 percent of males. After Margaret Wynn's "exclusive interview," Dorothy Mary Platt disappeared from the public eye altogether. The new polio vaccine, which was already inching Dorothy's and other names off headlines, was now the big news.

15

Wanda DiCenzi and Rose O'Donnell

First to Be Caught on Camera

In 1957, the St. Clair Savings & Loan bank was located on the corner of Clair Avenue and East 63rd in Cleveland, Ohio. The building still stands, a handsome brick building with the entrance located in the corner between two austere columns. Customers walk underneath decorative scrolling etched into the rotunda to enter the building.

Between February of 1956 and April of 1957, the bank had been robbed twice. Police Communications Superintendent of Cleveland, Thomas E. Story, saw an opportunity. As the police chief's son, Story knew the importance of staying one step ahead of the bad guys. There was talk of new technology: a "Photoguard."

The Photoguard was a new kind of camera system for military use but of late was considered for civilian security, including bank security. The camera itself was bulky, composed of gunmetal gray boxes with lenses and switches and thick-coated wires. It did not shoot video; it took pictures. They were not high-quality photos; they were grainy and would not show much detail. Criminal investigators tossed around the idea of making it an integral part of North American bank architecture. The Photoguard would not be easy to set up or remove, and the pictures were not clear. Still, it was better than allowing bank robbers to walk in and out unidentified like the place was giving away money.

Superintendent Story decided to check out the Photoguard contraption and, after doing so, elected to have a hidden camera installed in the bank. A Photoguard was installed in the St. Clair Savings & Loan bank on April 11, a Thursday, on a trial basis. The installers planned to return on April 12 to test it and make adjustments. Maybe it would work. Maybe it was useless. Turns out, it was tested by someone else.

Friday, April 12, 24-year-old Steven Ray Thomas shared a lunch table at a Sorn's Restaurant, located just a block west of Clair Avenue and East 63rd. Thomas sat with a Pepsi-Cola Bottling Company employee and two women: 19-year-old Wanda DiCenzi and 18-year-old Rose O'Donnell. The four talked amicably.

Unfortunately for three of those sitting at this table, another patron was also enjoying lunch at a nearby table at the same time. But he would not meet them until days later, and then it would be under very different circumstances.

Stories varied, but one has Steven Thomas offering the girls a ride around town in his car after lunch. They accepted. After driving around a bit, he pulled over, tied his handkerchief around his lower face, and produced what resembled a .32 Beretta handgun. "Let's rob a bank!" The gun was actually a starter pistol, but it looked real enough to get the job done.

At first, it was a joke. Somewhere between the guffaws, it became serious. They switched to Rose O'Donnell's car, a 1955 black-and-white Buick with a Dynaflow transmission that legally belonged to her boyfriend, Patsy Delligatti. Much later, investigators charged Patsy, claiming he received $100 for the use of the fast car for the getaway.

Folks at the St. Clair Savings & Loan bank were most likely starting to stifle yawns from their noon lunch breaks when the black-and-white Buick pulled up to the curb; a man and a younger woman stepped out of the car, leaving a young woman behind the wheel with the engine running. History was about to be made in a few short steps.

The man wore a long coat and hat over his suit. He was not particularly handsome. His hair was thinning at the sides, and his features were angular behind the handkerchief he had tied to cover his face. The girl wore her hair in a modern style, emulating young Elizabeth Taylor's

Opposite, top and bottom: **The first bank robbery caught on camera (1957). Two of the pictures captured by the Photoguard of Wanda DiCenzi and Steven R. Thomas robbing the St. Clair Savings & Loan bank. Wanda is behind the teller's window in a scarf and long black coat. Thomas is in the lobby, back to camera, in a long tan coat (courtesy Cleveland Police Historical Society, Inc.).**

curling, dark bob and penciled eyebrows. She wore a light scarf tied over her head, a long dark coat over her dress, and was carrying a paper bag tucked under one arm. They breezed into the bank, and then the man, later identified as Steven Ray Thomas, was brandishing a gun at the tellers. He began shouting and cursing. "Back then, nobody used the F-word," a former teller, who was 19 at the time of the robbery, recalls now. "But that guy comes in with that talk and there were a bunch of old Slovenian women in the bank."[1]

The second robber, 18-year-old Wanda DiCenzi, proceeded to walk behind the teller's windows, where she began to collect more than $2,000 in cash. There were a few witnesses, including customers, watching the duo proceed to rob the bank. They included one of the employees, a female with a bob of dark hair who wore stylish cat-eyed glasses.

Robbery completed, the man and woman walked out of the bank to jump into the car, and their accomplice drove them off. No doubt, they were feeling much richer. Later, they would divvy up the $2,376.63 that Wanda DiCenzi had stuffed into her paper bag.

Less than three hours after the getaway driver's stylish pump hit the gas pedal, bank managers were announcing into the television cameras that the robbers needed just to turn themselves in. Because unbeknownst to the trio and those who observed their thuggery, there was another witness. At the press of a button behind the teller's station, the Photoguard recorded the bank lobby area, capturing 25 feet of evidence. The "movie" it would make was sure to be a hit. The St. Clair Savings & Loan bank was about to produce a historical film; Steven Ray Thomas and Wanda DiCenzi were the show's stars.

The Photoguard had to be removed from the ceiling as investigators interviewed eyewitnesses. The 16 mm film was then processed and spooled onto a projector. A handful of detectives and investigators gathered in a room to watch the first photos taken of a bank robbery. Standing to the side, peeping behind their broad shoulders, the dark-haired female bank employee with the cat-eyed glasses was present, for it was she who had pushed the button to activate the camera. Her name is Elsie Zivich. Later she would tell a reporter, "I made history. I pushed the button that filmed the first bank robbery." But it was not because of the gun, she admits. It was because of the robber's language and behavior.

"I'm pushing the button so the police can handle this guy. And by golly, that was the big test."[2]

One of the detectives studied the film closely; then, he got up to walk over to the screen to peer closer at the image of the woman who was stuffing cash into the paper bag. He volunteered how he had seen this woman on Friday, April 12, when he had enjoyed lunch at Sorn's Restaurant, located just a block west of the St. Clair Savings & Loan bank. The woman who had robbed the bank had lunch at the same time as the detective. This woman was sitting at a table with other people near the detective's table. Cleveland was not a booming metropolis then, and folks stayed close to home in their tight-knit community. People often recognized faces or were familiar with others. The detective headed for Sorn's to talk to anyone who could identify the woman.

The images were broadcast on the national news in print and on television. Some news writers referred to the male robber as the "star" and the female robber as the "showgirl." Police Communications Superintendent Thomas E. Story had his picture taken standing next to the Photoguard. The still shots of the robbery showed the public just how brazen the robbers had been: the man in the tan coat, arm extended, pointing a gun right at the tellers' cage while two customers stood by. The female robber working behind the cage, her expression grim, as a teller watched helplessly with her fists clamped at her sides.

By now, the bank robbers were gone. Steven Ray Thomas had hopped a bus to Indianapolis. He was feeling safe until a stranger began a conversation, adding, "Did you see where they caught some bank robbers using picture cameras? Ain't that something!"[3] Mortified, Thomas sat in an Indy bar that night, head ducked low, peering at the television screen above the bar through the cigarette smoke, watching the grainy pictures of himself robbing the bank. It was with stooped shoulders and a heavy sigh that Thomas purchased a return ticket to Cleveland.[4]

While Steven Thomas was heading back to the scene of the crime, Rose O'Donnell was sweet-talking a 16-year-old girl from the west side. "I'll pay you fifteen dollars to hold this for me," she promised, passing over a bundle of money. The girl agreed.

Rose O'Donnell and Wanda DiCenzi partnered up, stuck out

their thumbs, and hitchhiked to a motel in Willoughby to lay low for a while.

With the now-famous robbers exiting the stage, the detective who recognized one of them from lunch headed back to Sorn's Restaurant for more than a blue plate special. He was showing the employees the female bank robber's picture. A Sorn's waitress recognized Wanda DiCenzi and told the detective there was a west-side restaurant that Wanda frequented.

The employees at the west-side restaurant didn't know Wanda's name, but they knew her face. The detective was directed to the Palace Theatre movie house because that's where this girl (Wanda) used to work, taking tickets and sweeping up discarded popcorn kernels and licorice whips.

The Palace Theatre movie house manager reported his employee's name was Wanda DiCenzi, from the questionable part of East Cleveland. The manager gave the detective Wanda's home address. The detective headed for East Cleveland.

Wanda lived with her parents. Wanda's parents told the detective Wanda had been missing for a few days. Following up on yet another lead, Wanda was located and arrested in a Franklin Boulevard Boarding House.

Rose O'Donnell rented a room in a home, and once they had identification on her, the detectives searched this room. They located a parking ticket that led them to the 1955 black-and-white Buick, the car her boyfriend Patsy Delligatti owned and the same type of car witnesses identified as screeching away from the bank with the bank's money.

Cops arrested Patsy Delligatti on the suspicion that he loaned her the car for the robbery. And while Rose's 16-year-old west-side girlfriend was savvy enough not to ask questions, she was also aware of Ms. O'Donnell's sudden movie star fame. The young girl called the cops. Investigators would manage to recover all but $800 of the stolen money.

In less than 36 hours, thanks to the wonders of the Photoguard camera, the click of a button, and a lot of detective work, the three bank robbers were sitting in front of the investigators, being processed into jail.

Steven Ray Thomas, who initially came up with the idea for fast cash, was booked in and his mug shot taken.

Why'd you do it? The cops asked him.

He told him that epilepsy kept him from holding down work.

Well, they reasoned, it didn't seem to keep him from holding up a gun.

He shook his head. "I got as far as Indianapolis, and those pictures were ahead of me."

Rose O'Donnell turned herself in when she heard the police arrested her boyfriend. Later she would say she had talked to Patsy Delligatti, and they mutually agreed "I should give myself up."[5] The whole affair had seemingly put a damper on her future. "Well, I was going to get married. I suppose that's all off now." Nothing like bank robbery and arrest to ruin the prenup.

Law enforcement officers and bank officials from all over the

Twenty-four-year-old Steven Ray Thomas, 18-year-old Wanda DiCenzi, and 18-year-old Rose O'Donnell read how they were the first in the world in 1957 to be caught robbing a bank using a new technology: video cameras (courtesy Cleveland Police Historical Society, Inc.)

country were now interested in the Photoguard, and this April 12 robbery, along with the photos, became the first hands-on training on bank robbery prevention and education. The story made news in *Life* magazine along with four stills from the robbery footage, Thomas's mug shot, and a casual photo of DiCenzi (April 22, 1957, p. 47).

The Photoguard's photographs of the robbery appeared on the local newspaper's front page, the *Plain Dealer*, while the trio awaited their arraignment. They were photographed reading the *Plain Dealer*'s account about their robbery, including the front page. None of them realized—again—they were being photographed.

Steven Ray Thomas, Wanda DiCenzi, and Rose O'Donnell were all charged with "Malicious Entry of a Financial Institution." All three pled "not guilty," with Thomas adding "by reason of insanity." The ladies' bail was set at $5,000 each; they paroled out within a year. Thomas would eventually plead guilty to armed robbery and receive a sentence of 10–25 years. In August 1958 Patsy Delligatti received five years' probation.

The original 14 still shots taken by the Photoguard are now in the Cleveland Police Department archives. The Photoguard can be viewed in the Cleveland Police museum.

16

Carolyn Sue McQueen

There Goes the Honeymoon

By any lovebird's standards, Carolyn Sue McQueen and her new husband, Gerald L. Molden, had a terrible honeymoon.

Sometimes a honeymoon is ruined because of the weather. Or plans just don't come together; something dubbed "Murphy's Law" comes into play. Maybe it's a lost ticket. Luggage seems to take on a mind of its own and travels elsewhere. But it wasn't the weather, or some unforeseen strange event, bags or a misplaced ticket that loused up Carolyn Sue's honeymoon. She was married for only 11 days because her husband turned her in to the feds when she robbed a bank.

Carolyn Sue left Cedar Lake, Indiana, behind to become Mrs. Gerald L. Molden. It was Tuesday, January 29, 1963, in Gary, Indiana, the same place immortalized in song by little Ronnie Howard in the movie *The Music Man*. But 18-year-old Carolyn Sue McQueen was not acting as she walked into the Tri-City Plaza Branch of the Gary National Bank. She wore a black leather jacket, blue denim pants, and purple shoes that matched her sweater. And she had a .22 pistol in one hand. Instead of singing, Carolyn Sue was ordering tellers to stuff money into her purse. She had a gun. She was not playing games.

Carolyn stuck up the teller; then, she left with $9,778 in her purse. Some witnesses believed she fled the scene by jumping into a vehicle with several other persons. Carolyn would later deny this allegation.

Soon after Carolyn relieved the bank of the funds, she went to her friend Francis Needham's home. She was with another woman whom

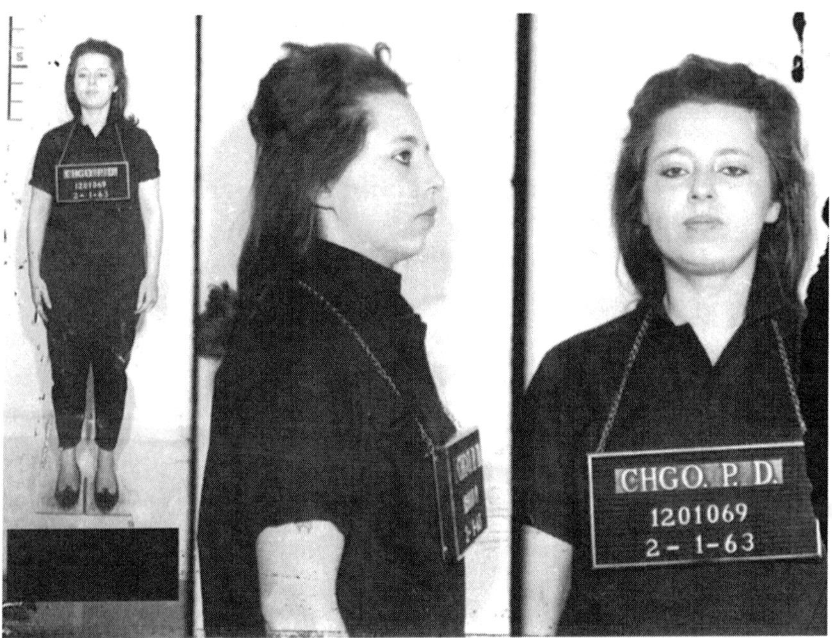

Carolyn Sue McQueen had been married 11 days when she robbed the Tri-City Plaza Branch of the Gary, Indiana, National Bank. She was arrested at a train station with another woman and a baby. Carolyn Sue was divorced soon afterward (Chicago Police Department mug shot, February 1, 1963).

Francis did not know. Francis was 17, single, and working as a waitress. Carolyn gave Francis a box and told her it was Francis's birthday present. When Francis opened her gift, she was staring at $2,990. Carolyn did make one request. "She asked [Francis] to buy her some new clothes. [Carolyn] left behind her old clothing, including Levis, a black coat, and a purple sweater." Carolyn had one more thing to tell her friend before departing. "She told Miss Needham she robbed the Tri-City Plaza Branch of the Gary National Bank at Gary Tuesday night."

On Thursday, Carolyn was preparing to hop a train at the Joliet Union Station. She held a one-way ticket to San Francisco in her gloved hand, dodging the homeward-bound commuters as she headed for her train.

As she stood gathering her purse and taking hold of her suitcase handle, FBI agents were collecting their handcuffs and taking hold of her arm.

If only the cops could have shown up five minutes later. Carolyn would have been on the westbound Santa Fe Chief train and pulling out of the station.

Carolyn was with a traveling companion, a 20-year-old woman named Caroline Moore, who was also from Cedar Lake. Caroline was holding her 18-month-old son, whom the media dubbed "Baby Eugene."

When they pulled Carolyn's suitcase and searched it, the agents found $5,500. Her purse matched the description the bank tellers had given, the same purse the tellers had nervously stuffed with $10 and $20 bills while a pistol stayed leveled at their noses. Later, investigators would recover the .22 pistol and the black leather jacket.

Carolyn learned that Francis Needham was either ungrateful, a snitch, or both because Francis had alerted Carolyn's new husband, Gerald, of the generous gift. She wanted to take it to the police, but being around that much money in a gift box made her "nervous." Gerald and Carolyn's uncle James Ritter picked up the box and took it straight to the Crown Point Sheriff's Offices in Hammond. Detective Barnard Bagley took the case from there. Gerald made damn sure the cops knew he had no idea about the bank heist. And he followed this declaration with the demand for a divorce.

The story spread quickly across the United States, focusing on the fact that Carolyn was 18, a "child bride"[1] and a newlywed of 11 days. A photo showed a tousle-haired woman, smiling slightly over her left shoulder at the cameraman.

Now the soon-to-be ex–Mrs. Molden was heading to Chicago for her arraignment. According to some accounts, Caroline Moore and Baby Eugene were also going along.

Federal agents reported Carolyn told the feds that she and Gerald had quarreled, so she stuck up the bank. The feds also informed the news media that Carolyn was unhappy in her marriage, so she robbed a bank. Other reports indicated Carolyn was going to leave Gerald, and she needed quick cash. How true any of this is, no one knows. It seems nobody bothered to interview the said bank robber.

Gerald filed for divorce. On September 6, 1963, it was granted: a short, one-page document freeing him from Carolyn and her legal troubles. The divorce decree is the sole remaining legal document of Carolyn's life in Indiana.

Carolyn Sue McQueen's legal troubles did not make the papers. Her arrest made exciting news, but evidently, the subsequent trial and punishment did not, because the story never resurfaced in the mass media.

The press never interviewed her; or, if they did, there is no record. Was she so unhappy in her marriage that she made a desperate break for it? What role did Caroline Moore play? All we have left are the headlines: Carolyn Sue McQueen, the "child bride," a newlywed of 11 days, was a bank robber who was turned in by her innocent husband.

17

Linda Marsh

There Goes Christmas

The photograph on page 49 of the December 22, 1968, Sunday edition of the *Boston Globe* appeared strangely out of place. There was no accompanying article. The photo sat between a story about an exciting bridge tournament and the reopening of three ports in Hanoi, Saigon. The image was of a woman in dark glasses, a long-sleeved dark blouse, dark slacks, and shoes. She was carrying a white bag, and she was hurrying out of a bank. The caption reads, "WOMAN ROBBER is snapped by hidden camera as she runs from the Farragut Cooperative Bank in South Boston following a $2300 armed holdup Friday. A man also took part in the robbery." Underneath this photo is the headline to another article: "Double Murder Motive Baffles Boston Police."[1] Readers and the police didn't know, but the photo of the "woman robber" and the headline of the "double murder" had much in common, and it wouldn't be long until no one was baffled, just sickened and saddened. Because no child should have to dodge bullets, and no child should have to watch his mother die.

It was Friday night, December 20, just a few days before Santa Claus was to visit a South Boston apartment on D Street where 30-year-old Marilyn N. Parker lived. Marilyn lived with three of her children: Norbert, four; Cyndy, ten, and Katy, five.[2] Her oldest, a boy of 12, was away at school. Their apartment was in a housing project courtyard located in what was known as a shady neighborhood. Marilyn had a roommate named Linda Marsh, 27. Marilyn was at home, with the kids in a back bedroom, just before midnight when there was a knock at the door.

Linda Marsh (with unidentified Boston police officer) was arrested in December 1968 for taking part in the robbery of the Farragut Cooperative Bank in South Boston. Days later, the cost would be heart-wrenching (courtesy Northeastern University Libraries, Archives and Special Collections Department).

Marilyn opened the door to find Donald D. Daigle, 39, standing on the porch with another fellow, both clearly drunk after barhopping South Boston. Marilyn's roommate, Linda Marsh, and a third man accompanied them. The group had a six-pack of beer. They no doubt sauntered in on unsteady feet. Donald introduced his pal as "Frank." He had met Frank at a café in the Broadway station of the train terminal, he explained, blowing whiskey breath into the tiny apartment.

Donald had recently been allowed to walk out of Walpole state prison, parole papers tucked under one arm, after a five-to-six stretch for a breaking and entering in Haverhill. Despite being from a well-heeled family who boasted a tony South Hadley Falls address, Donald liked to take things that were not his. Things for which his wealthy parents could have easily paid.

Donald and Frank began an alcohol-fueled conversation once in the apartment. Linda and Frank were in the kitchen, and the other fellow was headed for the bedroom to pass out. The clock had yet to strike midnight.

Norbert Parker, Marilyn's youngest son, came into the room with the adults when there was another knock on the door. Marilyn answered the door. This time, these guests did not want to stand around to gab.

Eyewitness accounts vary, but between three and five men were on the threshold. The men were wearing stocking masks and were shoving their way in, whipping out guns to fire into the home, and the air was full of smoke and lead, screams, and the shattering of window glass.

Marilyn fell dead, a bullet to the back of her head. Donald Daigle, who was standing near her, dropped when bullets began thudding into his body. Frank ducked and headed for a window when a bullet shot from outside the home whizzed past his ear.

Little Norbert stood frozen in the midst of the melee. Quick-thinking, Linda grabbed him and shoved him out of the way as bullets dug into the walls, drilled pits into the furniture, and shattered everything that sat on tables or hung on the walls.

It was over in seconds. By the time Frank and Linda could stand, the masked men had tossed their guns at the bodies and ran toward C Street and away from the little house. People in neighboring houses were crawling out from hiding and phoning the police with shaking hands.

When the ambulance and police arrived, they found a house that looked like a war zone. Norbert Parker had tottered to his mother; when he could not rouse her, he ran out of the house, wailing. His siblings, who by now had emerged terrified from the back bedroom, followed close behind. Marilyn was gone forever, leaving four children behind.

Neighbors were scooping up Marilyn's children and calling Mary Sheehan, Marilyn's mother, with the horrific news. Mary was on her way to gather up her grandchildren.

EMS rushed an unconscious Donald Daigle to Boston City Hospital with bullets lodged in his stomach and chest area. And Linda Marsh, who probably saved Norbert's life, went with the officers to the police station to assist with the investigation.

Donald Daigle held on, but he didn't last. He would die at 9:55 the next morning from his wounds. Police would not identify him until they took fingerprints when he lay on a slab in Northern Mortuary. To keep his anonymity, Donald did not carry any identification in his pockets, preferring to blend into any crowd.

Linda Marsh should have done the same because, at the police station, cops arrested her in possible connection with a bank robbery that had occurred earlier that Friday. It seemed someone had walked into the Farragut Cooperative Bank in South Boston on Friday, waved a gun, and walked out with $2,300. Linda matched the description of the female robber. She looked exactly like the woman in the photo taken by the bank camera, the same woman and photo that would appear on page 49 of the December 22, 1968, Sunday edition of the *Boston Globe*. Linda sat on a $10,000 bail with a hearing scheduled for December 27.

Linda was a tiny thing, standing perhaps five feet tall. She wore her dark hair short. A photograph in the December 21 *Boston Globe*'s issue shows one of Boston's finest towering over her, the top of her head barely reaching his broad uniformed shoulder. She is all smiles despite what she just went through. When booked in, she turned to the cameraman and stuck her tongue out, making a sour face.

Her future was swallowed up to history for there are no records of her life after being arrested. She probably saved the baby, Norbert Parker's life; she may have cost three adults their own.

Part V

"Power to the People!"

18

Undercover

"Someone willing to take action"

Some time ago, I was employed as an investigator for an esteemed company. Partnering with the FBI, we were investigating an animal rights group that had caused some significant disturbances overseas, one of which was a car bombing in Europe.[1] This animal rights group was now targeting corporations and individuals in our state. The FBI needed a local, so I went undercover as a potential new group member.

According to their emails and flyers, the animal rights group was to meet on a specific night in a local park to "strategize their plans" for the city and "determine the next move." They were welcoming volunteers and initiating new members. It appeared like a well-planned assembly. Online and on paper, they appeared to be a highly organized group of radicals, large in number, with a clear agenda. Law enforcement was on alert in town as this gang targeted people from individual businesses, attempting to destroy these people's properties. We needed to know what the group was doing.

The group was welcoming new members to join in, so I dressed the part—dirty jeans, T-shirt with radical slogan, eschewing a bra and makeup—and prepared for my role. An FBI agent and other investigators were standing surveillance.

I met the activists in the park that night. In reality, they were all in their early 20s to mid-30s, a ragtag group from wealthy families who were pretending to be of low socioeconomic status. One of them drove up in a shining new Lexus, and they all momentarily forgot their pretense and gathered around to admire the new vehicle, discussing the "old" Lexus in snobbish, tired voices.

They stood around in a circle, talking aimlessly about nothing in particular. They sounded like Ivy League college dropouts. The Lexus driver spoke at great length of the car wreck that had totaled their "old" Lexus, allowing them to purchase the "new" one. None of them discussed politics or anything about animal rights. One girl admired my T-shirt, and when I told her I had exchanged letters with Leonard Peltier, she came damn close to fainting with envy. Anyone doing any "real" activism was "*so* great."

Members reiterated their leader, who we all waited for, was "*so* great" that most of them could not find the words to describe him. I was expecting someone like actor Yul Brynner in the movie *The King and I*. When this leader finally arrived, I met a glib, somewhat articulate, young, charismatic man. He was skinny, in need of a shave and a haircut. He drove a rattletrap van, was clad in old clothes, but I could tell he came from a well-to-do background because of his speech and mannerisms.

Their "careful planning" was going to take place in a local bar. It entailed drinking much beer and listening to local, live music. This group was unorganized, built on bravado and extemporaneous ideas. Their ideology was based on emotion, imagination, and little fact. Each of them seemed to want to be poor and needy to show just how badly the poor and needy (in this case, animals) needed them. They were a handful of mismatched individuals of varying ages who seemed so disorganized, led by a kid, lying about having cells of their organization all over the world. Yet they were responsible for thousands of dollars of property damage, harassment and terroristic threats, theft, burglary, and a string of serious crimes in the United States alone.

I will leave out details for legal reasons, but someone's carelessness blew my cover. Now I became a target of the group. I lived cautiously for weeks, receiving hate mail from across the country when the group posted my name, address, and personal information (including my family members' names) on their webpage. The group terrorized my family and even my neighbors as they continued to threaten the targeted group in the city. Law enforcement officers patrolled to watch my family home. We put a safety plan in place, kept windows shuttered, and changed our driving patterns everywhere we went. I slept on the couch with guns handy.

I learned then: an unorganized group of radicals can be as dangerous as an elite crime gang. All that's needed is an idea and someone willing to take action.

19

Susan Saxe and Katherine Ann Power

Radicals

Philadelphia police officer Joseph Reid later reported he had to take a second look and then study the woman a bit closer from behind his patrol car's steering wheel. The woman he was watching was walking casually down the 10th and Market center city of Philadelphia, accompanied by another woman. This was March 27, 1975, and Officer Reid was about to make one of the most significant arrests of the century, ending one of the FBI's most intense manhunts.

He was watching a woman who had red-brown hair. A bit over five feet tall, she was about 150 pounds. Clad in tight jeans and a pullover blue sweatshirt, she strolled down the sidewalk with a second female. They did not seem to notice the Philadelphia police car nearby, or Officer Reid, who was now glancing at the "Most Wanted" flyer in his hand, the poster he had received during roll call for his 4 p.m. to midnight shift.

The FBI had reissued the flyer only the day prior; on a whim, the Philadelphia offices dropped off a stack of specific "Most Wanted" flyers to the Philly police departments, including the 6th District employing Officer Reid. The FBI suspected their quarry was in the center city area, but they didn't believe she'd be walking about in public.

Secure in his judgment, Reid pulled his cruiser over and parked, then approached the woman near the corner of 12th and Sansom streets. He stopped her to politely request identification. She was not carrying a purse and said she had no ID. She told him her name was "Walsh." When Reid looked her in the face, he knew who she was without a doubt; she had an unmistakable black spot in her left eye, close to the pupil, exactly as the FBI poster described.

Reid took the woman by the arm and placed her in the backseat of the patrol car. To be safe, he also detained the second woman. He radioed for his sergeant, who would confirm Reid's arrest.

Joseph Reid had just arrested Susan Edith Saxe, a domestic terrorist and bank robber who had been on the run since a September 23, 1970, bank robbery where one of her gang murdered a police officer. Upon arrest, Susan had nothing to say; "She was nervous as hell," an officer told the press.[1]

Saxe and the second woman, identified as Byrna Aronson, were taken to the Central Detectives Division to be fingerprinted and interviewed. Saxe produced identification at the police station, giving her name as Ailene A. Hellman, but the jig was up and too late to give fake names. Aronson, who was employed by the Philadelphia Civil Liberties Union, was released. She would not disappear on her friend.

Once in custody, Susan released a statement to the press, stating, "I am a lesbian, a feminist and an amazon," and pledged to keep fighting what she called "a despotic authority." Clearly, she was still a "radical."[2]

Susan Saxe had traveled a long road that had only lasted a few years to end up in a jail cell.

Susan E. Saxe was one of only eight women ever to make the FBI's "Most Wanted" list. She and Katherine Ann Power, along with a group of three others, robbed Boston's Brighton branch of the State Street Bank and Trust Company of $26,585 with deadly consequences. These photographs appeared on the FBI's Wanted poster in 1970 when Saxe had been on the run for years (FBI).

She had been born Susan Edith Saxe on January 18, 1949, in Hartford, Connecticut. An incredibly bright girl, she attended the esteemed Syracuse University, but the studies and classes were far too easy for her brilliant mind. She elected to attend Brandeis University, an American private research university in Massachusetts, less than ten miles outside of Boston.

Founded in 1948 and sponsored by the Jewish community, Brandeis University boasted a strong liberal arts focus. Alumni would include Pulitzer Prize winners, prime ministers, MacArthur Fellows, and a Nobel Prize winner. With her intelligence and drive, Susan Saxe could probably have been among such a prestigious graduating class. Instead, her name would end up on another list, called "FBI's Most Wanted."

She was a sociology student, class poet, an honor student, making the dean's list annually. She was also active in the National Strike Center[3] and became disgusted with the Vietnam War and all it encompassed, like so many others in her age group. She became involved with the student activist movement. "Power to the people!" was a statement she embraced with thousands of others.[4] One of those thousands was Susan's roommate, another sociology major, a young woman named Katherine Ann Power.

Katherine Ann Power was a former Girl Scout, Catholic school valedictorian, and Betty Crocker award winner turned radical bank robber. The FBI released this photograph (circa 1970) on her Wanted poster when she went underground (FBI Wanted poster).

Katherine Ann Power, born January 25, 1949, had six siblings and was from Denver, Colorado. Katherine grew up in a storybook middle-class lifestyle, joining Girl Scouts, winning a scholarship from Maycrest, considered the best Catholic girls' school in Denver. Katherine was a National Merit Scholarship finalist and was the recipient of a Betty Crocker award. Her family was deeply religious, their faces well known at the local Catholic church. Like Susan, Katherine possessed a sharp mind, having graduated valedictorian. She was already writing for the *Denver Post*. Fellow students recall Katherine had shucked that middle-class, Betty Crocker-loving Girl Scout uniform as soon as she arrived at Brandeis, trading it in for a braless orange smock, funky jeans, and bare feet. She and Susan were born to be comrades.

Katherine was soon one of Brandeis' honor students, a brilliant girl who became involved in the campus anti–Vietnam protests and the National Strike Center alongside Susan and their friends. A few of these friends would change Katherine and Susan's fate and help their educated lives become a fascinating story.

A paroled convict and returned soldier named Stanley Bond, 26, drifted into their world; Bond was taking classes at Brandeis on a special program offered to parolees. Like many of their protest buddies, Susan and Katherine had no actual, hands-on involvement with any war; Stanley's background gave him that mystique that intrigues girls involved in such radicalism. Stanley justified his criminal behavior by claiming it was "for the people," meaning females and minorities; despite being a pasty white guy, he considered himself a champion of the Black Panther Party. Susan and Katherine swallowed his stories. Katherine in particular was just mesmerized by Stanley.[5]

Through Bond, Susan and Katherine met two more wanna-be modern-day Robin Hoods: former convicts William "Lefty" Gilday, 41, and Robert Valeri, 21, also on parole. Short, slender Gilday looked more like a washed-up bartender in Chicago's seedy district. Valeri rounded out the group with what they believed brilliant input on how to change the world with his egg-shaped face and emotionless eyes. The group collectively decided arming the Black Panthers with guns and money would be the only way to end the Vietnam War. So where to get the cash?

Where else would an up-and-coming social activist go for big wads of cash?

On August 18, 1970, two of the male members of this group walked into the Prudential Savings & Loan Association at 2114 Central Street in Evanston, Illinois, at the noon hour. One brandished a sawed-off shotgun, the other a handgun. Both robbers produced bags. They robbed two tellers, who stuffed a reported $8,000 into the bags. The women's role, if any, was never published. The robbers fled on foot, which was the last any law enforcement saw of them until later arrested.

The group's movement is unknown until 11 a.m. Tuesday, September 1, 1970, when Stanley Bond and Susan Saxe, each carrying a bag, walked into the Bell Federal Savings & Loan bank at 7578 Haverford Avenue in Philadelphia. Susan, guarding the door, pulled a Molotov cocktail[6] out of her burlap bag while Bond approached the tellers' windows and demanded money.

Bond wore sunglasses with a jean jacket to match his pants. He wasted no time, producing a pistol and pointed it directly at a 19-year-old teller named Elizabeth. "This is a holdup," he told her. "Give me all your money. You have three minutes." He tossed his burlap bag at her. Elizabeth obeyed. The robber told her to pass it to the next teller, a woman named Betty. Betty removed cash from her till and then gave the bag to the third teller, Rosemary. Per the robber's orders, Rosemary's contribution filled the bag: $6,240. She quickly handed it over. Bond pulled the bag's drawstring tight, then he and Susan left the bank, Susan slipping the Molotov into her bag to later discard. A witness would say they walked east on Haverford to Overbrook Avenue "and disappeared."[7] A little boy would later point investigators to a brown paper bag on the street, the bag Susan had discarded. It held a wine bottle full of kerosene with a cotton wick.

Katherine and Susan's little group concluded that if a radical organization needed to rob banks to stop the Vietnam War, they had to have weapons. So, on September 20, 1970, the group burglarized a Massachusetts National Guard Armory of 400 rounds of ammunition, weapons, and a telephone switchboard. Katherine's job was to be a lookout, but she was so nervous she threw up as she watched her comrades torch the place, leaving $125,000 worth of damage in their wake.

All hell was about to break loose on September 23, 1970, on a lazy morning. The Brighton, Boston branch of the State Street Bank and Trust Company, located on Western Avenue and Everette Street, was about to be awakened. At about 9:30 a.m., two men and a woman came marching through the front door, pointing guns and demanding money. No one was sure which robber pulled the trigger, but several rounds went off towards the ceiling, and now everyone in the bank snapped to attention. The armed woman held a rifle pointed at three bank employees who sobbed and begged for their lives. That woman was class poet Susan Saxe.

The radicals departed with $26,585, slipping out the door. Later, one of the robbers would claim they thought it was a good idea to fire a few shots to keep anyone from following them. They were making a clean getaway....

Forty-two-year-old Boston police officer Walter A. Schroeder was one year short of retirement. He was the recipient of the Walter Scott Medal of Valor for his capture of three bank robbers three years prior, and his bravery was legend in the police force. So it was no surprise that Officer Schroeder and his partner, Patrolman Frank Callahan, were the first officers at the scene. Both officers were running towards a second bank entrance when Officer Schroeder observed the robbers dashing toward their getaway car; he stopped in the parking lot in an attempt to halt the robbers. The officer received a bullet to the back from ex-convict and getaway driver William Gilday's .45-caliber automatic machine gun. Officer Walter Schroeder crumpled to the ground, face twisting in pain. Officer Schroeder, father of nine, would not survive.[8]

Now they weren't just bank robbers but cop killers. Running like hell was on their heels, the group raced to leap into a second getaway car, abandoning the first. The car disappeared into the Boston streets. This getaway driver was former Girl Scout Katherine Ann Power.

The group would split up soon after. They temporarily ditched lofty ideas of saving the world from itself in lieu of saving themselves from the death chamber.

At the beginning of their investigation, detectives would find a purple dress at Logan Airport and a name on a flight list to Los Angeles: K. Power. And 60 minutes after Officer Schroeder crumpled to the ground, a "Kathy" Power had put a $100 cash deposit on a red Volkswagen.

That night, they caught Robert Valeri because he visited a resort lounge. He was either high or drunk or both as he sat down, uninvited, at an occupied table in the lounge. He made himself comfortable and flashed cash and a gun to the terrified couple whose evening he just ruined; they excused themselves to flee out a back door to their home where they called the police.

Robert sat on the lounge floor, playing with the gun with onlookers watching; then, he attempted to leave. Lounge staff took his keys and suggested he take a walk to sober up first. He took a walk—and kept walking, for when police arrived, he was gone. Police found him. Three hours after Police Officer Walter Schroeder drew his last breath in St. Elizabeth's Hospital, Robert Valeri would be arraigned in Brighton District Court. Robert turned snitch when he talked to the cops. He ratted out who was involved in the bank robbery as police officers quickly scribbled notes. The definition of "comrades" only went so far in Robert's book.

While the State Street Fund and Trust Company solicited donations for the Walter A. Schroeder Memorial Fund, and other businesses were making donations to assist the officer's large family, Stanley Bond was on an airplane headed for Colorado. The woman sitting next to him in the airport recognized his mug from the media. She quietly reported this resemblance to officials. Bond and the woman boarded the plane with the rest of the passengers without incident. Bond exited the plane in Grand Junction and boarded a flight to Chicago. The flight diverted on the pretense of repairs; as the passengers disembarked, a deputy sheriff was waiting for Bond. Officers frisked Bond and recovered three weapons and $10,000. In 1972, while awaiting trial, Stanley Bond was secretly building a bomb in his cell to aid in his escape; it detonated prematurely, and the explosion painted his cell walls with his remains.

Eventually, the cops caught up with William Gilday, who turned his arrest into a battle. Gilday led the police on a chase where he took hostages, including a grandmother and two children held at gunpoint. The cops captured Gilday.

The women would prove to be the most difficult of all to arrest. They did not give up.

Investigators searched Katherine's apartment shortly after the State Street Bank and Trust Company robbery. Investigators found a massive cache of guns, ammunition, military radios, and detonators; one of the pieces of evidence discovered and confiscated was a telephone switchboard. These items were all identified as stolen during the September 20 burglary of the Massachusetts National Guard Armory. That November of 1970, Susan and Katherine became numbers 16 and 17 on the FBI's "Most Wanted" fugitive's list.

The money that the women held, money earmarked for the Black Panther revolution, went to their survival: plane tickets, food, necessities. So much for power to the people.

Susan and Katherine stayed together, living in feminists' communes, drifting across the United States but never staying in one place for long. Then they went underground: they obliterated their identities, destroying anything that could identify them. They cut ties with anyone and everyone who knew them. College, families, friends—everyone. Out with the old. They changed their names. Then they said goodbye to one another.

Their faces were all over the police department walls, smiling from FBI posters. Still, they managed to hide until Susan was arrested that March 27, 1975, while meandering down 10th and Market in Philadelphia.

Susan Saxe went before the judge for a hearing in March 1975 for the 1970 robbery of the Bell Savings & Loan. In June, Saxe pled guilty.

She was tried in October 1976 before a jury for the State Street Bank and Trust Company robbery. It ended with a hung jury. In January 1977, Susan pleaded guilty in the Suffolk Superior Court to manslaughter and two armed robbery counts. As part of the plea bargain, the Massachusetts and Federal sentences would run concurrently.

Susan was sentenced to 12 years in Framingham State Prison. She received two years' time served. She would be eligible for parole in six years. Susan would release another statement to the press: "I plead guilty today for one reason ... that it is the surest and quickest way to end the hold this state will have on my life and my personal freedom. I have been harassed, hounded and vilified by the state for six and a half years and have been imprisoned for two years. I do not recognize the right of the state to a single day of my life, but I do recognize its power to take that and more. I will never abandon my political commitments in exchange for favors from the system."[9]

While incarcerated, Susan helped establish a children's play area for inmate visitation days and became a partner in a computer programming business ran by inmates called "Con'Puter Systems Programming." She told the media she was still a revolutionary, just not one with a gun committing illegal acts. Half of this statement was true.[10]

While Susan was releasing her statements to the press, Katherine Ann Power continued to move around the United States, landing briefly in Oregon. She had a new identity. She gave birth to a son. She enrolled in cooking school. In 1984 the FBI removed her from the "Most Wanted" list.

Ideals and causes had changed. William Gilday sat in prison. Stanley Bond was buried in pieces after his bomb-making efforts failed. Susan Saxe was somewhere in Philadelphia on parole; she had been released in May 1982 but was still facing charges stemming from the computer company she supervised from prison. Boston police officer Walter Schroeder's daughter grew up to be a detective on the same force where her father served; three of his other children were also cops. The 1970s died, and people forgot about saving the world with bank robberies and Molotov cocktails and "power to the people." Those flower children and radicals grew up and signed for mortgages and became soccer moms and insurance salesmen. Now Katherine was the Betty Crocker–normal she once aspired to be. She had a new name, Alice Louise Metzinger. She had a boyfriend who was a meatcutter and bookkeeper. "Alice" taught cooking classes, worked at restaurants, wrote for a local newspaper, and became part owner of a restaurant. She was seeing a therapist to help her with depression. And she prepared to marry her boyfriend. But something was amiss.

While dealing with a bout of depression, "Alice" confessed it all to her therapist: the dreams of stopping the war and saving America from itself. The robbery. The murder of a cop. The double life.

Trying to save the world from itself was a young person's lofty ideal. Murder was a serious crime. Alice Louise Metzinger was a nice woman, but Katherine Ann Power was a real criminal. And this is real life.

"Alice" agreed to self-surrender. It was time to tell the truth. Katherine had to come back and make right what she did wrong. And the death of Officer Walter Schroeder weighed heavy on her conscience.

On September 15, 1993, Katherine/Alice pled guilty to two counts of armed robbery and manslaughter in a Boston courtroom. Of the murder, she stated, "[Officer Schroeder's] death was shocking to me, and I have had to examine my conscience and accept any responsibility I have for the event that led to it."[11]

Of the robbery, "the illegal acts I committed arose not from any desire for personal gain but from a deep philosophical and spiritual commitment that if a wrong exists, one must take active steps to stop it, regardless of the consequences to oneself in comfort or security."[12]

Katherine/Alice received a sentence of 8 to 12 years for the bank robbery, 5 years and a $10,000 fine for the National Guard Armory theft and fire. She spent her time in prison continuing her education. The system released her in October 1999 on 14 years' probation. She married her boyfriend, who adopted her son, and continued her studies. She became an instructor and has continued philanthropy for persons with AIDS.

Katherine/Alice has evidently learned it doesn't take a bank robbery to create change for the better.

20

The Symbionese Liberation Army

Stealing Patty

If a cover girl existed for female bank robbers, it would be heiress Patricia "Patty" Campbell Hearst. Despite spending only a few years of her life involved with the domestic terrorist organization that kidnapped her, generations will forever remember her as "Tania of the SLA."

The "United Federated Forces of the Symbionese Liberation Army (SLA)" was a revolutionary left-wing organization operating between 1973 and 1975. The group consisted of one black male prison escapee, a smattering of middle- to upper-middle-class white men and women, and, in 1974, a kidnapped Hearst.

The "symbiosis" was in name only, for the group borrowed words, phrases, and ideology from Pan-African solidarity movements, Cuban and South American Marxism, Mao Zedong, Germany's Baader-Meinhof gang, and Italy's Red Brigade. "The words were scarcely understood by the SLA members who uttered them and totally ignored by the public who heard them."[1] *Symbionese* was not even a real word.

Upon its creation there were six females and six males in the SLA. Mary Alice Siem, one of the females, would leave after death threats from the self-appointed "General Field Marshal" escaped con Donald DeFreeze, who named himself Cinque Mtume (DeFreeze mispronounced it "Sin-*Cue*"). When they ditched their lives and went underground, SLA members took on new identities, names of revolutionaries they admired. Angela "Gelina" DeAngelis Atwood, Patricia "Zoya" Soltysik, Camilla "Gabi" Hall, Nancy "Fahizah" Ling Perry, and

Emily "Yolanda" Harris were the female members. The male members were Bill "Teko" Harris, Emily's hot-headed husband, and Willie "Cujo" Wolfe, the idealistic young man who wanted to create change. All but the Harrises and Hearst would eventually die in a 1974 shoot-out with law enforcement.

But first, there was a bank robbery.

The first robbery committed by the SLA was a public relations coup (Cinque pronounced it "coop") to show off their newly acquired member, their kidnapped victim Patricia Hearst, who DeFreeze had renamed "Tania." The robbery had to be unique, the group decided. This time, the robbers wanted the cops to know who the bad guys were. It would be "the people" against "the pigs" (a catch-all phrase for law enforcement members, but also the government, wealthy citizens, and just about anyone held in disdain). The ill-gotten gains came secondary.[2]

Angela Atwood and Bill Harris selected which bank to hit. It would be the Hibernia Bank at 1450 Noriega Street and Twenty-Second Avenue in San Francisco, California.

They must have been a sight: the gruff, arrogant Bill Harris with the cheerful little Angela at his side. Before scouting banks to rob, Angela "General Gelina" Atwood, born in 1949 in suburbia Americana, had cheered on her high school football team as captain of the cheerleading team and as voted "Most School Spirited." Her friends remembered her as a lovely girl with gorgeous eyes and perfect skin, always active in student groups and known for befriending the "outsiders" in school. She was a talented singer who had starred on stage in many high school musicals and plays. The future leftist was an education major when she became involved in politics at Indiana University, eventually moving to Berkeley with her then-husband. She carried her theater skills—and armloads of stolen props—into the SLA by providing wigs and theatrical makeup to be used as disguises. And it had all led to the day she was at Bill Harris's side, selecting a bank to rob, toting an automatic weapon in her groovy, fashionable purse.

Camilla Hall and Emily Harris were both given the task of using stolen credit cards to rent cars for the operation. Stolen credit cards were an SLA staple. Stealing credit cards was one of the few ties between these two women. No two people could have been more opposite than "Gabi" Hall and "Yolanda" Harris.

Angela DeAngelis with her future husband, Gary Atwood, watching her stroll at Indiana University in 1970. They would marry the following year and separate in 1973 when she assisted in creating the SLA and became Angela "General Gelina" Atwood (courtesy Indiana University Archives).

Born in 1945, Camilla was a gentle, trained social worker, an artist, and (now, finally!) an out-and-proud lesbian who left a pious life of loving parents, mission work, and comfortable Minnesota life to eventually move to Berkeley, California. She met and fell madly in love with a woman named Patricia Soltysik. Soltysik's family adored Camilla, enjoying her gentleness, guitar playing, and were the recipients of her artwork. They saw her as a shy woman, quiet, sweet.[3] Camilla's politics were peaceful; she preferred to take part in food boycotts, monitor political situations, discuss philosophy, to be that silent voice in the peace movement. Bombings, guns, and angry rages were not her style. Yet because she wanted to stay with her beloved, Hall had followed Soltysik into the SLA. When Hall went underground, she left everything in her apartment and gave away her artwork.

Emily Montague (b. 1947) hailed from Baltimore, Maryland. She was the only girl child in her family; she had three brothers. Emily grew up in an upper-middle-class neighborhood. Her school report cards always covered with As, she sported the school pep squad's uniform.

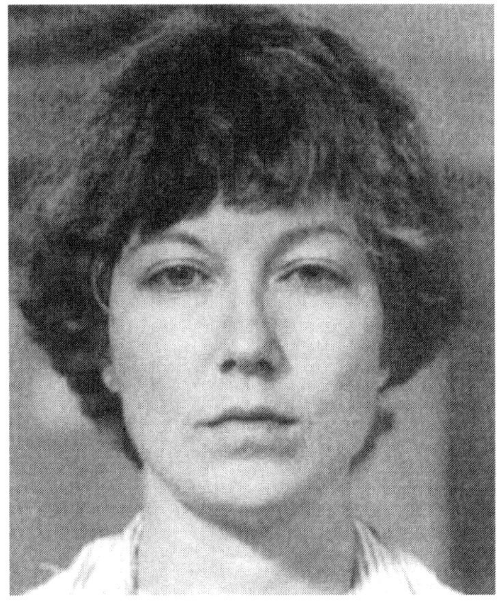

SLA two-time bank robber Emily "Yolanda" Harris. The FBI released this photograph in Harris's Wanted poster. Highly intelligent and from an upper-middle-class background, she reveled in living in squalor and peppered her language in expletives to "act poor" (San Mateo Sheriff's Office mug shot, September 1975).

Once she began classes at Indiana University, she pledged a sorority. She met and married Bill Harris. Emily, small in stature, with a soft voice, was highly intelligent and serious about her studies. She quit her job to begin communal living with uneducated people in the high-crime area of Oakland. Emily became involved in radical politics while obtaining her language arts degree.

She met Angela and Gary Atwood at Indiana University, becoming such good friends that Emily and her husband Bill would move to Berkeley with the Atwoods. Emily was rabid about the "revolution," expletives now a constant in her vocabulary. Fuck the pigs and fuck the fucking capitalist bourgeois! She would rage. The blacks and the poor needed the SLA. *Needed* them. Of this dependency on her whiteness, Emily/Yolanda was sure.[4]

Donald DeFreeze had appointed himself the chief planner; it only made sense: he was an uneducated black man and an escaped convict; thus, he alone was genuinely aware of the struggle, he explained. He was also genuinely aware of the taste of plum wine. Although the leader forbid alcohol and drugs in the SLA, General Field Marshal Cinque declared himself the exception. The SLA members adored him. "I wish I was black!" Bill Harris would sometimes rage. "God, I wish I was black!" But white people, Cinque explained, just could not get their shit together. Thus, a black man had to lead and educate the SLA.[5]

Patricia Soltysik, born in 1950, was another high school success, despite being one of seven children who stayed unhappy at home. Strangely, few public photos exist of her. In high school, she graduated in the top tenth percentile and was student body treasurer. At Berkeley on a scholarship, she became involved in politics during her studies. Patricia "Pat" Soltysik was intelligent, an artist who wrote poetry and dabbled in watercolors. Her writings are clever and deep.[6] Initially, she planned to be a lawyer but drifted into staunch feminism and radical revolution. She ditched school for a program to educate prisoners. When DeFreeze escaped, a mutual friend hid him in Soltysik's house. She and Emily Harris would later be credited for the assassination of School Superintendent Dr. Marcus Foster in 1973 for, in their twisted logic, becoming a fascist. During their relationship Camilla had nicknamed Patricia "Miss Moon"; Patricia liked it so much she had her name legally changed to "Mizmoon." She had to constantly correct her family until they called her "Mizmoon" in lieu of "Patricia." Patricia/Mizmoon was one of the founders of the SLA.

Ex-cheerleader, Goldwater Republican, and Sunday school teacher Nancy Ling "Fahizah" Perry, born in 1947, was of upper-middle-class background. She was Honored Queen in Job's Daughters before attending Whittier College. Nancy transferred to Berkeley, where she majored in English. Then the society girl went far left when she met and married a black jazz musician, worked as a topless blackjack dealer, fought mightily with her husband, and became involved in drugs. She was forced to drop out of college when financial aid dried up. She lived in her car for some time. Friends knew her as someone who was not highly intelligent, rife with physical problems, easily swayed by whatever man she was dating, and attracted to black men (a somewhat cultural taboo in these times). She adopted the sound and dialect of street blacks (a blindfolded Patricia Hearst, in her first months after the kidnapping, thought Fahizah was indeed a black female). Fahizah was tiny, fierce, and scared Princess Hearst, whose closest association to a mean girl, prior to the SLA, was a fight with her sisters.[7]

Atwood had found the ultimate stage where she could write and star in her own drama. Emily Harris had taken honorable ideas and twisted them into some bizarre, self-serving philosophy. Soltysik was deeply committed to reform by revolution, and any kind would do. Smitten Hall would follow Soltysik anywhere. Perry was at a crossroads in life. These women were perfect fits for left-wing terrorism, and their next act, after killing Marcus Foster, was about to happen. Power to the people, man![8]

It was Donald DeFreeze who oversaw the debut of Hearst/Tania at the Hibernia Bank robbery. The "outside" team consisted of the Harrises, Wolfe, and Atwood. The "inside" team consisted of himself, Soltysik, Perry, and their prize: Patricia Hearst. The always-bumbling Hall's job was to open the bank's front door to allow the robbers' grand entrance. Then she was to drive them out of there.

The Very Special Guest Star of the show was Patty Hearst, who was to make a loud speech and let all the pigs know she had moved on to become a revolutionary. Cinque made her practice the big speech.

At about 9:50 a.m. on April 15, 1974, preacher's daughter Camilla Hall swung open the Hibernia Bank front door, allowing heavily armed DeFreeze, Hearst, Perry, and Soltysik inside. Then Perry dropped an ammo magazine and knelt to scoop it up as DeFreeze jumped over her to shout that this was a holdup, and motherfuckers best hit the floor.

An employee punched the silent alarm at 9:51 a.m., and two high-speed cameras began shooting four pictures per second to create a strange, jumping motion picture totaling 400 pictures. Perry was screaming "SLA!" swinging her gun at the people while Soltysik leaped over the partition and then hopped over the prone employees to scoop up cash. Hearst forgot the speech Cinque trained her to announce, but according to witnesses, she did remember to warn everyone she *was* prepared to blow motherfucking heads *off*.[9]

Then two customers walked in the front door, and Perry let off a round of machine gunfire. One of the men took a shot in the buttocks and the other in the hand. They dove out the door and later recovered from the wounds.

The inside group filed out, $10,660 richer, stepping over one of the bleeding victims and hopping into the car where Hall sat behind the wheel. Then they were gone.

The SLA had just robbed their first bank. Later, they would send out a "communiqué"—an audiotaped confession—to ensure everyone knew who it was that took the money. They had Patricia Hearst record a communiqué to ensure the public knew she was the one cradling the M1 carbine in the lobby of the Hibernia.

WANTED

SAN FRANCISCO POLICE DEPARTMENT

37 - 74 BANK ROBBERY - ARMED 18 APRIL 1974

WARRANTS OF ARREST HAVE BEEN ISSUED FOR THE BELOW PERSONS IN CONNECTION WITH THE ARMED ROBBERY OF THE HIBERNIA BANK, 22ND & NORIEGA STREETS, ON MONDAY, 15 APRIL 1974. THESE SUBJECTS ARE TO BE CONSIDERED HEAVILY ARMED AND EXTREMELY DANGEROUS.

DONALD DAVID DE FREEZE
AKA "CINQUE" 11/26/43
5'9",150 lbs., Blk/Brn

PATRICIA CAMPBELL HEARST
WF 2/28/54
5'3", 110 lbs., Lt Brn/Brn

NANCY LING PERRY
WF 9/19/47
5'0", 95-105 lbs., Brn/Brn

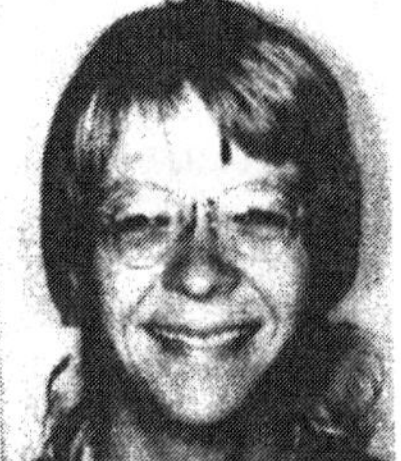

CAMILLA CHRISTINE HALL
WF 3/24/45
5'6", 125 lbs., Blnd/Blu

PATRICIA MICHELLE SOTYSIK
AKA "MIZMOON" WF 5/17/50
5'5", 135 lbs., Brn/Brn

INFORMATION FOR ROBBERY DETAIL
CASEY/GOYTON CASE 7402957

DONALD M. SCOTT
CHIEF OF POLICE

The Wanted poster of five Symbionese Liberation Army (SLA) members after robbing the Hibernia bank featured female members Patricia "Tania" Hearst, Nancy Ling "Fahizah" Perry, Camilla "Gabi" Hall, and Patricia "Zoya" Soltysik. All but two of the SLA female members would die terrible deaths fighting for their beliefs. Also pictured: Donald DeFreeze (San Francisco Police Department, 1974).

Some historians believe Hearst suffered from Stockholm syndrome and became a sworn member of the SLA. Others believe she willingly cast off her legacy of wealth and privilege to join. Still others insist she joined to survive, under constant threat of death. Whatever the real story, the FBI had Hearst's mug for bank robbery.

In May 1974, because of a stupid stunt pulled by Bill "Teko" Harris, Patty "Tania" Hearst was stuck with the Harris duo in a no-tell hotel just outside of Disneyland in Anaheim, California. When they turned on the television to relieve the tension in the room, the scene playing out live on-screen was more tension-filled than any stunt pulled yet.

The police had been alerted that the SLA was holed up in the Los Angeles suburb of Inglewood, California. More than 400 of LAPD's finest, FBI officials, and members of the Los Angeles County Sheriff's Department, California Highway Patrol, and Los Angeles Fire Department surrounded a bungalow at 1466 East 54th Street. They were now ordering the occupants to give it up: drop weapons and come outside.

Thus began one of the most massive police shoot-outs in U.S. history. Law enforcement exchanged gunfire with the members of the SLA terrorist group, who refused to surrender. Television news cameras taking cover from the fracas caught live a plume of smoke rising from the bungalow, flames bathing the sky, and then the building burning to the ground. Donald DeFreeze, Angela Atwood, Patricia Soltysik, Camilla Hall, and Nancy Ling Perry were either shot to death or died from burns and smoke inhalation. Autopsies revealed all of the SLA members had worn gas masks. Even as the flames licked their bodies to scorch and melt their skin, the SLA members continued to fight. In a strange and sad moment, investigators found the skeleton of a little cat beside Camilla Hall's body in the rubble and a letter to her family with some of her poetry in her knapsack.[10]

There were no law enforcement or civilian casualties. A reported total of more than 9,000 rounds (estimate of 4,000 SLA and 5,000 by police) were all caught LIVE by news cameras for the public to observe in living color, including Patricia Hearst and the Harrises; according to Hearst's memoirs, they watched from the seedy hotel room through tears and amid screams of expletives.

When they were not continually bickering, the very annoying Bill Harris and his equally irritating wife Emily, with Hearst in tow, hooked up with established radicals, including one Kathleen Ann Soliah (pronounced SOH-lee-uh). During this time, another bank would lose funds at the end of a gun, causing a tragedy that would have sickening repercussions for years to come.

21

The New World Liberation Front

"Expect the Unexpected"

The activists had renamed Berkeley's Willard Park "Ho Chi Minh Park." This once serene patch of greenery in southeast Berkeley was now the place to gather for rallies, for speeches, for "the people" to come together. To experience "power to the people."

There had been memorials held in the park for the Symbionese Liberation Army's slain members after the May 17, 1974, shoot-out between "the pigs" and the SLA. Judging by the turnout, the SLA spirit lived on in the hearts and minds of left-wing radicals.

On June 2, another organized memorial to the SLA's slain members was taking place. The woman who stood before the microphone onstage at Ho Chi Minh Park spoke passionately of Angela Atwood, a fellow Berkeley student and the speaker's best friend. They were both in the local theater where they had shared the stage, the speaker recalled. The woman said her beloved Angela "Gelina" Atwood and her comrades "were viciously attacked and murdered by 500 pigs in LA while the whole nation watched. Well, I believe that Gelina and her comrades fought until the last minutes, and though I would like to have her with me here right now, I know that she lived happy and she died happy. And in that sense, I'm so very proud of her. SLA soldiers—I know it is not necessary to say, but keep on fighting. I'm with you and we are with you…"[1]

Then, gazing at the crowd from behind her aviator-style mirrored sunglasses, the woman's voice rang out over the crowd. "I am a soldier of the SLA!"[2]

The woman who spoke so fervently was Kathleen Ann Soliah. The FBI was clandestinely taping her as she presented. Maybe she knew she was on camera; perhaps she didn't. Soliah had made it clear she was a card-carrying member of the "Fuck you, pigs! Power to the people!" movement.

Kathleen (b. 1947) hailed from a conservative Lutheran family living in Minnesota. When she was eight years old, the family pulled up stakes and headed for sunny California, shedding off the single-digit winters and welcoming the palm trees and dreams.

"Kathy" had been a Girl Scouts counselor. A pious family, they were all regular churchgoers. She was "pep chairman" on the pep squad at her high school, cheering on the Palmdale High School Falcons. She was popular on the high school stage, having scrubbed off many layers of stage makeup from school plays. Kathy was the quintessential "normal" teen. She would graduate from the U of California in Santa Barbara, a school where she learned to love two things: the world of extreme politics and a man named Jim Kilgore.

With Jim, she made the trek to the mecca of radicalism: Berkeley; Kathy's brother Steve would later join them. It was here Kathy and Angela Atwood became best friends. Angela tried to sponsor her into the SLA, but Kathy and Jim did not want to join. The Kilgores followed the SLA in the media, cheered from the sidelines, but that was as close as they wanted to be.

Kathy and Jim were just as angered by what was going on around them as many of their friends. The 1970s just seemed to be so fucked up, they all agreed, and there was nowhere to go but down. It was going to take some radical movements to wake up America. Kathy and others like her were quick to argue their points: Richard Nixon was sitting in the Oval Office, but he did not end the war. Watergate was proof you couldn't trust the establishment, which meant from the White House on down. The cops were out to get you, mainly if you were black and poor; the prisons were teeming with uneducated, poor blacks, which proved that point. The old geezers had screwed the economy for the younger generation: between 1973 and 1974, the stock market had lost half its value. The Kilgores sat in their car with beads of sweat coursing down their faces, sometimes for an hour, in line with other vehicles to use a gas pump; gas lines were ridiculous thanks to the oil embargo. No one could afford a damn thing with inflation at 12 percent. And the bourgeois, white, filthy rich male was running it all, the Kilgores and their ilk told one another.

The streets seemed meaner, too. There was something new out there, people called "serial killers" who struck with random violence, killing people who were just minding their own business. Someone in a spooky costume calling himself "Zodiac" was sneaking up on couples and murdering them as they were smooching in the car or picnicking on the lake. In October of 1973, black Muslims, "the Death Angels," were shooting whites randomly. A few victims were kidnapped and tortured, and it was grisly. Reported ties between the Death Angels and the Nation of Islam scared everyone. It stirred up old nastiness and created new problems between blacks and whites. There were no real leads on either Zodiac or the Death Angels, fueling the angry, age-old chant, "Why can't the police *do* something!"

The cops, the political figureheads, the older people, none of them seemed to be able to "do something," the radicals theorized. It was up to their generation to "do something," even if it meant a bomb, a gun, or propaganda disguised as truth. So, Kathy, Steve, and Jim created a "cell" and called themselves the Revolutionary Army. They were involved in setting off explosives—never to hurt anyone, but to make statements. Kathy Soliah had always loved the stage. Now the world was her stage. And she had a serious lead. Someone had to take control and wake up America![3]

Going underground meant severing ties with family, but Kathy kept a mail drop box in case she needed to get in touch with anyone. Her father was a conservative man, a veteran of World War II with old-fashioned values, like believing a woman should save her virginity until marriage. So he was very upset to learn that Kathy was living with Jim Kilgore. Still, he and his wife loved their children very much. Kathy's parents did not understand much about Steve and Kathy's political ideas except that they hated them. And Kathy's parents were stalwart in their beliefs, so they didn't care to learn, even when the kids tried.

To pay for their food and shelter and bombs, the Revolutionary Army elected to have honest jobs, so the boys were house painters, and Kathy worked at a bookstore. Through this "outside" work, they created ties with more radicals: Michael Bortin, Willie Brandt, and Wendy Yoshimura. Eventually, a third Soliah would join them: Kathy and Steve's sister Josephine, whom they affectionately called "Jo."

Emily and Bill Harris had read about Kathy's statements at Ho Chi Minh Park, and they knew how close Kathy had been to Angela. In disguise, Emily met Kathy at the bookstore. They arranged to meet at a local church, hidden from the public. The remaining SLA eventually teamed with Soliah's group and a few other radicals. Thus, the broken SLA began a partnership with the Revolutionary Army and became the New World Liberation Front.

The New World Liberation Front (WLF) was no more organized than the SLA, for meetings turned into bitch sessions about who wasn't doing what. Bill Harris wanted to kill pigs, and the WLF planted bombs not to kill but strictly to make statements. Bill wanted to strut about and boss, and the WLF would not allow it. Emily was manipulative. Patricia Hearst, now full-fledged Tania, was the wallflower. And in the middle of it all, they were hungry because there was no money. They ate a lot of horsemeat and mung beans because they were cheap. They were stuck together in a smelly, cramped apartment because the former SLA believed showing their faces meant sure death by the FBI or the PD or the government. Always, always there was a bullet out there with your name on it, per Cinque. Bullshit, the Revolutionary Army members countered, *we* have jobs out there.[4]

When the WLF did decide to act, they began to set off bombs. Patricia/Tania joined in on that action, but she wasn't very good at building explosives, so her bombs never detonated. Bill Harris pretended to be an expert; in reality, he relied mostly on guesswork when he was patching together a bomb.

An underground organization needed money to operate. And where does one obtain a lot of money without working for it? You go to the bank. Finally, an action they could all agree on!

Jo Soliah took a clerking job at a local bank so she could get the inside scoop on operations. Emily Harris scouted for a bank and came up with the Guild Savings and Loan just outside of San Francisco. On February 4, 1975, Bill Harris and Patricia Hearst did a second scouting of the bank. Once the group agreed on the bank, the meticulous planning began. And one of the agreements was that Bill Harris not be directly involved, a decision based on his arrogance and stupidity.

On February 25, 1975, Michael Bortin and Jim Kilgore successfully robbed the Guild Savings and Loan of $3,700, with Kathy Soliah as a lookout and Emily and Patricia assisting in transferring the weapons and the money. It ran smoothly: no one was hurt, the tellers gave up the money, and the robbers escaped, rich and unharmed.

It worked so well that they planned a second robbery.

Patricia took a solo trip to Marysville, California, to case a Bank of America and made copious notes right down to managers' physical descriptions. Still, the group took a vote and decided the Crocker National Bank in Carmichael, a suburb near Sacramento, would work better. They were seasoned bank robbers, the bank had no security cameras, and they had this whole theft thing down pat. It would be too easy.

Kathy planned her dress: a green turtleneck sweater, dark trousers, and hiking boots. She carried a carbine and a pistol in a straw bag. Emily wanted to tote a shotgun, so she was practicing, pointing and thrusting it, trying variations of what she was going to shout at people, words like "move!" and "get down on the floor!" Jim Kilgore warned her not to take the shotgun; it was not a good gun for a bank robbery, and the shotgun Emily coveted had a hair-trigger. Emily, her husband siding with her, told Jim to just shut the fuck up and worry about himself. She knew exactly what the fuck she was doing, had it under control. So, fuck off.

Jim complied.[5]

Perhaps the group should have reviewed their plans that one of them had typed out. Typed to the side of the list of "how-to's" was "EXPECT THE UNEXPECTED."

But first, there was a considerable argument over Emily not being the team leader who entered the bank. What the fuck? Bill raged. She discovered the bank they were going to rob! Some of the members said Emily didn't have the physical presence that was needed to intimidate people. Then someone else said that was sexist bullshit. It turned into an argument over feminism. But it was only fair—Emily was a member, and everyone should get to have a part in the robbery. Emily was an experienced bank robber—wasn't she a brave soldier in the SLA? After much shouting, cursing, manipulations, and accusations, hardheadedness determined that Emily would be the robbery lead.[6]

This was a bad, bad decision.

The group rented cars using stolen identification cards. This idea had the potential to turn into a cluster because the plan was somewhat convoluted, with so much vehicle switching and so many people involved. It turns out that this wouldn't be the problem.

On the morning of April 21, 1975, eight members from three apartments scattered to four different cars: Michael Bortin, Emily, Jim Kilgore, and Kathy, labeled the "invasion team," were in a stolen Thunderbird. Bill Harris and Steve Soliah, holding guns, were in a stolen Mustang, waiting outside the bank for backup. Wendy Yoshimura was in one of the rental cars used as a "switch car." Patricia, armed with a carbine, parked nearby to aid in the escape.

Michael parked the Thunderbird near the Crocker National Bank, and the robbers stepped out, holding their weapons close. The plan was to be in and out of the bank in 90 seconds. They headed towards the door with purpose, while three innocent female customers were also walking towards the entrance. The robbers would have walked into the bank before these customers, but Emily halted production because, for whatever reason, she stopped to look at her watch. So, as they walked into the bank, Michael opened the door for the three customers, one of which was carrying an adding machine. "Thank you," this lady with the adding machine told him.[7] They were the last words she would ever say.

The kindly woman with the adding machine was 42-year-old Myrna Opsahl. She was there to deposit the weekend's offerings from the church she attended. It was a task the church ladies divided, and it wasn't Myrna's turn, but she volunteered when the woman who was supposed to make today's deposit couldn't go. Myrna's life was church and family. She and her husband had been medical missionaries, and now her beloved husband, a doctor, had a practice at a local hospital while she kept the house and raised their four children. "I love you" was always being said in their home and always told with sincerity. Myrna was kind and well mannered. So, when the gentleman who opened her door was now in the bank lobby screaming, "Everybody on the ground! Get the fuck down on the floor!"[8] She must have been both horrified at his behavior ... and scared.

While customers and bank employees dove for the floor, Kathy Soliah ran for the tellers. Jim Kilgore took his place to guard the door.

Emily took her spot, pulled out her hair-triggered, sawed-off shotgun from under her coat, and began counting off … "Fifteen seconds!" Then she noted the only people who had not hit the carpet were Myrna and her two lady friends. Emily roughly ordered them to the floor.

As Myrna's friends moved to the floor, Myrna hesitated. She still held the adding machine. Conceivably, she didn't know if she should set it down, or where, or if she should—

"Emily raised her shotgun," one historian describes the scene, "and the weapon discharged with a tremendous explosion." *Boom!*

Everyone, even the robbers, froze to stare at Emily. Her shotgun still pointing at Myrna, smoke lazily wafting out of the barrel, and Myrna Opsahl was slowly crumpling to the floor, a big hole in her side dripping blood.

And then it was business as usual. Bortin jumped up on the teller's counter, screaming at Myrna's friends to keep their noses down, to not look at Myrna and the pool of blood that was seeping into the carpet. Kathy was now grabbing up money, stuffing it into bags. Emily was shouting out the times. "Thirty seconds!" Thanks to Jo's instructions from her tenure at a bank, Kathy knew right where to look for money.[9]

Bank teller Lindy Aberssen[10] was pregnant, but the robbers forced Lindy to lie in a position that would not protect her unborn baby. Michael began yelling at Lindy, asking for traveler's checks. As Lindy tearfully explained the bank did not have them, Kathy swung her heavy hiking boot to deliver a kick into Lindy's stomach.

Kathy would continue to grab the money, and Michael would continue to shout until Emily told them it was 90 seconds, time to go. Then all three scampered out the door, stepping around Myrna. They walked hastily to the appointed getaway vehicles, switched out as planned, and made a clean getaway back to the apartment.

An ambulance rushed Myrna and the pregnant teller to the hospital. Myrna's physician husband came to her aid, but there was nothing he could do except be with his wife when they pulled the cold, impersonal sheet over her sweet face. The pregnant teller whom Kathy had viciously kicked ultimately lost the baby because of the trauma from the heavy boot's impact. Back at the hideout of the New World Liberation Front, no one cared.[11]

Jim Kilgore was angry with Emily for screwing up their entry time by stopping and fucking around with her watch. He was also furious at her for being lackadaisical with her gun. She was what Jim always accused her of—careless. But, he reasoned, something spared his life: if Myrna had not been in the way, Emily's accidental shot would have hit him instead, and for that, Jim was grateful.

Emily blamed the gun. She reminded everyone of how the trigger had malfunctioned during dry firing practice. And anyway, who cared? "So what if she got shot?" Emily snorted. "Her husband is a doctor. She's a bourgeois pig." Her husband, Bill, backed her up, holding up the shotgun shell recovered from the crime scene. "The murder round" he was calling it. Then he would agree with Jim's claim. "If it hadn't been for good old Myrna, one of our comrades would be dead."[12]

After following thousands of leads and spending even more man-hours and dollars locating the group, the FBI arrested Bill and Emily Harris on September 18, 1975, as the couple was jogging. Bill froze in fear, but Emily ran, screaming and cursing. Patricia Hearst and Wendy Yoshimura were arrested the same day as they lounged in their hideout apartment.

The Harrises wrote syrupy and sexual notes to one another in jail, but Emily divorced Bill once released from prison. Emily received an eight-year sentence for the Hearst kidnapping, incarcerated at the California Institute for Women, where she spent the first half of her term in solitary confinement. She studied computer programming. Bill and Emily Harris served about six years each in prison.

Upon her release in 1983, Emily began dating women and ran a successful consulting business. After his release, Bill took a job as a receptionist with a law firm, then obtained a private investigator's license. In 1998, he married a well-respected attorney and became what he hated most: a suburban soccer dad, a bourgeois pig, just like many of his ex-radical comrades had done.

Hearst was convicted on March 20, 1976, of bank robbery and using a firearm during a felony commission. She received seven years in prison. In January 1979, President Jimmy Carter commuted Patty Hearst's sentence; that same year, Patty married one of her bodyguards. In January 2001, President Bill Clinton granted her a pardon. She is now an actress, involved in charities and shows champion dogs.

Wendy Yoshimura received a sentence of 1 to 15 years for illegal possession of explosives. She served her time at the Frontera state women's prison. Released on parole in September 1980, Wendy is now an artist who lives quietly in the San Francisco area.

Steve Soliah returned to housepainting after his acquittal in the Carmichael bank robbery. He died from a stroke in 2013. Michael Bortin became a fugitive after Patricia's arrest but surrendered in 1984, served 18 months on a parole violation, then married Jo Soliah; Jo remained free of charges. Jim Kilgore had fled to Africa but was extradited to the United States in 2002. He pled guilty to the Carmichael robbery and explosive-related charge and was released from prison in 2009.

Following the September 18, 1975, arrests, Katheen Soliah went further underground, crossing the United States. She returned to her home state of Minnesota. She changed her identity and called herself Sara Jane Olson. She began a completely new life, marrying a doctor, living in a posh house, and raising three children. Sara and her husband traveled to Africa to do medical missionary work. She became all the things the old Kathleen had hated and preached against: a bourgeois pig of the

Kathy Soliah assisted in an April 21, 1975, bank robbery with horrific results. She was on the run for about 30 years. She was caught when *America's Most Wanted* aired her story (FBI Wanted poster).

establishment. But some of Kathleen Soliah still peeped through. "Sara Olson" was involved in some politics, charity and volunteer work, albeit from a minivan.

She named her daughter "Emily."

Sara/Kathleen returned to her former love: performing in local theater. Her face was all over town, but this time it wasn't on Wanted posters; it was advertising the next theater production. Did she ever wonder, *Oh, Angela Atwood, if you were only here…!*

Kathleen Ann Soliah/Sara Jane Olson might have washed her hands of bombs, guns, the SLA, the New World Liberation Front, and—yes—even Myrna Opsahl and Lindy Aberssen. But the FBI had not washed their hands of Kathleen. All leads dead, the feds turned to mass media.

22

Sara Jane Olson

AKA Kathy Soliah's "Witch Hunt"

America's Most Wanted (*AMW*) was a television show on which host John Walsh profiled crimes committed by fugitives who were at large, asking the television audience to call in with any clues or information as to where the fugitives were hiding. Walsh, best known for being the father of a little boy who had been abducted and later found dead, was a victim's advocate who was instrumental in changing laws to protect children. *America's Most Wanted* debuted on television in 1988 and initially profiled murderer David J. Roberts, an escaped convict. Within four days of the broadcast, police captured Roberts as a direct result of the show. *AMW* was a hit, and Walsh was a celebrity vigilante.

On May 15, 1999, when Americans turned on the television show to see what criminals they could help catch this week, they learned about Kathleen Soliah. They learned how this tall, thin woman was responsible for an attempted bombing of a Los Angeles police car. After the show, 19 tips came in. One of them sounded promising.

The tipster explained this really nice lady was living in a suburb of St. Paul, Minnesota. She was one of those moms where kids liked to go hang out; the mom was always baking fabulous desserts for school events or her kids' teams. She was the first to volunteer to help others. She did volunteer work and was an outspoken advocate. People could count on her. But she looked an awful lot like the woman on the *AMW* show....

One month later, almost a day to when the show aired, Sara Jane Olson, aka Kathy Soliah, wore handcuffs. She was one mad bomber-turned-homeroom mother. "This is a witch hunt. ... I am being transformed by the Los Angeles District Attorney's Office into a model of anti–Americanism and thuggery." She was seething.[1]

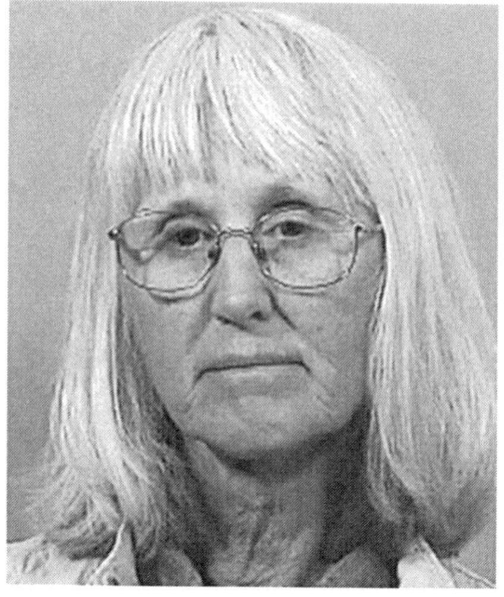

Sara Jane Olson was a suburban housewife and mother when arrested. She was popular for her baking skills, performed in local theatre, and did volunteer work. When she was arrested, it sent shockwaves across the nation (California Department of Corrections, Chowchilla Prison mug shot, March 17, 2009).

Olson was charged with conspiracy to commit murder, possession of explosives, explosion, and attempt to ignite an explosive with intent to murder. After she posted bond, she began to work feverishly on her defense. The "perfect mom" wrote and sold a cookbook, *Serving Time: America's Most Wanted Recipes,* to raise money for her defense. She hired defense attorneys who were famous for defending radicals.

However, she had some explaining to do about her past to her friends and fellow soccer moms. So she did what Sara Jane Olson did best: cooked up some wonderful dishes, had close friends over who brought food, gathered together the group and announced who she really was and where she had really been. It was akin to a Tupperware party for the coming out of ex-radicals.

And then it seemed like the world was coming to an end when two U.S. passenger airplanes were hijacked and flown into the twin towers of the World Trade Center in downtown New York. A third hijacked plane crashed into the Pentagon. Passengers thwarted the fourth hijacked plane to prevent crashing into Washington, DC. Close to 3,000 people died, and over 6,000 were seriously wounded. The combined attacks were masterminded by a radical extremist group of Sunni Islamists called al-Qaeda. It took place on September 11, 2001. The experience is also called 9/11.

9/11 made foreign terrorism real, and it made Americans realize the U.S. was vulnerable to attack. The threat of the 1970s' domestic terrorism had passed. Now it was time to worry about extremists from other countries.

Sara's case took a backseat to the terrorist attacks on September 11, 2001. Then it picked up and continued for Sara Jane Olson, and she would use the 9/11 attacks to her advantage in her statements.

She may have legally changed her name, but she was still Kathy Soliah, and she always loved the stage. Enter controversy and scene-stealing actress, stage leftist. Sara made a statement to the press: "It became clear to me that the [9/11] incident would have a remarkable effect on the outcome of this trial ... the effect was probably going to be negative. That's really what governed this decision, not the truth or honesty, but what was probably in my best interests and the interests of my family."[2]

On October 31, 2001, both parties reached a plea bargain, and Sara pled guilty to two counts of possession of explosives with intent to murder. The defense dropped the rest of the charges.

But Sara's statement to the press had angered Superior Court Judge Larry Fidler because she was admitting she lied in court. He ordered another hearing for November 6. On this date, he asked her, more than once, if she was guilty of the charges. She replied that she had not made the bomb, possessed, or planted the bomb placed under said police car but *did* aid and abet, so she pled guilty to that charge. Seven days later, she filed a motion requesting to withdraw her guilty plea. She just couldn't plead guilty because she wasn't guilty. She wanted a trial.

Judge Fidler offered to let Sara testify under oath about her role in this case, but she refused. In January 2002, there was an audible gasp in the courtroom gallery as the judge sentenced Sara Jane Olson to two consecutive ten-years-to-life terms. The judge reminded her the Board of Prisons could change the sentence. Her attorneys offered great news for Sara and her suburbanite friends: sentencing laws and good behavior could have an effect on decreasing the time Sara would have to sit behind bars.

It seemed as though everyone had forgotten the fact that Kathy/Sara had kicked a pregnant woman, causing the woman to miscarry, during the robbery of the Crocker National Bank in Carmichael on April 21, 1975. And it appeared the court was brushing aside the murder of Myrna Opsahl, the sweet mother of four killed because she had volunteered to deposit her church's offerings that morning. Kathy/Sara did not pull the trigger herself, but that did not make her entirely innocent. She had offered no apologies and shown no remorse; thus far, she was just complaining about mistreatment by the right-wing machine.

But Myrna's family had not forgotten about Myrna, and they wanted vindication. Their mom laid in a pool of her own blood while the robbers stepped over her, and she laid on the operating table while their daddy, Myrna's husband, stood over her, helpless. The Los Angeles District Attorney's Office wanted Myrna to have her day in court, too. Now, with new evidence obtained through modern technology, it was time; Myrna's family and the DA's offices pushed Sacramento to reopen the case.

It had taken close to 28 years, and it meant pulling former SLA members back into court. The city had demolished the Carmichael bank building years ago but not the memories of those who were there. In 2002, it finally happened. Myrna Opsahl was going to have her day in court.

The courtroom doors opened for Myrna's surviving victims, shuffling feet and creaking wood as people took their places, the press vying for the perfect camera angle.

Now using a different name, Emily Harris was there; she sported the same haircut as she wore in her mug shot from so long ago, looking puffy in the face. Bill Harris was cocky as ever, assured he could beat the case. Michael Bortin, looking haggard at 54, and Sara Jane Olson, now facing another charge, were present as well.

Sara decided to give press interviews, focusing on her martyrdom and not her guilt. Again, the star of the show is…!

All of the defendants were pondering the case going to trial, the weight of the evidence, the time it would take, the jury … it did not make sense to roll the dice. The guilty parties were in their 50s. They had lives now, children, families, jobs. Screw it. Plea bargain time. What's the prosecution offering?

Emily, Bill, Michael, and Sara's attorneys were bargaining with the prosecutors to make a deal everyone could live with. Each pled guilty to second-degree murder. Bill received seven years of imprisonment. Michael and Sara each received six years.

Emily, who fired the shot, received eight years. On the day of the robbery, Emily had said of killing Myrna, "So what if she got shot? Her husband is a doctor. She's a bourgeois pig." Today in court, she spoke aloud to her victim's son. "I've thought about your mother a lot. Your mother was never an abstraction to me. It's absolutely unacceptable that this happened. I will be sorry for the rest of my life."[3] Of her eight-year sentence, Emily served four and was released on parole in 2007. When released, she had a difficult time trying to restart her business.

Sara Jane Olson (nee Kathleen Ann Soliah) strolled out of prison when they accidentally released her in 2008 after a parole date miscalculation. She was able to spend five days in the free world until rearrested. Finally, the ex-radical walked out for good in 2009 after serving seven years in the Central California Women's Facility in Chowchilla. She returned to suburbia to disappear, finally, into the dusk of the backstage.

Bill Harris served close to five years. By then, his second wife had divorced him, and his children alienated him. He moved away to start anew.

Jim Kilgore was extradited from South Africa and charged with the murder of Myrna. In 2004 he took a plea deal and was sentenced to six years for the crime. He was released in 2009.

No one else received a charge in the death of Myrna Opsahl. With the sentencing of Jim Kilgore and the closing of the Opsahl murder case, the family was expected to have closure.

Part VI

What Little Girls Aren't Made Of

23

Mean Little Girls

Or Mean Little Brains?

As a criminologist who has devoted close to 30 years in studying crime, I have always insisted "there is nothing meaner than an adolescent girl." This usually draws guffaws from an audience; at the same time, it brings nods of agreement. Considering teenaged females and crimes they commit—from schoolyard bullying to murder—in comparison to the same crime committed by boys of the same age, crimes committed by females have a cruel streak, a psychological twist. Compare murdering a peer, for example. Girls are more cunning; they plan and scheme. Yet even when they swear one another to secrecy, they will usually turn immediately to break their own pact. Why?

Nature or nurture? Both. And either.

As one example, in the report "Females in the Justice System: Who Are They and How Do They Fare?" Bright et al. note there are common risk factors associated with female juvenile delinquency:

- Maltreatment and poverty
- Mental health diagnosis
- Family and caregiver problems
- Living in disadvantaged urban areas
- Foster or group care
- Substance abuse

Female crime appears to be reactive; "violence among female youth can be a response to a broken or threatened relationship … offending may correspond to male partners' influence. Running away may at times be a link between a girl's family problems and later offending behavior."[1]

A teenaged girl is in a precarious place. Physically, she is dealing with the new onslaught of puberty. Humans place much emphasis on the body—"fat" versus "thin," how a woman "should" look. The introduction of hormones and emotions that come with menstruation. Changes in the skin that create acne. The fact that girls mature faster than boys. Emotionally, it is a time for abstract thinking, desiring independence from parents, an interest in relationships, questioning of sexuality. It's a time between childhood and young adulthood. And then there's peer pressure, learning about oneself. "Am I a leader or a follower?" The pressure of the future looms ahead: What do you want to do? College? Trade school? Marriage? Mental illness or emotional disorders start by age 14. Suicide is the third leading cause of death in 15–19 year olds.

Television true crime shows, books, and movies feature female teens and adolescents who commit heinous crimes, such as the murder of a peer. While this type of crime does occur, it is still rare. (This is why it was made into a book or movie—it makes for an interesting story!) Still, "serious" crime remains a "male crime." A study on girls (younger than age 18) in the juvenile justice system released by the U.S. Department of Justice revealed less than one-third of all youth arrests are of girls, "their involvement varied by defense." Females account for 40 percent of arrests for both larceny theft and liquor law violations, 37 percent for simple assaults, and 35 percent for disorderly conduct. For robbery, females account for only 11 percent. Thus robbery remains a "male" crime.[2]

Evolution has ensured that men and women developed distinctively. Females have often had to survive by their wits since the beginning of the human species. Males are more often physically built to survive by power: stronger physique, higher respiratory functioning for prolonged running and jumping, larger bodies. While both males and females possess instinct, women's instinct is considered fine-tuned; we call it "women's intuition." Some believe that because women do not have the brawn, they must have the brain: the ability to figure out survival outside of physical fighting. They believe this continues today: men are physical. Women scheme. When they feel jilted, men will fight. Women will think. A punch-out in a bar versus a key down the side of a car. Women are emotionally driven. The female versus male emotional response has been studied over years: "Numerous studies have shown that, compared with men, women usually experience more frequent and stronger negative emotions."[3] This observation is cited in one study that observes "women show relatively stronger emotional expressivity, whereas men have stronger emotional experiences with angry and positive stimuli."[4] This also might explain why incarcerated females are known to be overly emotional and dramatic, much more so than men.

But once girls are entered into the legal system, are they entering a revolving door? In the last decade legal experts have discussed creating "juvenile female courts" because "historically speaking, the American juvenile justice system [is] formed in a manner intended to cater predominantly to male offenders.… The end result is often a quick dismissal or inadequate managing of [female offender] cases, leaving the core issues unresolved."[5] Some argue this sets the precedent for a female juvenile to grow to become the victim of domestic violence, hinders the girl from obtaining an education or skill set, and limits their parenting skills—in short, sets them up for failure.

There is a legal argument that juvenile justice systems are setting the adult age as 18 when the human brain does not mature at 18. Harp (2017) has noted how "neuroimaging studies" show the adolescent brain develops through 18 past the 20s. "Some advocates and practitioners … promote raising the age of juvenile court jurisdiction to 24.… Maturity is unique to each person."[6]

The juvenile brain is guided more by emotion and reaction, the part of the brain called the amygdala. The amygdala develops earlier than the frontal cortex, the section that controls reasoning and logic. Thus when we ask the kid, "why did you *do* that?" and we get "I dunno," we really are getting the truth.

An adolescent's world is about the "here and now." The focus is on committing the crime and its immediate reward. There are no consequences of criminal behavior, and this includes schoolyard bullying to vandalism to murder. Afterward there is that cocoon of false safety a child carries with them even when the evidence is there, and it is the same as when they were small; "I'll get away with it because I can lie / fool them / keep a poker face." When presented with evidence, there is almost a "pretend" stage of "it didn't happen," including "it was all a dream" (denial to self) or "I don't want it to be real" and/or "It wasn't my fault" (blaming others).

For an adolescent mind, a bank may be perceived as a cash cow waiting to be milked. Young people may not understand exactly how banking systems operate. Few care the average take on a bank is less than $1,500 (a large amount of money to an adolescent). Tellers no longer keep an untold amount of cash on hand, ripe for the taking, but few people comprehend this or are aware—including some bank-robbing adults. It's a simple process to young minds: People go in to put money into the bank. People take money out. There are no "real" police guarding; no one will stop you. And the mantra of the juvenile criminal everywhere: "I won't get caught."

Put these facts together—the lack of proper resources for juvenile females in the justice system, the immaturity of the juvenile brain, and a juvenile's misconceptions regarding banks—and there is a recipe for the crime.

In the last decade, there is an alarming number of juvenile bank robberies. Some are masterminded by adults who believe they will not be held accountable, as the adult didn't physically walk into the bank. And some of the robberies are actually planned and executed by the juveniles themselves.

By the same token, as reckless and clueless as juvenile criminals can be, given their state of circumstances, a young person holding a weapon and demanding cash might be perceived as far more dangerous than any adult.

24

Chelsea and Elysia Wortman

Twin Twin Robberies Robberies

Chelsea and her fraternal twin, Elysia, would later admit they said a prayer. Then they looked at one another through the eyeholes of the masks they wore, took deep breaths, and headed towards the New Jersey bank.[1]

Chelsea had a trash bag. Elysia had her brother's BB gun. They walked into Barnegat's Sun National Bank and shouted, "This is a holdup!"

The twins walked straight up to teller Carolyn Smithers,[2] the bank manager. Elysia pointed the gun at the teller and demanded cash as her twin sister shook the trash bag open.

"Is this a joke?" Smithers asked, looking from one of the girls, who was wearing a ski mask, to the other who had a stocking pulled over her head.

"No, we ain't fucking joking! Give us your money!" One of the girls snarled.

Money was dumped into the trash bag, and the robbers started out; then the one holding the trash bag stopped, taking two steps back. "Is that all of it?" she asked incredulously.

"The bank doesn't keep a lot of money on hand," Smithers told her.[3]

That seemed to satisfy the skinny robber. Both thieves hurried out with $3,500 to the getaway car, a 1992 Buick Skylark. Their driver, Kathleen Wortman Jones, hit the gas. Kathleen was their mother.

Kathleen had to drive them because the sisters were not old enough to have a license. Sun National Bank had just been held up by two 14 year olds.

The girls would later testify that it was family hardship that forced them into the bank on October 29, 2002. "I saw that my family was upset. The money was needed." Chelsea would say.[4]

The twins were born on December 5, 1987. Elysia went by nicknames Le, Le-Le, and Leesh. As with most twins, the girls were referred to as "Chelsea-and-Elysia," as if one, and they had "a twin thing" as their family called it, that special connection other siblings cannot share.

Their family constantly lived paycheck to paycheck, just surviving. Now situations were dire in the Jones household, according to Chelsea, and robbing a bank for fast cash seemed like the best solution. Kevin, their stepfather, and Catherine were filing bankruptcy in a desperate attempt to save their home. Creditors were constantly phoning threats, preparing to foreclose. To save money, 12 people were crammed into their $94,000 four-bedroom ranch style home: the twins, their mother, Kathleen, who had been a teenaged mom. Kevin Jones, 37, was the girl's stepfather of seven years. Kevin had always worked menial jobs as a laborer, to include construction, while slinging dope on the side. Then he was popped and spent three years in the slammer for dealing cocaine. Kevin was a big guy at six foot four and 310 pounds, and now he couldn't work because of congestive heart failure. The twins' siblings lived with them: a sister and brother and two stepsisters. Then there was Kevin's mother and Kevin's brother. Two family friends, one being a former coworker, rounded out the brood. The twins had been at the house full time since being kicked out of school two years prior. Chelsea already had a bad reputation for her criminal behavior and bad attitude. So now she had more time to kill, sitting around at home and listening to the constant family troubles.

With privacy a luxury, it was easy to overhear one particular conversation between Kevin and "a lawyer, saying bankruptcy proceedings were stalled, which meant they could still lose their home." The phone rang a second time, and Kevin was negotiating "about an overdue phone bill." Both twins were privy to these phone calls. Chelsea and Elysia decided they had to help their family. If someone didn't take action, they would lose their home. Then where would they go? This is when Chelsea says she hatched the robbery plan. "I decided to rob a bank."[5] Stepsister Devinee agreed to be an accomplice.

Chelsea's mother, Kathleen Wortman Jones, 34 at the time, refused to believe Chelsea was serious about committing the crime. Chelsea allegedly told her mother regardless if Kathleen would help or not, the bank would be robbed.

Fine, Kathleen said. Someone had to drive them anyway.

Chelsea took her brother's BB gun and used nail polish to paint over the orange tip so it would look realistic. Then, as Kevin slept, the twins and their stepsister Devinee slipped out of the house and headed for the Sun National Bank, Kathleen behind the wheel of her Buick.

It was a five-minute ride to the bank. Suddenly, Devinee chickened out.

Whatever, the twins must have said. But they weren't about to turn tail. They dropped Devinee off at the house. Then they returned to the task.

Kevin says he learned of the robbery after the fact. His wife and daughters came home, tossed the money onto the kitchen table, and said, "we did it." Kevin would later testify, "I was raging, telling them to get the fuck out of my house." Then his advice turned practical: he had everyone trash the clothes they had worn during the heist. But keep the money because that would get them out of the dire straits they were in. Then he took his wife, Devinee, and the twins to Atlantic City.[6]

Kevin and Kathleen took some of the money to Caesar's Palace Casino. The idea was to launder the stolen money, investigators would later claim. The twins went shopping with some of the loot, meandering through Ocean One Mall.

Kevin Jones would later argue there was no way he could turn in his wife and daughters for the crime. And now the family actually had money to play with! But the joy didn't last long. Two days later, instead of sitting down at the dinner table, the family was sitting down at the jail book-in. Cops had shown up just as the Jones family was preparing to eat their evening meal and had hustled Kathleen and the twins out the door while investigators searched the house.

Le-le pretty much sealed the deal when Kevin's mother began protesting the arrest as the cops escorted the look-alike bandits out the door. "Grandma, shut up!" she shrieked at the old woman. "Me and Chelsea robbed the fucking bank!"

Investigators recovered $2,500 of the stolen money.

As detectives questioned them, the twins remained tough, then "softened up," a detective recalls. Chelsea attempted to take all of the blame. Chelsea was a dichotomy—a sweetheart who felt responsible for everyone; then she could also be vicious, a lover of hard-core rap and the street style. Elysia was described as "more introverted," a "fan of ballads, sketching, and cooking." Though she was emotionally immature, "I don't think she understood what would happen if they got caught," said a friend.[7]

The females were charged with bank robbery. Kevin was charged with money laundering, obstruction of justice, aiding and abetting a felon, and endangering minors.

Kathleen would plead guilty and receive 15 years.

Chelsea remained the cool one, even when taking the stand in court. Elysia was just angry at her parents for getting her in this situation. And then Kathleen wrote a letter to Elysia, asking her to lie to protect her parents from prosecution. Kathleen had to testify against Kevin; the law of spousal immunity did not apply because of the child endangerment charge. But on the stand, getting Kathleen to say anything bad about Kevin was like pulling teeth. And while in juvenile detention, the girls had received a letter from their mother that read in part: "If we all say we weren't going to Atlantic City to launder, just to get away from the area, and the discussion occurred on the way home, [Kevin will] get off. But please remember that if they try to make you testify, don't let them make you say anything that will hurt me or Pop."[8]

The twins ended up taking a plea bargain. In exchange for pleading guilty and testifying against Kevin, they would each serve four years in a juvenile facility. So they testified. On September 24, 2003, they were transferred from the juvenile prison so each could sit in the witness box to give their testimony.

The girls were only 15, but they were tigresses on the stand. Chelsea testified first. She wore her brunette hair tight against her head, wrapped in a bun. She told the court she was "determined" to go through with the robbery in an effort to prevent the foreclosure. Her mom had told Chelsea, "'You're not going to do that [rob].' You'll get in trouble.' I let her know 'if you're not coming, I'm still doing it.'"

When the prosecution showed Chelsea a still bank camera photo of her robbing the bank, she identified herself with a smile. "It's me."

Her sister took the stand. Elysia's hair was darker, and freckles dotted her long, angular face. Initially, she was a little smartass, giving snippy answers to the prosecution. Her bravado gave way, and she was in tears after describing the aftermath of the robbery. "Want a tissue, Chelsea?" Her stepfather's attorney asked her.

"I'm not Chelsea!" she snapped.

Elysia let the court know just how angry she was and where her anger was directed. "I'm mad at him," she glared at Kevin. "And I'm mad at my mom for getting me into this situation."[9]

Testifying against their stepfather must have been bittersweet. Their biological father left them when the twins were young. Growing up, they lived in a home that was reportedly clean, neat, and orderly. They sang in church choir, and strangers noted their excellent manners. But in their teen years, the family began experiencing money problems, which led to in-fighting. Because their stepfather was black in a predominantly white town, they felt out of place. A bout with mononucleosis kept them out of middle school for a chunk of time. Then the twins lost interest in school altogether. Anger just built inside them, "fuck you" replacing "yes, sir" and "please and thank you." So, Kevin Jones was the only father figure Chelsea and Elysia knew—for better or worse.

Kevin was looking at 30–50 years behind bars but eventually was given four years in exchange for pleading guilty to obstruction of justice.

And the family home that the twins had risked their lives to save? It went into foreclosure in 2003. But before it could be sold, it caught fire and burned to the ground.

The saga was not over for the bank-robbing twins.

They were sent to Valentine Residential Community Home in Bordentown, New Jersey. Chelsea started a job in the facility's salon and Elysia was painting murals on the detention center's walls. They began attending school and church.

In August 2004 Elysia, now 16, and another girl her age must have decided they had had enough and walked away from Valentine. Their flight from custody was short-lived; they were scooped up by the law less than 24 hours later when someone ratted them out. The girls were dropped off at the Burlington County Jail for women. It was back to court for Leesh and a more secure facility, this time with "escapee" stamped on her paperwork.

Elysia Wortman became one of the 38,364 people in 2010[10] who committed suicide when she took her own life on January 16. She is remembered as a kind person, an accomplished artist who loved to cook. She left a family and many friends who loved her. She was 22 when she died.

25

Moxham, Johnstown, Pennsylvania

The Youngest Female Robber Caught

As of December 6, 2005, the First National Bank in the Moxham section of Johnstown, Pennsylvania, had been robbed four times in the past five years. This included an April 2001 high-profile case when a lone male robber, clad in a baggy sweatshirt and baseball cap, walked into the branch and got away with $2,954.[1]

The case drew national attention because police initially searched for a male suspect. But the thief was actually a female disguised as a male. She was Johnstown resident Jacqueline George, and she would eventually receive a 37-month sentence in federal prison.

And on December 6, 2005, there was about to be yet another high-profile case at the Moxham branch. This would be twice as notorious as Jacqueline George's cross-dressing heist.

About noon that day, a smooth-faced black male of medium height, dressed in a baggy red sweatshirt and oversized khaki pants, a cap pulled snug down on his forehead, entered the bank and sauntered up to one of the tellers. He asked politely for a piece of paper. Video recorded him walking over to a customer table, where he was observed scribbling out a note on the paper.

The young man did not seem to be satisfied with what he had written, so he went back to the teller and requested another piece of paper. Then it was back to the customer table to write on this second piece of paper.

Evidently, this was not up to par either, because the fellow tossed it into the trash can.

Both notes were now tossed, and the young man walked up to the teller and calmly ordered the smiling employee to hand over the money within a certain amount of time. The bank was being robbed again; this robbery made number five.

As the robber fled on foot, the teller contacted bank management.

Shortly after, witnesses outside of the bank observed a young girl near a trash container, tossing some clothing into the bin. The girl was discarding an oversized red sweatshirt and a ball cap.

Once police arrived, they reviewed the videotapes of the robbery and told the bank management the robber was not a male.

But no one blamed the tellers. One day you are helping customers deposit their paychecks or checking their balances, the next you are wondering if you get to go home that day. "You can definitely see how the tellers, going through the stress of a robbery, would have thought she was a boy," one investigator offered.[2]

Investigators canvassed the neighborhood and discovered the robber had been inside and outside a nearby convenience store, and it was all captured on surveillance video. The notes and discarded clothing were recovered and tagged as evidence.

Later, investigators would learn the robber asked for the pieces of paper to practice writing out demands for the money: how to say it, what to say. On the second note, the wording changed a bit. Then the notes were just discarded, and the robber flew by the seat of her baggy khakis.

The suspect was arrested later that same evening by Johnstown police at a relative's house in the Hornerstown neighborhood. She was charged as a juvenile and held at the Cambria County Juvenile Detention Home. Why was she charged as a juvenile?

The girl that robbed the First National Bank in the Moxham section of Johnstown, Pennsylvania, unknowingly gave the bank both a national news story and a national record. She was 13 years old. As of 2005, she was the youngest female on record to be arrested for robbery of a United States bank.

At the time it seemed impossible a 13-year-old child would walk into a bank to rob it. Five years later, the idea of what was "impossible" would change.

26

Symmes Township, Cincinnati, Ohio

The Youngest Female Robber at Large

January 5, 2010, was a Tuesday, and around 3:19 p.m. business was slow. It was cold outside, cold enough for heavy jackets and caps. A blanket of snow kept most folks inside for the day. So, there were no other customers when the two girls walked into the 1st National Bank on 9051 Fields Ertel Road in Symmes Township, Cincinnati, Ohio.

There was one teller, and she looked up and smiled at the two girls who walked into the bank, the doors closing quietly behind them. "One girl appeared to be 14 to 16 years old, about 5 feet 4 inches with a heavy build, and the second girl was about 12 years old and 5 feet 1 inches, and both girls were black."[1] Video shows the bigger girl wearing a hooded top and blue jeans. The younger girl, slimmer, wore a baseball cap snuggled down to hide her face.

The teller's face went from smiling to incredulous when the heavyset girl produced a note on a yellow, lined sheet of paper: "Don't look up or alert other tellers or you will die. I'm not by myself. All $100's, $50's and $20s. no dye pak [*sic*]."[2] It was no joke. These two kids were robbing the bank. The note implied if the teller did not comply, someone was going to get hurt. And these girls weren't even old enough to graduate high school.

Nonetheless, per policy, the teller complied immediately by removing the money from her till and passing it over, bills that included "bait money."

Taking the money but leaving the note, the girls turned on their heels, walked quickly out of the bank lobby, exited the building, then ran in an easterly direction. They raced past a local Comfort Inn towards a group of tan and red brick apartments. The young robbers were $3,000 richer.

Per protocol, the bank was locked and closed immediately. Law enforcement and banking officials were notified. Sirens and red and blue patrol car lights interrupted the otherwise quiet neighborhood.

When police arrived, they were directed to the log books where the bait money's serial numbers were logged. Now that the bait money was out the door, it was officially "hot money." If the hot money was located, the robbers could be traced. (Some banks also keep copies of bait money.)[3]

Where it was the norm to see an occasional police car cruising Fields Ertel Road, now the number of police vehicles more than doubled, with cops from two different counties. Overhead, a police helicopter could be heard, its blades *whup-whup-whup* overhead. Canine police vehicles were called in, and sniffer dogs eager for work hopped out of the backs of trucks and cars, tongues lolling and tails wagging. Time to go to work![4]

An investigator asked about surveillance video but was disheartened to learn the videocassette player and the videotapes were old and a very grainy, jerky, fuzzy video was obtained. At first glance it appeared the heavyset girl, standing at the teller window, was holding a cell phone to her left ear. No, the teller explained nervously, the robber was pulling on the edge of the hood of her sweatshirt, probably trying to avoid being videotaped. Still, there was video. A picture was taken from the video of the robbers and given to the media.

The search was on. It just seemed there was no way one intelligent adult could escape this manhunt, much less two kids. Police were confident; with sniffing dogs, cops in the air, a mass ground search, videotape, and good physical descriptions, silly teenaged girls would be crying for mercy as soon as handcuffs were placed on their little wrists—within, say, hours.

Unfortunately, the cops were wrong.

The girls were dubbed "the Baby-Faced Robbers."[5] Investigators started with local schools. Handwriting samples were obtained from nearby Sycamore High School and Green Elementary, seeking a match to the robbery note and for latent prints. Dead end.

1/05/10 PL Tue A00
3:18:40P 240 L
CAM 1

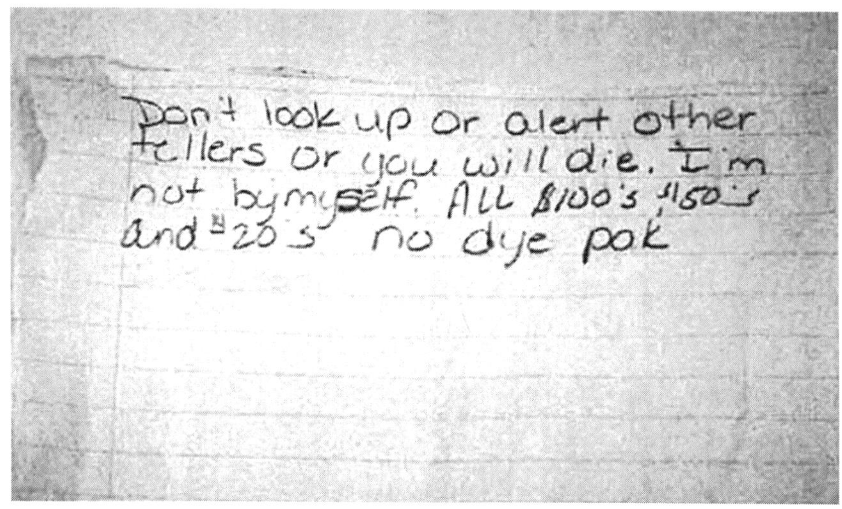
Don't look up or alert other tellers or you will die. I'm not by myself. All $100's $50's and $20's no dye pak

Bank robbery note used by the two girls in the January 5, 2010, 1st National Bank in Symmes Township, Cincinnati, Ohio, robbery (released to the public by the Hamilton County Sheriff's Office).

There was a good suspect, but she claimed she was at home "playing Monopoly" with her friend when the bank was robbed. Yes, she insisted. It was with the same multicolored paper money that came with the game, not real greenbacks.[6]

There were leads from the local Crime Stoppers to follow. All of them panned out.

By July 2018, the case was on "Inactive" status, meaning it was waiting for new evidence for future investigation.

Until someone comes forward or investigators turn up a new lead, "the Baby-Faced Robbers" remain at large at this writing. One of them may have set a record for being the youngest person in the United States to have robbed a bank. In order to qualify for this title, she'll have to prove her age by showing her ID, the same as if she were legally withdrawing money.

Opposite, top and bottom: **On January 5, 2010, two girls robbed the 1st National Bank on 9051 Fields Ertel Road in Symmes Township, Cincinnati, Ohio, of close to $3,000. They were between 12–16 years old at the time of the robbery. At this writing, they remain at large. Any information should be called in to the Hamilton County Sheriff's Office at Crimestoppers 1-888-352-3040 or crime-stoppers.us (released to the public by the Hamilton County Sheriff's Office).**

If you have any information on the January 5, 2010, robbery at the 1st National Bank on 9051 Fields Ertel Road in Symmes Township, Cincinnati, Ohio, please contact the below officials. You can remain anonymous.

Hamilton County Sheriff's Office 513-946-6400

or

TriState Crime-Stoppers
P.O. Box 14330
Cincinnati, Ohio
45250–0330
Tips: 513-352-3040 or (1-888) 352-3040
http://crime-stoppers.us/

27

Oakley, Ohio

"She skipped school to rob a bank"

On Monday, April 14, 2014, the 16-year-old girl robbed a bank. On Tuesday, April 15, she stood, crying, before the judge, her attorney at her side. The prosecution was listing the charges.

"I'd like for my client to be released," said the teen's attorney, "so that she will be able to go to school."

"Well," the judge surmised, "she skipped school to rob a bank." And with that, the girl was led away to the Hamilton County Juvenile Detention Center.

That Monday, just before noon, the slight, white female dressed in dark clothing had walked into the PNC Bank on Paxton Avenue in the Oakley neighborhood of Cincinnati, Ohio. She passed a note to one of the tellers, and in the note she warned she had a gun. The girl scooped up the loot and walked out of the bank. Then she seemingly disappeared.

It took less than an hour to locate her, thanks to a GPS tracking device in the money. She was at Kenwood Towne Center Mall. It was a short-lived shopping spree.

The girl was no stranger to crime. On April 1 she had been in the courtroom on a plea bargain, pleading guilty to a theft charge in exchange for dropping two charges, one being a drug charge and the other "unlawful use of a vehicle." She had also been issued a violation for trespassing. She was on probation when she robbed the bank.

In mid-May, the 16 year old was back in court making yet another plea bargain. This time it was for the PNC Bank robbery. Rather than be charged as an adult, she pled guilty to robbery with an implied weapon.

She received 18 months and probation. And she stated it wasn't her idea to commit the crime. A man had called her to set up the robbery. "Want to make $1,000?"

On the same day, the girl with the chipped, pink nail polish apologized to her victim, the teller who received the robbery note. "I just want to apologize," she told the teller. "I don't have any excuses. But I do want to apologize for threatening and doing what I did."[1]

Hopefully, there will be no more skipping school. It just doesn't seem to pay off.

28

Fall River, Massachusetts

Down the Street from Lizzie

Fall River, Massachusetts, has a former internationally famous criminal resident, the subject of one of history's biggest unsolved crimes. There is even a ditty that many a little girl has sung while jumping rope:

Lizzie Borden took an axe
And gave her mother forty whacks
When she saw what she had done
She gave her father forty one

In 1893, the "trial of the century," Lizzie Borden would be acquitted for the ax murders of her father and stepmother at the family home on Second Street. Today, the murder house is a popular bed and breakfast. The double homicides are the subjects of books, movies, stage plays, and true crime discussions worldwide: did Lizzie bludgeon them to death, or was she innocent? Her father was wealthy, one of his positions being president of the Union Savings Bank. Lizzie and her sister profited greatly from the crime, inheriting their father's assets.

On February 20, 2019, another crime made headline news in Fall River, Massachusetts, involving females and bank profits. But this crime was no mystery, and their profit did not last long. And the public was just as shocked at the identity of the perpetrators as they were when the wealthy, demure Ms. Borden was accused in her day.

The single-story, red brick Bay Coast Bank at 81 Troy Street in Fall River is a six-mile drive from the home where Lizzie Borden allegedly committed the crimes. On that February 20 at about 3:45

p.m., Bay Coast Bank alerted police of an armed robbery. Employees told responding officers that the perpetrator was a young female, about 5'6" wearing black leggings and a dark blue sweater emblazoned with the New England Patriots football team logo. The girl was holding her hands together as if she "was concealing something," She had handed the teller a note "demanding money or she would blow everything up and kill everybody."[1] She received the cash and ran towards Troy Street.

The detectives reviewed the video of the robbery. There were also cameras posted outside the various local businesses, so it was possible to track the robber as she ran out of the bank, around the piles of snow where snowplows and industrious business owners had cleared streets and sidewalks. The robber then was observed hopping into a dark-colored Toyota Camry. A second female was driving. The cameras made it easy to view the Toyota's license plate. It was registered to a house on Mulberry Street.

Mulberry Street is a three-minute walk to Lizzie Borden's old home.

A surveillance of the Mulberry Street house located the dark-colored Toyota Camry in the backyard. When investigators knocked on the front door, no one responded, though officers could see people through windows. So the cops busted through the door. A detective glanced over at one of the persons in the house, did a double take, and recognized the girl as the getaway driver. But now she was wearing the Patriots sweater. Upon questioning, it was discovered she was 15 years old.

Officers learned there was a basement apartment, so they made their way downstairs. There was a bathroom in this apartment, and out of the bathroom came the robber, wearing black leggings and a different shirt. She was taken into custody. She was 14 years old.

"Both are charged with armed robbery," the media reported. "Their names are not released due to their ages."[2]

At this writing, the girls have yet to appear in court. Perhaps, like Lizzie Borden, they'll be acquitted. They've already made history in Fall River by being the youngest female bank robbers on record in the city.

29

Urbana, Illinois

Jumping Off the Bridge

"If all of your friends jumped off a bridge, would you jump, too?" is a chastising that makes every adolescent seethe over this parental pearl of wisdom. (Somewhere there must be a bridge where a stream of followers are following leaders, and the bodies below are probably so stacked by now that jumping from the bridge is just a step off.) In this chapter, the saying is in regards to a crime. "If all of your friends robbed a bank, would you rob one, too?"

The Heartland Bank & Trust Company on Philo Road in Urbana, Illinois, seemed to be a hot spot for female bank robbers. Urbana's Alicia M. Smith robbed the bank at 3:05 p.m. on Friday, October 3, 2013. She ended up turning herself in to police the following day and was promptly arrested for aggravated robbery. Alicia was 18 years old at the time of the robbery. She glares into the camera in her mug shot, as if resigned to her fate. But she would not be the only female to be sharing the "Female Robs Bank" headline. The next headliners would be a convoluted story of copycats, friendships, blood relations, failed family ties, and juvenile delinquency, all in one lurid headlining crime spree that lasted three months.

Janelle Moss[1] was the product of the juvenile justice system, and at 16 years old, she was already having adult-sized problems. Janelle's mother had six other children, and their ages ranged from one week old to six years. Her mother lived in St. Louis. Janelle's grandmother cared for another one of Janelle's siblings.

Janelle had a boyfriend, Ernest,[2] 14, who lived in Urbana, Illinois. His 23-year-old sister, Symone Simmons, was living about ten minutes away in Champaign. Symone herself had a story. Her mother was in prison for murder. Symone had four kids, aged nine months, two years, eight years, and nine years old. Symone had managed to obtain her high school diploma and a job after surviving a rough childhood.

Symone's friend Tia Woods, 19, was dating Symone's cousin. Tia was a pretty girl. She had her nose pierced through the right side with a post, and a ring in the cartilage between her nostrils. She was a student at Parkland Community College in Champaign.

Janelle, Ernest, Symone, and Tia all hung out together. Symone would later tell the court she wanted to help Janelle, who at the time was broke and needed cash. Somewhere along the story, someone had an idea for fast, easy money. Later, each would blame the other as to who was responsible for the idea.

Janelle was already on probation for "Mob Action." The probation was in another county, but evidently she wasn't too worried about it when she sat with Ernest, Symone, and Tia, planning a bank robbery. Allegedly, one of the older females suggested the juveniles commit the actual robbery because juveniles could not be charged. That seemed to make sense to all four.

According to Ernest's later testimony, Symone and Tia talked him into the bank robbery. They would give him a disguise so he would "not get caught," and they provided a gun. They had selected a long-haired black wig, a gray hoodie, and a vest in camouflage. "We don't have a statement from him as to whether the gun is real," First Assistant State's Attorney Steve Ziegler would later tell the press. On December 18, 2014, "he says that the friend[3] drives him to an apartment complex nearby where he gets ready, goes to the bank, does the robbery, then goes back to the friend's apartment nearby." Ernest robbed the Heartland Bank & Trust Company on Philo Road. "The majority of the money goes to Simmons and her friend. He gets a minor amount of money that he splits with [Janelle] his girlfriend."[4] But he didn't cover his face, so the bank cameras obtained nice, clear photos of Ernest holding up the female teller. The amount of money was insufficient, so on January 21, he robbed a Mr. Gas Plus, also in Urbana. Two other boys assisted him.

Because Ernest had robbed a bank, now Janelle decided she wanted to rob a bank, too. So on February 13, the same friends met at Tia's apartment where Symone and Tia furnished Janelle with an orange hoodie and a wig. Then Tia drove Janelle to the Heartland Bank & Trust Company on Philo Road, the same bank Ernest had robbed almost two months before. (If you're going to follow someone off a bridge, pick one you know.)

In a strange coincidence, Janelle would rob the same teller that Ernest had robbed. Janelle walked into the bank around 3 p.m., stuck a BB gun into the female teller's face and, shoving a plastic bag at the frightened woman, demanded money. After the robbery, Janelle ran from the bank and headed for an apartment complex that was surrounded by a fence. Janelle was not an athletic girl; she lacked grace in scaling the fence, so she was dropping a trail of money that Urbana police would later recover. During the robbery, Symone and Tia texted one another as to Janelle's performance and various locations as she moved.

Symone, Tia, Janelle, and Ernest split the money from Janelle's heist. Tia would later testify her total take from both robberies was $875. They went to the mall and Symone bought herself, among other things, a television and some shoes. Janelle made some purchases for herself.

Soon after, Janelle left town to go live with her mother in St. Louis. Later, her mother would testify she had no idea that Janelle had committed any crimes. She told officials that she enrolled Janelle in school; records would reflect this was a lie.

On March 13 in St. Louis, Janelle was arrested on a warrant. Evidently, young, sweet love had gone sour because she spilled the beans on Ernest and both bank robberies, and Ernest was arrested on March 17. Friendship dissipated, so Symone was arrested, and all three were charged with aggravated robbery, as officials did not know if the gun was real. For the teller who had the gun stuck in her face not once but twice, it didn't matter, but to file legal charges it was an issue. (Later the gun was discovered to be a pellet gun.) Judge Tom Difanis set Symone's bond at $500,000.

Janelle also named Tia Woods as an accomplice. When she ran from the bank on February 13, it was most likely Tia's apartment she was running to for shelter.

In April 2015, charges alleging that Symone coerced Ernest into robbing the bank were dismissed. In return she would plead guilty to aggravated robbery for persuading Janelle to rob the bank.

Meanwhile, Janelle was in juvenile detention awaiting trial and was not a model prisoner. On April 25 she threatened a staff member and received a write-up. In May she went before Judge Difanis to plead her case. Janelle explained that she did plead guilty "because I knew I did something wrong," but she was forced to rob the bank because Symone was making threats if Janelle didn't comply. "She told me if I don't rob the bank for her, she was going to kill me and my family."

Her attorney argued that Janelle was truly afraid of the older Symone. Janelle deserved a chance. What about sentencing her to probation, living with her family in St. Louis where she could be enrolled in school?

The assistant district attorney asked Janelle what she did with the money she stole. Janelle said, "I gave some to Symone and then I went shopping."

Judge Difanis wasn't buying her story of being threatened. "She was promised money, which she did get and did spend," the judge said, looking down from the bench.[5]

The prosecution and the judge agreed: Janelle was beyond the control of her family. And the teller was the true "scared" person. This was a woman who had guns held to her face.

Janelle was sentenced to 15 years in juvenile prison, but Janelle could not be held after she turned 21.

Tia Woods was arrested April 1, 2015, in an apartment during an unrelated investigation. A warrant was being served, and Tia was at the wrong place; but for cops, it was the right time. "Who are you?" officers asked her as a matter of protocol.

"Tia Woods," the 19 year old answered.[6] The pellet gun used in the bank robberies was located in the apartment and seized as evidence.

Tia was charged with two counts of aggravated robbery. She cooperated with the investigators, admitting she supplied the wigs and disguises and drove both Ernest and Janelle to Heartland Bank & Trust Company for each robbery. For this she received a portion of the stolen money, doled out by her friend Symone. The judge would set her bond at $50,000. Tia posted bond and went to live with her mother in Chicago, leaving Parkland College to enroll in a cosmetology school in the windy city. She kept a low profile, stayed out of trouble, found a job, began some volunteer work at a grade school, and waited for her day in court. She had agreed to testify against the rest of the clan. Friendship does not run deep when you are sinking.

Tia and her attorney would eventually strike a plea bargain. Two counts of aggravated robbery and two counts of contributing to the delinquency of a minor would be dropped. One count would be lowered to "robbery." On September 14, 2015, Judge Harry Clem sentenced Tia Woods to four years of probation, including 150 hours of public service. "I believe everyone should have one opportunity to make one really bad mistake and to atone for it," Judge Clem told Tia Woods. However, he warned her, the teller who fell victim to the robbery "will remember that for a good long time." Tia was going to be a convicted felon for life now. Still, she had a "sterling academic record in high school" and "enormous family support."[7]

Symone went before Champaign County Judge Harry Clem in August 2015. "I didn't see any money from that bank robbery," Symone testified about Janelle's robbery. No, she was not texting Tia during Janelle's robbery. No, she didn't buy a television or shoes with the ill-gotten gains, just one outfit. And, hell no, she didn't "persuade the teens to conduct the holdups because they would be sentenced less harshly as juveniles" no matter what witnesses or any text message had to say.

Symone told Judge Clem, "I deeply regret having any involvement in the charges that brought me in front of you." She said the five months she served in jail had given her time to think. She decided she wanted to be a mother to her children.[8] The judge didn't believe her. Symone jumped off the figurative bridge right behind her friends. He sentenced Symone Simmons to five years in prison for aggravated robbery.

For his role in the December 18 bank robbery, Ernest was sent to juvenile prison. In exchange for his pleading guilty to the gas station robbery and testifying against his sister and Tia Woods, the bank robbery charge was dismissed.

Everyone in this story paid a heavy price. A young mother, a bright scholar, a troubled girl, and a boy not yet old enough to graduate high school will forever be marked as convicted felons. A bank teller will be emotionally scarred for life. Children will miss their mother in formative years. The little group of friends and relatives fell victim to greed.

Part VII

Diapers and Electric Bills

30

Stealing to Buy Necessities

"Literally Robbing for Pampers"

Studies from the last decade reveal when an adult woman walks into a bank with the sole intention of walking out with a bag of stolen money, she will use the money to purchase and pay for fundamentals. While male bank robbers are robbing for the thrill, to fund an addiction, or to flash cash to impress, females are buying diapers and paying their electric bills or feeding an addiction. Some of them are at the end of their financial rope, while others need money to quell the screams of their drug manias.

Rosemary Erickson is a forensic sociologist and crime prevention expert who has studied female bank robbery. Erickson has noted the crime has changed from a group of males coming into a bank as a "take-over" robbery to an individual passing a note to a teller—a crime much more "suitable for women" due to the "nonviolent nature." Most importantly, "[women] are more likely to be robbing for personal financial needs. Being homeless, or single and alone, especially if they have children … they are literally robbing for Pampers."[1]

An analysis of the U.S. Census data conducted by Wider Opportunities for Women (WOW) reveals older women are at much greater risk than men of economic insecurity, struggling to pay for basic needs such as shelter and food. Forty-two percent of all women, 66 percent of Hispanic women, and 63 percent of black women lack economic security. "Older women rely on Social Security for the bulk of their income, but they receive smaller payments; the median women's payments lag behind men's by $4,500 a year."[2]

The 2019 "Income and Poverty in the United States" publication by the United States Census reveals that, although there has been an increase in numbers, the 2019 real media earnings of men is $57,456 versus the real median income of women is $47,299. While median income for households has increased (7.3 percent for family households, 6.2 percent for nonfamily households),[3] single-family households still lag behind significantly in median income. And while pay for females is higher and poverty rates have lowered nationally, "median income for households maintained by women was lower than that for married-couple family households and those maintained by men in 2018."[4]

Given those numbers, perhaps it should be no surprise that bank robberies by women have risen 25 percent, with the FBI reporting 6.2 percent of all bank heists today being committed by women. That's up from 4.9 percent in the beginning of 2002.

But three out of four bank robbers are caught, thanks to new technology and the investigation by both local authorities and the FBI. Still, 83 percent of the robbers believe they will not be caught. This leads to robbing a second time, maybe a third time[5] because the money doesn't stretch as far as it should.

Most are caught so many hours after their first robbery. If not the first robbery, then after the third the robber's career as a thief is over. Law enforcement will inevitably be placing handcuffs around the wrists, reading the Miranda rights, completing the reports. Robbing a fourth bank is usually not in the future because after the first or the third time, studies show the robber will be caught.

At least, most of them are.

31

Naomi Betts

A Lot of Time, Money, and Attention

Naomi Betts was probably confident that she had gotten away. After she committed the robbery of the Fifth Third Bank in Indianapolis, Indiana, in October 2003, she was now staying with her family in Sikeston, Missouri, a city with a population of a little over 16,000. While it might have been easier to disappear into the masses of the Indianapolis metropolis, she must have trusted her family and friends in Sikeston, a little over 300 miles away. Indy boasted a population of over 863,000; still, Naomi might have been constantly looking over her shoulder because the city was covered with Wanted posters of her. Law enforcement had the entire city looking for her face, as caught on video robbing the bank.

Since the October 9 robbery, law enforcement broke state records in spending costs in the attempt to find and arrest Naomi Betts and her accomplice. Over $500,000 had gone into radio, newspaper, and television ads in the search for her.[1] Who knows if she could trust her so-called Indianapolis cronies who might be coveting that reward?

The police were all over the news, informing the public how, on October 9, 2003, a black female had walked into Indianapolis' Fifth Third Bank with a black male accomplice. The male selected a deposit slip at a counter and appeared to be completing it. The female stood in line at the teller's window. As the female finally stepped up to the teller's window, the male moved to the doorway. The teller smiled pleasantly at the 5' 4", 200-pound woman who passed a note. The teller's eyes scanned the note. "I have a gun. Give me the money. No dye packs" it read in part.[2] When the teller looked back at the woman, she was now looking at a gun in a robber's hand. The teller complied with the demand.

Now carrying an undetermined amount of cash in her bag, the female left the bank, followed by the male. Only then did they run. They were both observed hopping into a 1980s' dark-colored, four-door Cadillac with the male driving. And that was the last witnesses saw of her.

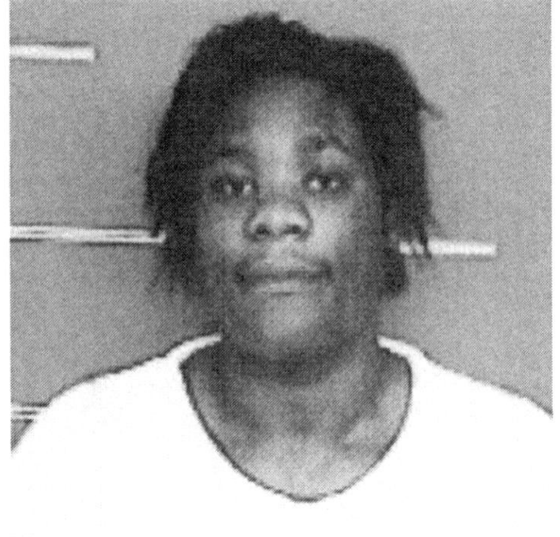

Naomi Betts was caught when her crime aired on television's *America's Most Wanted*. She robbed the Fifth Third Bank in Indianapolis, Indiana, on October 9, 2003, at gunpoint (Sikeston Public Safety mug shot).

The robber had made no attempt to hide her face during any phase of the robbery. It should have been an easy arrest.

Shortly after the robbery, the expenditures began in the search for the short, chubby female who robbed the bank and her getaway driver. And law dogs were coming up with zilch. As time passed, more and more money was spent trying to identify the thieves. Someone *had* to know something and would come forward for the large reward! Investigators on the case were surely becoming disheartened and their supervisors becoming red-faced. All that money spent on catching one robber, and they still could not find one clue? The investigative team finally turned to television for assistance. They sought the help of *America's Most Wanted*.

America's Most Wanted (*AMW*) remained a popular weekly, 60-minute television program hosted by victim advocate John Walsh. Based on the concept of "Watch TV—Catch Criminals," *AMW* featured dramatizations of unsolved crimes, asking for viewers to call in tips to a hotline if they have any information to help solve the depicted cases. By the time it went off the air, *AMW* assisted in capturing more than 1,100 criminals and reuniting 43 missing children with their families. The show would run until 2012, and there were several spin-off shows.

On May 22, 2004, *America's Most Wanted* aired the segment on the October 9, 2003, bank robbery in an attempt to identify the unknown female and male who robbed the Fifth Third Bank. Photographs taken by the bank's security system of the female and the robbery in progress were shown on-screen. After the show aired, several tips were received. Most of those identified the female as Naomi Betts. One of those callers explained Betts and her male accomplice might be driving a green Dodge minivan. "Naomi is either from Sikeston or Charleston, Missouri," one caller added.

Another caller swore the robber was Melinda, Naomi's sister. The two looked so much alike that sometimes it was difficult to tell one from another, the caller explained.[3]

Both sounded like good tips, given the details in the information. Police surveillance confirmed that a Naomi Betts possibly did reside at 1234 Bonner Street[4] in Sikeston, Missouri, and a minivan matching the caller's description was observed occasionally parked at the residence. The Bonner Street address was the home of Naomi's mother, Myrtle.[5]

Investigators in Sikeston were notified, and they began to research both Melinda and Naomi. Naomi Betts had an active warrant out of Miner, Missouri, for Failure to Appear from March 2003. They relayed the information to the Indianapolis police department and the producers at *America's Most Wanted* were also called. The producers wanted to do a few follow-up interviews, and they wanted the grand prize: to film the capture of the bank robbers and add the footage to one of their shows.

America's Most Wanted producer and reporter John Turchin, along with a film crew, arrived in Sikeston on May 25. An Indianapolis police department robbery detective arrived two days later with a warrant in hand for the arrest of Melinda Betts in connection with the bank robbery. They were joined by an officer with the Sikeston Department of Public Safety. The case was finally gaining momentum.

Was it Naomi or Melinda who walked into the bank and brazenly handed the teller the note, demanding cash? The surveillance footage at the bank was not telling; either sister could have been the robber, they so closely resembled one another.

The only addresses that could be located for Melinda Betts

were in Charleston, Missouri. So the investigators, with the *America's Most Wanted* crew trailing, headed out for the 20-minute drive east.

Once in Charleston, officers arrived at each known address. They interviewed the residents, asking for Melinda's whereabouts, and were given the same answers.

"She was here a few days ago for a funeral, but she left. Maybe went to Indiana...."

"Melinda did come here for a family funeral, but she's gone now. Gone back to Indiana, I think." Along with these interviews, they received more addresses where Melinda might be living.

The crew packed up and drove back the way they came, east to Sikeston.

The group arrived back in Sikeston on Thursday, May 27, at about 3 p.m. to check the new addresses.

Melinda's whereabouts were undetermined, but there were two addresses the investigators were betting on for Naomi. And Naomi Betts had that 2003 warrant out of Miner for Failure to Appear. Two surveillances were set up at two separate addresses, one being the home of Myrtle Betts, the mother of Naomi and Melinda. Another dead end?

Then the call came in: either Naomi or Melinda was standing outside of 1234 Bonner. But when officers arrived, Myrtle met them outside on the carport. She was proving blood to be thick, because she refused to give up anything. No, her daughters were not there. No, not Naomi. No, not Melinda. But then a screen door creaked open, and a familiar face peeped around the corner, resigned to fate and loyal to her mother's safety. You're looking for me, she told them, coming out onto the carport. I have a warrant out. Yes, out of Miner. I'm Naomi Betts.[6]

Naomi Betts was arrested at the home of Myrtle Betts on an outstanding warrant and taken to jail. *America's Most Wanted* cameras caught every moment, giving Naomi her 15 minutes of fame. Naomi gave *AMW* cameras the bird as she extended her middle finger in response.

A search of the home revealed Naomi, the father of her children, and her children had evidently not lived there long enough to unpack.

Their clothing was stuffed into trash bags that lay in a middle bedroom. So was a single spent 194-1 Winchester 9 mm shell casing.

It appeared the stolen money was not used for luxury. Living with her mother, out of trash bags, and on the run—Naomi Betts was not spending her ill-gotten gains on good wine and an apartment with a view.

Naomi was interviewed by investigators about the bank robbery while in custody on the warrant. She admitted it was her, not her sister Melinda, who had robbed the Indianapolis Fifth Third Bank in October 2003. She gave up the name of her accomplice. And she had confided in two friends who, when later interviewed, admitted they knew about the robbery.

At this writing, there are no criminal records, and Naomi Betts, with the exception of a Wikipedia page, is no longer of interest in the media.

It was a lot of time, money, and attention caused by a 22-year-old girl who had robbed a bank.

32

Ashley Carrington

"Used It to Pay Bills"

When a Riviera Beach Police Department officer pulled a car over for a routine traffic stop, the officer probably had no idea what it would lead to. But then, many federal arrests are made via "routine" stops. It was September 29, 2015, a date which stands out in Ashley Carrington's mind.

Floridians Matthew Taylor, 31, and Ashley Carrington, 20, of Riviera Beach appeared to be the average driver and passenger. What was not average was the chunk of money in the vehicle, part of $19,260 the duo had forced the Capital Bank at the 4800 block of North Federal Highway to part with just two hours before the officer had signaled them to pull over.

Carrington was in trouble, to be sure, but it was trouble that would keep growing: the solid-built, light-skinned black girl was five months in on a three-year stint of federal probation.

"For what?" the officer asked.

"Robbing banks."

Incredulous, the officer might have noted the plural. "How many 'banks'?"

She was truthful when she told him she had robbed three.

The FBI took over the case that evening as Ashley was sitting behind bars, dipping a spork into jailhouse chow.

Matthew Taylor and Ashley Carrington snitched out their partner in crime, a male named Chester Robinson, 28. Chester would turn himself in the next day, his bank-robbing spree cut short by being ratted out. He also told the truth when interviewed.[1]

Ashley Carrington, at age 19, was a serial bank robber. She was on federal probation when she was arrested for robbing a fourth bank (FBI release of bank robbery in progress, Broward County Sheriff's Office, Florida, mug shot, September 2015).

The trio each came forward to individually discuss the morning's activity with officers. The day before the robbery, each told law enforcement officials they had conducted surveillance of the Capital Bank in the 4800 block of North Federal Highway. The next day, Ashley, now a seasoned bank-robbing pro, strolled up to a teller's window and handed the woman a note: "you have 30 secs to empty all draws no pack/no dye."

"Give me all the money," Ashley had ordered the teller, who was quick to do so. The teller also gave Ashley bait bills from a top drawer and, at the same time, activated an alarm.

"Give me all of it," Ashley snapped.

The rest of the till went into the bag.

A few windows over, Ashley's male accomplice was doing the same. Money from another till was being scooped into a white trash bag. A total of more than $19,000 walked out the door with both robbers.[2]

The day after this robbery and the traffic stop, Ashley Carrington stood before Judge Seltzer and announced she needed a few days to hire an attorney. The men were on their own—court-appointed lawyers for them. Federal prosecutors determined the three to be flight risks. Ashley settled down in the women's unit of the Broward County Jail, making her bunk, eating from a plastic tray, and schlepping about in the hard, plastic slippers issued to her. She was an old hat at the jailhouse system. She had just been released in April from the Palm Beach County Jail after serving a year, when her mom had snitched her out, and Ashley was arrested in May 2014 for robbing three banks in Broward County. And the more banks she robbed, the more threatening the demand notes became.

On May 15, she attempted to rob the Wells Fargo bank branch on Northlake Boulevard in Palm Beach Gardens. She passed a note to the teller: "I HAVE A BOMB EMPTY ALL THE DRAWS [*sic*] NO DYE PACKS OR TRACKING DEVICE NO POLICE OR KABOOM!!!" But it went awry when the teller dropped a bomb of sorts on Ashley. The teller called another teller over to assist. Ashley left the building, caught on surveillance video but leaving empty-handed.

She must have decided to try her luck again, because the same morning at 9:37 a.m. she walked into Lantana's SunTrust Bank, passing a new note: "I HAVE A GUN GIVE ME ALL THE MONEY OR I WILL KILL EVERYONE." This time, it worked, and she left the building, again caught on surveillance video, but this time leaving $1,726 richer.

Either the money didn't last long or greed overrode common sense, because on May 27 just past 9 a.m., Ashley walked into the PNC Bank in Lake Park. She wore a T-shirt emblazoned with the rap artist Lil' Bow Wow over jeans. This time, the note was far more cryptic: "I HAVE A GUN! ... IF YOU DO NOT MOVE IN 30 SECS IM GOING TO START SHOOTING CUSTOMERS." The take was much better: $6,931.

Considering the average take in a bank robbery is about $1,200–1,500, this robbery was quite successful, except it had to be split three ways, because this time she had two accomplices. Never mind it was Ashley who walked into the bank with a threatening note, which could result in a federal charge with a maximum sentence of 20 years.

The cops released the photos of her robbing these banks, and she was dubbed "the Lil' Bow Wow bank robbery suspect" due to her choice of wardrobe.[3] The camera recorded her image, documenting her every move, just as it had prior.

On May 27 and 28, the FBI released the images of all the bank robberies to the media. This is when Ashley's mother made the call: "That sure looks like my daughter." She wasn't trying to be a snitch or gain a reward: "Ashley needs help." Her daughter was homeless and suicidal before she robbed the three banks. Maybe, by being locked up, Ashley could get the help she needed.

When Ashley was a little girl, she says, "[she] dreamed of being a singer." Her reality was living in cheap apartments, living month to month on what little money she had, with her kids in tow.[4]

Ashley agreed to assist prosecution by formally pleading guilty, and she received a sentence of two years and nine months in the federal system. She also snitched out a few other bank robbers.

This was far more serious than the crime she had committed on March 31, 2014; she had taken four air freshener refills from a Publix grocery store in West Palm Beach. She was arrested. Ashley pled guilty to retail theft the next day. The little girl who had dreamed of being a singer was now an adult, and her life of crime was beginning.

She said the bank robbery idea was hatched when she and a few friends, including her live-in boyfriend, were discussing it one night. At first, Ashley took it as "a joke." Then it became very real. But between pressure from a boyfriend/accomplice and the need for cash, the "joke" began to look like a good idea.[5]

Ashley would eventually plead guilty to one charge. She admitted she did rob all three banks. She cut a deal and Assistant Federal Public Defender Robin Rosen-Evans requested a lenient sentence. According to her attorney, Ashley was "suicidal and homeless" prior to the 2014 robberies.[6]

In a 2019 interview, Ashley Carrington said she robbed the Capital Bank on North Federal Highway with accomplices because she was trying to keep her relationship with her then-boyfriend, doing whatever it took. When she would initially walk into a bank, she felt "scared and nervous." She says of one robbery, "I felt bad for the lady [teller] because she was scared." As for the money, she insists, "I used it to pay bills." There were no fancy clothes or cars, no drugs or extravagant restaurants. Just food, water, rent, and electricity. She does not discuss the previous robberies.

In prison, she wrote of having no concrete plans except to get out and avoid men who would attempt to sway her into breaking the law. She spoke of finding work and taking care of her family but without detailed plans. She was placed in segregation for fighting, insisting the fight was not her fault, and she was not involved.

Ashley Carrington did her time and was paroled to a halfway house in Florida. "I'm not going to get involved in any more trouble," she insisted.[7]

Part VIII

A Cane in One Hand, a Gun in the Other

33

The Granny Bandits

Truth About the "Golden" Years

The advertisements of beautiful, loving grandparents enjoying their golden years surrounded by soft light and smiles is fast becoming a myth in the United States, if it ever existed at all. Studies have reported that not only does life become more difficult for too many adults over 50 years old, it can lead to illegal acts just to survive. A report titled "Aging and Housing Instability: Homelessness Among Older and Elderly" (September 2013) predicted, "It is estimated that elderly homelessness will increase by 33% in 2020.... By 2050, the elderly homeless population is projected to increase more than double, with 95,000 elderly persons expected to be living without stable housing" (p. 1). The study identified two pathways to the homeless situation for those over 50: chronic homelessness and "living on limited, fixed incomes—including Social Security and/or Supplemental Security Income—elderly persons experience severe housing cost burden more frequently than the general population, potentially resulting in housing loss" (p. 2).

Affordable senior health care is available only to those in a higher income bracket; the more money a person has, the better the living facilities. As for persons over 55 who rely solely on social security or a limited income for housing, there is "an average wait time lasting approximately three to five years" to be placed in affordable housing facilities. To supplement their income, studies show that some senior citizens may resort to crime.[1]

Daisy[2] is a 65-year-old woman living in a small apartment complex located in a Tennessee town with a population at just over 5,000. The majority of Daisy's neighbors are over 60 years old and living on social security and disability. A few have lost long-term jobs because of layoffs in a failing economy and are not considered "job material" due to age or limited skillsets. A scant few are widowed or retired. Many of Daisy's neighbors sell their prescription drugs for extra cash. "I can sit on my porch and watch them do it," Daisy says matter-of-factly. This activity scares some of her neighbors, causing them to become shut-ins.

The grandmothers and grandfathers who are selling their painkillers and opioids to friends and family of their neighbors are not trying to compete with local drug lords or street gangs. "They need grocery money or rent money," Daisy explains. "Their [government aid] checks aren't cuttin' it. And they're raisin' the rent on us next month." When asked about public housing, she explains that many of her friends are on a waiting list, but the waiting list is over three years' long. The public housing in this town has another set of problems. "Everyone's afraid because of the crime there." Daisy says she knows one elderly public housing resident who has been victimized by numerous burglaries, an easy target due to age and the number of medications she has on her property. For Daisy and her friends, their other choices are a senior retirement community, which none of them can afford, or the nursing home, "but we don't qualify for that" due to their better health. "So [residents] sell their pills."[3]

Sharon Walsh, director of the University of Kentucky Center for Drug and Alcohol Research in Lexington, is cited as explaining, "We know that some elderly patients use their prescriptions as a strategy for increasing income.... People, especially in rural communities, they don't see anything wrong with selling or sharing prescription medications. It's a culturally accepted thing."[4]

Charlie Cichon, executive director of the National Association of Drug Diversion Investigators, states, "If [seniors] discover they can make $20 a pill on the street, then it becomes a temptation to supplement their income."[5]

In the study "Older Criminals and the Crimes They Commit," Hegstrom et al. cite Kyle Kerchier's article in the *Research on Aging*: "There are 'elderly-specific' theories of law-breaking that identify several causes of illegal behavior that are 'unique' to older persons" (1987, p. 260). Hegstrom notes, "The hypothesis holds that there are variables that cause the older person to commit an offense." One of those variables is loss of income. Another is dependency on chemicals (alcohol, prescription drugs) due to sudden life changes.[6] In "White Haired Criminals: An Emergent Social Problem" (1984), G. Feinberg notes older criminals are committing crimes as "they must often transit several roles at once: death of a spouse, physical disabilities, change in residence and the like" (p. 48).[7]

Addiction Center is a content-driven "informational web guide for those who are struggling with substance use disorders … created by our team of researchers and journalists … fact-based and sourced from relevant publications, government agencies and medical journals." The information for "Causes of Addiction in the Elderly" notes that triggers can be health related, such as trouble sleeping, or life-changing events, such as loss of income. There is an inherent danger for people over 65 in using legal drugs or drinking alcohol, because they "have a decreased ability to metabolize drugs or alcohol along with an increased brain sensitivity to them." Without realizing it, these people can become addicted.[8]

Substance abuse is also a factor in senior suicide, the risk of which grows higher with age. The highest suicide rate is persons aged 85 and older; the second highest suicide age group is 75–84 years old. And the attempts are far more lethal—for every four attempts there will be one suicide. Medicare covers only 50 percent of mental health care compared to the 80 percent of physical health care coverage. Mental health problems often worsen in response to medical issues the elderly suffer, such as a stroke, diabetes, cancer, and Parkinson's disease.

Lack of affordable housing and health care for lower-income persons, social security and disability or loss of job, drug addiction, and mental health problems left untreated can force seniors into a situation where illegal activity may seem like the best option. Or, because of their mental and medical state, such a serious crime may be a call for help.

The need for cash to pay bills or to pay for medication, to fund an addiction, or a lot of cash is seemingly the answer to all problems—these are reasons the elderly population turn to bank robbery. And when the older women rob a bank, they are inevitably dubbed "the Granny Bandits."

34

Rowena Leonard

No Capone and No Irish Terrorist

Life must not have been going so well for Rowena Leonard. It started off as frightening, it changed quickly to crap, and now here she sat in shit creek, floundering away.

It was June 5, 1987, in Chicago. Rowena, 45, had made plans to rob a bank. She was carrying a plastic bag that held two different styles of wigs and a change of clothing. Rowena also carried a .22 six-shot revolver. She parked her car by an elevated train stop so she could just hop on the train and go, blending in with the crowd. She had dressed nicely so as not to stand out.

At this point in her life, Rowena had a business that was failing: she was the president of a dying real estate company with more money going out than was coming in until the bank had foreclosed on it. Adding to that, her mom's health was failing, and money wasn't available for doctors' visits and medicine. At 45, she must have been feeling older than Methuselah—emotionally, perhaps she was. Robbing a bank must have made sense. Just one time, just $100,000, and maybe all would be right; it would all be okay.

Rowena looked more like a kindly aunt than a hardened criminal. Glasses overrode her soft, fleshy, triangular face, and her short hair was coifed. Approaching 50, she was growing rounder. On the day she robbed the bank she was dressed in an almost matronly style suit and blouse with a big, floppy bow tied at the throat. She wore little jewelry except for conservative earrings and pendants.

Now she was walking into the National Bank at 30 North Michigan Avenue in Chicago, Illinois, the gangland city that had been home to mob kingpin Al Capone and other notorious gangsters. Rowena, however, turned out not to be much of a gangster.

Once at the teller's window, Rowena Leonard told the teller that she was an Irish terrorist and she had a bomb. She quietly showed the teller the .22 six-shot revolver. Then she told the teller that two tellers needed to hand over $500,000 each or Rowena was going to blow the place to smithereens with her bomb. One teller handed over $33,000 and simultaneously hit a silent alarm. Rowena must have settled for this amount because she and her reported "bomb" departed the teller's window as quickly as she arrived. Or, at least she tried.

Rowena had made the mistake of arriving during the lunch crowd, when everyone was trying to get into and out of the bank quickly before they had to rush back to work. She had to worm her way through the crowd to reach the exit. In this crowd was Chicago patrolman Anthony Bonder, who was there to conduct some quick personal business.

After pushing her way through the mass of humans, now Rowena had to shove her way out the door. Officer Bonder, who had been alerted that the lady had just robbed the bank, was also now pushing folks aside. While two officers joined Bonder outside on the pavement, Rowena was ducking and dodging through the downtown city streets of Chicago. Al Capone would have shook his jowly face in shame. *Tsk, tsk, what a sloppy bank job.*

Rowena stopped outside of the bank. So did her pursuers, because now she had a gun to her head.

"Easy there," Bonder called out to her. "Just put it down, easy."

"Just shoot me right now!" The well-dressed woman shouted at him. Then she dodged into the crowd and disappeared.[1]

Four cops were hot on her trail. Rowena skidded to a stop on North Wabash Avenue, right in front of Marshall Field's department store, where the better dressed were coolly coming out of the front doors, sunglasses in hand. Outside, they mixed with the lower classes: the street people and the middle-class folks who were rushing back to sit behind desks and stand behind the counters to wait on society.

And so here she was. Rowena Leonard, nondescript, married woman from Pontoon Beach, Southern Illinois, pulling a gun out of her purse, putting the muzzle to her head.

The cops came to a halt, simultaneously calling out to her to please, don't do it! Their own hands went to their holsters. "Please, ma'am, put the gun down!"

Rowena, desperate, kept the gun to her head. Then she pulled the trigger.

Click. Nothing.

She pulled the trigger again.

The *boom* sent those shoppers from Marshall Field's, the four cops, and even the unwashed on the pavement who were begging for coins, scattering for cover.[2]

When the cops recovered, they found the bullet had grazed her skull. Rowena's ears were probably ringing. But she was *alive.*

While Rowena was stretched out on the pavement surrounded by cops and waiting for an ambulance, the National Bank at 30 North Michigan Avenue was evacuating and shutting down, police tape cordoning off the entire area. Rowena's claim of being an Irish terrorist with a bomb was not taken lightly. The Irish Republican Army (IRA) had been active in the last few years, what the British Army was calling the "terrorist phase," by committing high-profile bombings. This included a 1981 bombing in Shetland Isles during Queen Elizabeth II's visit, the 1982 dual bombing at a British Army ceremonial parade at Hyde Park, the Brighton Hotel in 1984, and multiple attacks on British troops. And now the IRA's movement was spreading across the globe to include the United States. The IRA were heavily armed courtesy Muammar Gaddafi of Libya.[3] Rowena had probably gleaned some of this information from the news, thus her use of the "Irish terrorist" scare tactic. Did she know it would turn downtown Chicago into a maelstrom?

Drivers were surely alternately snarling and cursing as the roadblocks went up and already busy traffic rerouted, and commuter trains were shut down and changed over to the elevated. The police bomb technicians and arson unit arrived, ready to investigate.

By now, the eye of this tornado of madness was in an ambulance, a middle-aged woman with a gunshot wound surrounded by a heavy police presence.

Rowena was immediately carried to Northwestern Memorial Hospital where she was listed in serious condition. When her medical diagnosis read "fair," she was moved to Cook County Hospital. Rowena didn't have much to say to anyone during this time. She was placed under heavy guard by Chicago police officers. As soon as she was declared ready, her next stop would be the county jail and then before a judge to determine her bond, if any.

Once she was released from the hospital, Rowena Leonard was charged with armed robbery and armed violence. Her bond was set at $100,000. She bonded out and went home, where she stayed in and stayed quiet, having little to say to anyone outside of her family. She did give at least one interview, explaining how badly she felt for the fear she had caused in the teller and in the police officers.

Her mother, Cordell V. Fisher, granted *The Pantagraph* newspaper an interview. "She just wanted to build Pontoon Beach and make it a beautiful place. Things just went bad, and I think she just cracked." Fisher lived with Rowena and Rowena's husband, Lewis, in the run-down subdivision of Pontoon Beach, where no one even suspected Rowena would pull such a stunt. "It was such a shock to me. Everybody thought a lot of her."[4]

Lewis, like Rowena, was the epitome of conservative. He wore dark suits and stiff white shirts. His receding hairline gave way to dark hair that was combed straight back, the remnants of hair on top also slicked back. Both he and his wife appeared to be more of the "Ozzie and Harriet" type than the slick, hip television characters on the current hot shows *Knot's Landing* and *Family Ties*.

On June 18, 1987, a Cook County grand jury indicted Rowena with armed robbery and armed violence. Rowena was there with her forgiving husband, Lewis.

Rowena tried to play the female card during the October trial, when she pled "innocent by being a female." She claimed she was legally insane due to a hysterectomy the year before the robbery. "I really didn't know what I was doing," she told the judge. But the judge turned down her plea for a minimum six-year prison sentence; he ordered her to serve eight years. "But for the grace of God," he told her sternly, many people could have been killed or injured by her shenanigans. She could be looking at 30 years, he reminded her, but this was her first arrest, so he was being lenient.[5]

Rowena's story faded from the newspapers, and, eventually, she returned to her quiet suburban life. Robbing the bank was her first and only attempt at the criminal lifestyle. She left the gangster life of Chicago to Capone and company.

35

Gail Cooke

(We Think That's Her Name)

It was November 2019, and a woman was leaving the Federal Bureau of Prisons with a bag of her meager belongings under one arm. The woman was in her late 60s and wore her graying hair short. She was far from frail, and in her eyes there was a certain brashness. She had just completed a sentence for robbing a bank. This bank robber's name was Gail Cooke. Or her name might have been Gail Van Cleave. It was possibly Gail Thorton. "We were never sure what her real name was," admitted one investigator involved in the case. Gail was a master at identity theft. She was no master at bank robbery.

It was August 13, 2010, when Gail Cooke, aka Van Cleave, walked quietly into the Lake Tansi Branch of the Cumberland County Bank on Dunbar Road in Crossville, Tennessee. She was dressed casually in a sports visor pulled down over fuzzy hair, a pullover shirt, and denim shorts. To the teller who called her over to their window, she probably looked just like any other customer who was tolerating the Tennessee sun as best she could. But when this customer pulled a gun, the teller most likely changed their mind.

The woman was demanding money, and the teller did exactly as all bank employees are trained to do: give the money; don't be a hero. The gun-wielding woman left without another word. Witnesses would later place her exiting the bank parking lot in a black, late-model Volvo. All of her actions were caught on video.

Bank robbery is considered a "victimless" crime, but tell that to a teller who has looked down the barrel of a gun, regardless the size of the gun, regardless if the gun is a working AK-47 or a lime-green water pistol. Ask anyone who has ever been robbed at gunpoint, "what type of gun was it?" And the first answer you get is "big!" A .44 and a BB gun look the same from the business end.

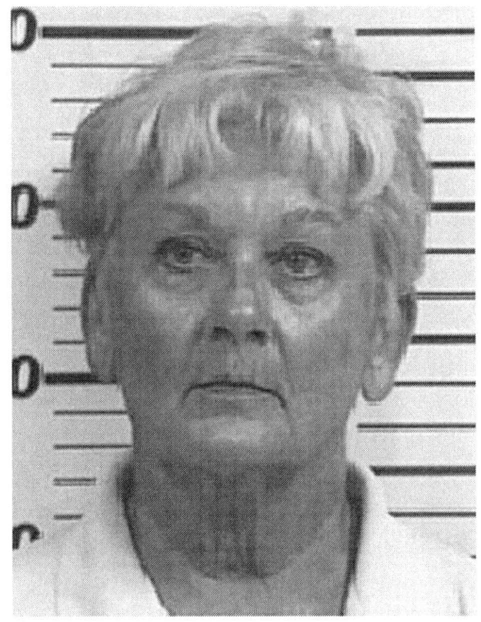

Gail Cooke/Van Cleave was dubbed the "Grandma Bandit" by the Cumberland County Sheriff's office in Tennessee. She robbed the Cumberland County Bank's Lake Tansi branch at gunpoint (Cumberland County Sheriff's Office mug shot).

The crime fell in the jurisdiction of the Wilson County Sheriff's Department, so these officers responded. The bank was shut down and witnesses separated and interviewed one by one. Because the Cumberland County Bank was FDIC insured, the FBI was notified. The Sheriff's office contacted bank security for a copy of the security camera footage. The video would clearly show the robbery and the perpetrator. "It wasn't shocking to me that an older woman would rob a bank," one investigator admits, "after years in law enforcement, nothing shocks you. Surprised? Yes."[1]

Cumberland County Sheriff Butch Burgess dubbed the thief the "Grandma Bandit."

Prior to the robbery, an elderly woman had stopped at a Walmart Murphy USA gas station near the bank area to gas up her 2008 black Volvo; she drove off without paying for the gasoline. In 2010 such theft was possible because of the structure of the gasoline pumping systems, and she was able to steal gasoline in this fashion two more times. Surveillance cameras videotaped her every move. Later, the woman in the Volvo would be charged with three counts of theft of property.

A BOLO ("be on the lookout") was released for the black Volvo. Patrol officers were given a description with license plate information.

Investigators used the information off the Volvo to learn the name of the vehicle's owner, a Gail Cooke, and her address. From a prior subpoena, it was discovered Gail was receiving checks from Louisiana and was using a credit card in the same state. The card was also being used at an Econo Lodge in Lebanon, Tennessee.

The Econo Lodge was just off I-40 in Lebanon, an area where clusters of hotels and gas stations await truckers and travelers seeking a night's rest, hot coffee, gasoline, or maybe just a stop to shake off the road noise.

Warrants were drawn to include a search warrant for the black Volvo should it be located. Officers arrived at the hotel on Wednesday afternoon, August 25. And there in the parking lot sat the 2008 black Volvo.

The law enforcement officers discovered what room Gail was staying in. Armed with the search warrants and aware she had a gun, they waited. When Gail stepped out of her room, she was quickly and quietly apprehended.

A search of her room and of the Volvo revealed Gail had been traveling for the last few months, burning up the miles between East and Middle Tennessee and Louisiana. She fell to sleep each night in the bed of whatever hotel room was affordable and available, eating fast-food meals and free continental breakfasts, as they were offered at the motels. The odometer on her 2008 Volvo never stopped turning. It was a flotsam life. And everywhere she went, she took on a new name.

Investigators found several sets of identification in her hotel room. Criminal history checks of the names would later show lengthy criminal histories. There was one identifying her as Gail Cooke, the name which the Volvo was registered under. As Gail Van Cleave, she had been arrested in Athens, Tennessee, for shoplifting. She had also used an ID with the name Gail Thorton.

She had charges of armed robbery for the bank, and three charges of theft of property from when she drove off from the Murphy USA gasoline station. The FBI was to handle the bank robber charges.

Lebanon was in Wilson County, so Gail would be held in the Wilson County Jail until she could be transferred. After she was booked in, she sat down with investigators but refused to speak with them. "She didn't want to talk to us," one of the officers notes.[2] So off to a cell she went, scratchy blanket under one arm with jail-issued shower shoes and plastic-wrapped necessities in her fist.

Cumberland County officials would eventually travel to Lebanon, Tennessee, Wilson County, to transport Gail back to Cumberland.

Bond was set for Gail Cooke at $400,000. Her sentence hearing was scheduled for September 29, 2011. It was expected she would plead guilty and receive a sentence of seven years. Otherwise, the case could go to court, which meant more time sitting around the county jail until the trial and a possible sentence of 25 years with a fine of up to $250,000. Gail was now 59 years old. Every year behind bars adds about seven years to the physical body and mind. And no matter how many times they call a low-security prison "Camp Cupcake," a prison is still prison. The plea bargain sounded like the better deal.

Gail's attorney did explain the federal court wasn't like the state court. In the federal court, pleading guilty to a set term means serving that term 100 percent, maybe a little time off for good behavior. None of this "percentage off" for this or that.

So on Friday, July 8, 2011, Gail Cooke went before the judge and formally pled "guilty." Her sentencing hearing was set for September 29. That was the legal system: wait and then wait some more.

On September 29, Gail went before the federal judge and was sentenced to seven years. She now belonged to the Federal Bureau of Prisons, inmate number 20364–075.

36

Josephine Sari

The "Hooded Bank Robbing Granny"

Initially, they thought she was in her 40s–50s and reported it as such in social media. The Willingboro, New Jersey, police were using Facebook to post photographs of the woman they dubbed the "Hooded Bank Robbing Granny" in an effort to identify and capture her before she robbed again.

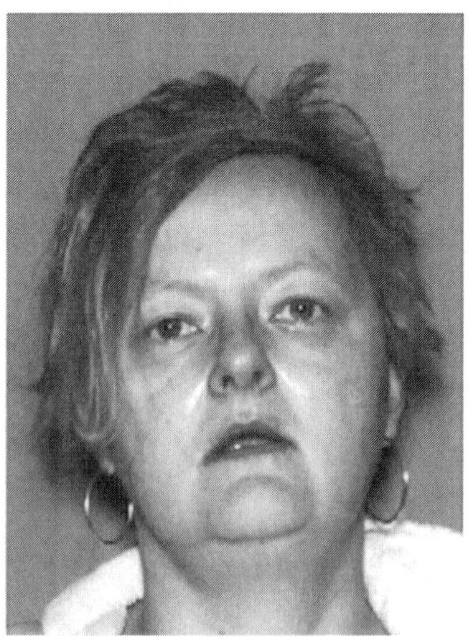

At 42, Josephine Sari's crime spree lasted two days. She robbed three banks on May 13 and 14, 2016, in Hamilton, New Jersey (Willingboro, New Jersey, police mug shot).

Her crime spree was short-lived.

Rakesh Patel owned the Quick Shoppe on Beverly-Rancocas Road in Willingboro, New Jersey. He was working one night in early May of 2016 when an older woman walked in. When he looked up from the register, the woman was brandishing a screwdriver, announcing that she was robbing him and to give her the money in the register. Patel asked her why she needed the money. "She told him it was because her daughter was sick."[1]

When her store-robbing career fizzled out, her bank robbery career began. On May 13,

Josephine Sari's disguise, a dark scarf, covered only one side of her head. She was dubbed he "Hooded Bank Robbing Granny" by the media in 2016 (released by Willingboro, New Jersey, police to the public).

2016, the same woman walked into the Wells Fargo bank in Willingboro, 4306 Route 130 North, and presented teller Lou Wells[2] with a note. It was not the note that was so strange but the woman's appearance. She was about 5' 6", a white female with light-colored hair, dressed in saggy, gray slacks, a black, short-sleeved blouse, and wearing large, dark sunglasses. The short sleeves and neckline of her blouse revealed sagging biceps with crepe skin. She carried a large, unusual-shaped lime-green purse. The strangest part of her "disguise" was a black scarf she had draped over her head: it covered one side of her head but not her face.

The teller placed the money into the green purse, and the robber walked out the door. The security camera videotaped it all in color.

Witnesses placed her walking towards a Goodwill store. It was just past 11:41 a.m.

Per protocol, the Wells Fargo bank was locked and closed. The Willingboro, New Jersey, police responded. Witnesses were separated and interviewed. Willingboro police officers began the task of filing their reports.

But later that evening, the same woman entered a Hamilton TD Bank on 1130 Whitehorse-Hamilton Square Road in Hamilton Township, about 20 miles away from the Wells Fargo. Again, she was clad in the saggy, gray slacks, black, short-sleeved blouse, and large, dark sunglasses. The black scarf was draped over her head, still covering only one side of her head but not her face. She presented a note, and the teller filled the green bag with cash. The robber departed. And again, a security camera videotaped it all in color. The protocol was repeated: bank locked and closed, police responded, witnesses interviewed.

The robber must have felt secure in the routine, because that next morning on May 14, dressed in the exact same clothing, including the black scarf covering half of her head, and with her trusty green purse, the woman walked into a TD Bank on 3470 Quakerbridge Road located about five miles away from one of the banks she had robbed the previous day. Again, a recording device silently whirled as she robbed the teller and departed with the green purse full of money.

The Willingboro, New Jersey, police arrived and made a report. They obtained photos from the recorder. This time, investigators received permission to post it to the department's Facebook page along with a request for anyone recognizing the suspect to call a hotline number.

A tip led the officers to a woman named Josephine Sari, a 42-year-old woman who lived in Chesterfield, New Jersey. Officers went to her home, but she was not there. Instead, they found her at another location.

Sari was arrested and taken into custody. Her bond was set at $200,000 cash.

Josephine pled guilty to the bank robberies and to the robbery of the Quick Shoppe in Willingboro and was sentenced to probation and to pay out fines and restitution. She eventually agreed to enter and complete the Mercer County Drug Court Program, indicative of a possible drug-related problem. The "Hooded Bank Robbing Granny" had been caught. Maybe she has found any help she needed.

37

Gail Simpson

Big Pun's Little Mama

Christopher Lee Rios (b. 1971) has the distinction of being the first Latino rap artist to have an album certified platinum as a solo act. He began his career in the hip-hop underbelly of New York, truly living the life of crime that he rapped about. He went from homelessness to becoming one of the most revered artists in the genre. His net worth was estimated to be at $5,000,000. At 300 pounds, the 21-year-old Rios, who now went by the name "Big Pun[isher]" was a force to be reckoned with in many ways. Unfortunately, it was also his downfall. At 28 years old and almost 700 pounds, he succumbed to a heart attack and died in 2000. The sadness of his passing was exacerbated when it was discovered his friends at the recording studio had reportedly bilked Rios and his family of millions, leaving the family destitute at Rios's passing.[1]

Reportedly, one of the reasons Big Pun had left home as a young man was the family dysfunction that he was raised in.

This included a time in 1993 when his mother, Gail Angelique (Tirado) Simpson, was arrested on six counts of unemployment fraud and one count of grand theft. Her fines were paid by 1999, but her criminal career was far from over.

Gail Simpson's first attempt at robbery was not a successful one.

April 26, 2014, was just another day at Sam's Beauty Supply in Homestead, Florida. Owner Kaied Turabi was preparing to ring up his customer's purchase. The customer, Sandra Apple,[2] was waiting at the counter, her mind wandering over what else she had to do that day. It was about 4:30 p.m. when the shop's door opened and another customer, a short, chubby, black woman dressed in white pants and a pink blouse, came into the shop.

The tiny woman walked up behind Sandra and placed what looked like a kitchen knife against her throat. Thinking it was a prank between friends, Kaied ignored the scene, told Sandra her total amount due, and accepted her credit card.

Sandra felt someone walk up behind her, and when something pressed against her throat, her first thought was to wonder what was happening. A friend must be playing a prank! And then the woman behind her said, "Give me all the money in the cash register or I will slit her throat!"

Kaied smiled at the prankster and continued bagging up Sandra's purchases. He glanced up and saw his customer's eyes; they were wide with fear. This woman wasn't laughing or joking with the knife-wielding woman. She was *scared*. Sandra Apple had realized this was not a friend with a strange sense of humor. She didn't know who the robber was, but she sure knew there was a knife at her throat.

"Okay, okay!" Kaied told the robber. "Here!" From where the robber stood, it was looking like payday: the man behind the counter was opening up the register. So when Kaied Turabi came up with a handgun instead of a handful of cash, the robber was completely thrown off.

Kaied came around the corner, waving the gun at the robber, and Sandra yanked away from the woman and grabbed the knife out of her hand. Sandra then called 911 while Kaied held the robber at bay.

When the police arrived, the would-be robber identified herself as Gail Angelique Simpson, 62 years old, of Homestead, Florida. She was transported to the Miami-Dade jail.

A detective arrived to speak with Gail. As she was being read the Miranda rights, Gail told the detective, "I'm taking a lot of pills." She volunteered the fact she had a psychological history and then admitted she wanted to kill herself. She was transported to a Ft. Lauderdale hospital for evaluation.

On May 5, there was no Cinco De Mayo celebration plan for Gail; she was in custody in the courtroom, and while she was there, she was served an arrest affidavit for probation violation. She was not given a bond. When she gave her personal information to the clerk who completed the paperwork, the impact of her son Christopher's, aka "Big Pun's" financial despair at his death revealed the desperation of his family. Instead of an address for Gail, the clerk had written "homeless."

Just a few weeks later on September 23, employees at the Wells Fargo bank at 8850 S.W. 24th Street in Miami, Florida, were inevitably glancing up at the clock, knowing they would soon be winding down their day, when a customer walked in at 3:30 p.m. The customer was a tiny black woman, barely five feet tall, wearing a brown blouse and black slacks. She wore large glasses and stylish dangling earrings. She paused at the customer's counter, then walked up to the teller's window. When the teller asked, "How can I help you today?" Gail Simpson passed a note that read, "No funny business I know where you live and I will kill you. I know how you get to work and what route you take. Someone will come for me in 15 minutes."

The teller's brow puckered, and she asked gravely, "Where do you want me to put the money?"

"In the white envelope."

Left and right: **Mother to a millionaire rap star, Gail Simpson robbed a bank in Miami, Florida, on May 5, 2014. The robbery occurred while she was on probation for attempted robbery of a beauty supply store while taking a hostage. She was 63 (Miami, Florida Police Department mug shots).**

The teller removed a white envelope from a neat stack at her station, opened her till, and removed $800 in various denominations. Quickly, she placed the money into the envelope and passed it over. Then she watched the customer walk out as quietly as she came in.

Gail Simpson was still outside of the bank when the Miami-Dade police cruiser rolled up only minutes later. She matched the exact description given by the teller and still had the white envelope full of cash. The cash was returned to the bank. Once again, Gail found herself being transferred to jail.

For the talented and successful Big Pun, it is a sad ending to a man who rose up out of the streets to entertain millions of fans all over the world. The saga continues for his mother, Gail Simpson, who, as of this writing, remains entangled in the legal system. A net worth of $5,000,000 is so far away from a jail cell.

38

Emily Coakley

Oldest Female Robber on Record

Emily Coakley was convinced: The TD Bank where she had an account had shorted her $400, and she was there to get her money back. She had lived long enough to know when someone was messing with her! And if they wanted a problem, well, she was about to give it to them.

According to what she would later tell the police, Emily did not want it to come to this, but the teller did not listen when she patiently explained her situation: on November 20, 2017, Emily had entered the TD Bank at 38th and Market in West Philadelphia to make a withdrawal. She had slowly pushed her walker up to the teller's window, pausing to sit in its chair while the money was carefully counted out for her.

Once home, Emily counted out the cash. Puzzled, she recounted the money; she believed the cash was short $400.

So on November 21, Emily returned to the TD Bank at 38th and Market, pushing her walker ahead of her. She wore a dark sweater over her clothing, with a red bandana tied over her head and a dark cap over the bandana. Once again, she slowly pushed her walker up to the teller's window. Tapping one of her brightly painted red fingernails on the counter, Emily explained that the bank had shorted her $400 the day before.

The situation was investigated. She was told that no one had shorted Ms. Coakley; there must be a mistake. Words were exchanged: kindness on the teller's side, anger on Ms. Coakley's end. That was when the old woman decided they wanted a fight, and she was going to give it to them.

With one hand on her walker for support, Emily Coakley pulled a .38 revolver out of her coat pocket and demanded the teller give her the $400 that was due. Now.

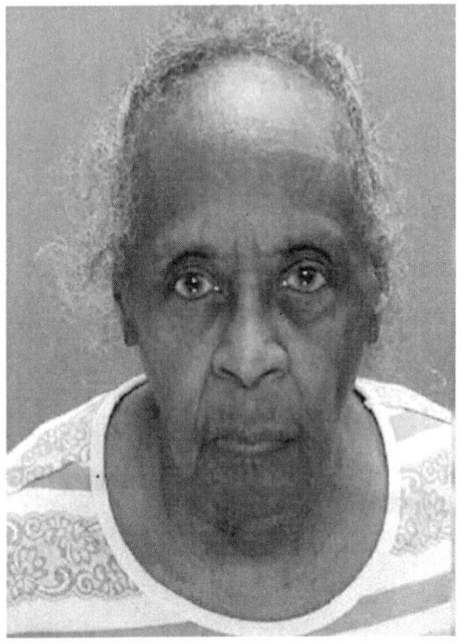

Emily Coakley became the oldest female bank robber on record when she was charged with robbing the TD Bank in West Philadelphia in 2017. She leaned on her walker while wielding a gun at the teller (Philadelphia Police Department mug shot).

One of the bank employees hit the silent alarm to notify police.

Police officers arrived. It didn't take much effort to get the gun away from Emily. To their relief they discovered the .38 was unloaded. Emily had the bullets in her bag.

Emily's family arrived while she was being held at the bank. They tried to calm her down to no avail.

Law enforcement listened to her, but they could not stop her rants.

Emily was escorted out of the bank building to a waiting police cruiser. She treated everyone around her, including a photographer, to a sour expression as she slowly pushed her walker with one foot, her knee resting on its seat; she was still angered with TD Bank. Then she was driven to jail for processing.

She was released on her own recognizance. In hindsight it is comical, but when a woman is outraged and swinging a gun around, shouting threats and accusations, no one cares if she is 86 or 26.

On November 22, 2017, Emily's list of charges read:

1. Robbery—inflicting serious bodily injury
2. Firearms not to be carried without a license
3. Carry firearms in public in Philadelphia
4. Theft by unlawful taking / movable property
5. Receiving stolen property

6. Possession of instrument of crime with intent
7. Terroristic threat with intent to terrorize another
8. Simple assault
9. Recklessly endangering another

Eventually, Emily's attorney would plea bargain the case. Counts 1–5, 7, and 9 were withdrawn, and she pled guilty to counts 6 and 8. Emily was placed on one year of non-reporting probation.

Part of her punishment was to pay $446.25 in court costs to the Municipal Court of Philadelphia County; $5 of court costs was allotted, as in all cases, to the "Firearms Education & Training Fund."

Emily Coakley was born August 12, 1931. She was 86 years old the day she attempted to rob Philadelphia's TD Bank. While she was not successful, this makes her the oldest known woman bank robber at this writing.

Part IX

Who Needs Television When We Have Reality?

39

Voyeurs

America's Obsession with Fake Reality

Just how real is "reality television"?

"It's very real," explains one television producer who has worked with several production companies that have created and produced reality shows. "The trick is, filming never stops. After some time people forget the cameras are there and just become themselves. Of course, there is a lot of editing. And [the audience] is only going to see the dramatic parts, the suspense, sometimes rearranged for 'dramatic purposes.'"[1]

"Reality television" includes shows that follow famous families, singers, or actors as they go about "daily lives." Many times dialogue is loosely scripted on these shows (e.g., sisters are told they should fight and the mother should take a side; the father is told to make a house rule that will confuse or embarrass the family). Sometimes, even the houses are not real: a model home (not the families' actual home is used for the set) or an actual movie set is used. And those appearing on these shows (or "stars") have agents who know how to get them publicity, good or bad: Will JoJo patch things up with Kari? Is Toni showing a baby bump? Tune in!

Television has made voyeurs out of viewers with the invention of reality television. In the 1950s, real families watched fake families solve problems by working together, always with soft scolding and easy answers. Dad always knew best. Mom deferred to Dad, and sometimes she helped solve the problem, too, but always behind the scenes of the drama and without recognition. In the 1970s, large, blended families repeated part of the formula. No one became abusively angry—no hitting or cursing, and it all worked out in the end. Then television families—particularly the powerful and wealthy—started showing cracks: alcoholism, abuse, even a good "whodunnit." Soon, television audiences became hungry for what was real: problems never solved and people staying angry; they curse and throw things. Viewers wanted realism without a soundtrack or canned laughter.

Enter reality television. Viewers began to spy on families or preselected groups and watch how the other half lives. They get to pick and choose what woman should pick what man to fall in love with and who should stay on the island. In short, they play God. The boring parts of people's lives are skipped over, and we get to the meat of it: who is sleeping with whom, what expensive houses and cars are owned, and what good fights are happening behind those closed mansion doors. But is it enough? Will the American public grow immune to reality television, like everything else, and seek something meaner, tougher?

Viewers can now be law enforcement officers without the training and the application. They can be thrown into prison without committing a crime. Side by side with police, corrections officers, inmates—new shows allow the viewer to be in a netherworld of the criminal element. Still, the viewer can get up to get a drink, a snack, or change channels if it all becomes scary or boring.

It's called "the train wreck effect": when people see a train wreck and can't help but gawk. This is a natural response built into our psyche, some psychologists explain. "The data ... stimulates the amygdala [which then] sends signals to the regions of the frontal cortex that are involved in analyzing and interpreting data." The brain utilizes this data to determine "fight or flight." The process is so fast that we then continue to stare, secondly, "as a way to face our fears." Looking at disasters—be it the aftermath of a hurricane, a mass shooting, or even a horrible argument—makes humans "automatically give more attention to a negative event" stimulating our empathy, "and we are programmed as humans to be empathetic."[2]

A study by the American Psychological Association reveals humans react and learn more from negative experiences than positive ones. Negative experiences demand more attention.[3] Thus the old newspaper and television parable "if it bleeds, it leads." The same with reality television.

Simply put, reality television is digging into our psychology and neurology for response without our knowledge.

Then "real" reality steps in, and the public remarks, "Just like on TV!" It isn't television. It is better than television; *it's real.* But this time, it's unbelievable. It's so damn interesting and crazy.

Now, that's better than reality TV. It's real life. But it's just like a movie.

Except no one can believe it's real.

40

Betty Oldham

LSD and Bank Robbery

She was a nice little girl, but the neighborhood kids knew you didn't mess with her. Just because they all lived in the South didn't mean she was sweet as sugar.

Her name was Betty Oldham, and she was one of those girls that, when one looks back on her history, they will say she had a "normal" childhood. Except she had a propensity to turn to fisticuffs when she saw fit. Perhaps it was because being raised with brothers she learned she had to stand up for herself. Or she did not want to conform to the southern belle stereotype.

She had several boyfriends in high school and remained a "nice girl," and if the boys tried to take it a step further, they felt her wrath. Betty was not beyond saying what she thought or following through with a promise to duke it out.

She graduated from high school in the early '60s, when the United States was experiencing drastic changes politically and socially. Women and minorities were working to find their voices. Protesters took it to the streets, the press, the colleges. Mom and Dad's rules went out the window along with "square" values and old-fashioned thinking. Tie-dyed clothes, liberal use of drugs, free love, and a nomadic lifestyle were beckoning many young people. To Betty Oldham, it called loud and clear. She headed for south California, where the call was the loudest.

Marijuana and LSD were readily available, and Betty was ready to try both. It was in a cloud of pot that she walked into a bank with a stolen gun and dreamily demanded money. She was so high that tellers did not want to startle or anger her, so they complied. They were also so shocked to see a woman robbing a bank that it was surreal. Betty walked out with $4,400 and went to buy drugs. When she sobered up, she would tell people that she had no idea how she got the money and didn't remember donning the wig and big sunglasses as a disguise.

The second bank robbery was in 1971. The '60s had passed by, and, as the saying went, if you remembered them, then you weren't really there. Betty Oldham decided if the first robbery had been as easy as they told her it had been, with a little planning this second one should be a breeze. Just in case, she took a hit of LSD before marching into the bank waving a .44 Magnum, demanding money.

The tellers did not hit any silent alarms. They didn't have to.

Shoving her way through customers, Betty stomped over to the first teller, laid a bag down on the counter, and ordered the bag be filled with cash.

While Betty was busy waving the gun, two employees made a dash for the exit. She swung the .44 and popped off a round but the shot went wild. Two more shots, and chaos erupted.

Employees and customers shot out of the bank through the doors like projectiles while the bag sat empty on the counter. Betty stood there, the gun at her side. There was no Plan B.

The cops were now pouring into the bank, so she backed herself into a small office. Now, of all times to get fucked up, the LSD kicked in.

Panic and hallucination and all things caused by LSD started, and Betty began to cry and shake. It was a bad, bad trip.

"Throw the gun out!" Now there was a cop on each side of the office door, positioned outside.

"Come out with your hands up!"

"Throw the gun out the door! Come out with your hands up! NOW!"

Instead of complying, Betty Oldham placed the .44 Magnum under her chin, the end of the barrel tight against her skin, and squeezed off a round as the cops and the onlookers stared in horror.

There were screams from the observers as she crumpled to the floor, the gun hitting the carpet with a solid *thunk*.

Betty Oldham was listed in critical condition when she arrived in the emergency room. The bullet had traveled through her mouth, up along her sinus cavities, splitting the optic nerve. Then it tumbled pell-mell through her brain before exiting the top of her head.

It took months of therapy, but she was able to walk with an aid and by feeling her way along the path. Her eyesight was limited to near blindness. She lost her voice and bodily functions. Her few pleasures were rare family visits and sitting by a sunny window in the hospital for the criminally insane where she became a lifelong resident.

No mug shots or criminal court records exist of Betty Oldham because the bank robbery charges were dropped. It would not have mattered. Betty never remembered who or where she was after placing the gun under her chin and pulling the trigger.[1]

41

Carolyn Sue Turner

"What I Did on Summer Vacation"

August 8, 1989, 3 p.m.

Alice Mitters[1] pulled the car to a stop in the parking lot of a shopping center in Clarksville, Tennessee. Her good friend and roommate, Carolyn Turner, was sitting in the passenger seat. Carolyn was disguised; she wore a fake beard and a dark wig over her short, neat, blonde hair. She had donned a baggy shirt and pants to cover her slender, athletic frame. Alice was not alarmed; Carolyn was here to play a practical joke on some girl named "Cathy." Practical jokes were a staple with Carolyn.

Carolyn got out of the car and trotted out of sight. Alice would later recall how Carolyn once showed up at the beauty shop that Alice owned, dressed in a gorilla costume. They all had a great laugh. But now they were about 65 miles away from where they both worked in Smyrna, Tennessee. Carolyn was driving a rented Toyota Corolla and had asked Alice to drive them to Clarksville. It was a long drive just to play a practical joke. Still—

And then Carolyn was back at the Toyota, jumping into the passenger backseat and slamming the door. "Let's get the hell out of here!"[2]

Alice drove out of the area and was headed back for Smyrna, with a panting, nervous Carolyn crouching in the backseat, cowering on the passenger side. That's when Alice noticed the lights in the rearview mirror. Blue lights flashing on and off. Police cars, trying to pull her over.

Carolyn told her to keep driving, not to stop. "Just keep driving! Keep driving!" she shouted as she was yanking the fake beard off of her face. But Alice, a law-abiding citizen, was not about to try to outrun a bunch of cops, with lights now flashing across the Toyota and sirens blaring. She pulled over as soon as she could.

And then there was a huge gun in her face. Cops yelling. "Hands on the steering wheel! Get your hands on the steering wheel NOW!"[3]

Alice was terrified. Carolyn was still crouched down in the back seat, on the passenger's side, bits of fake beard still clinging to her face.

When the police had each of the women separated and in handcuffs, Alice learned what was going on. Her good friend, Carolyn Turner, had not driven all the way to Clarksville to play a practical joke on some girl named Cathy; Carolyn had just robbed the Bank of Dickson, and Alice was considered an accomplice.

Alice was held for five hours. She had no idea that she was "aiding and abetting" a serial bank robber. She told investigators all she knew: that Carolyn had some money problems, possibly related to prescription drug usage. Yes, Carolyn loved practical jokes, dressing in costumes. She knew Carolyn as a roommate. Carolyn had never revealed a dark side—she was completely trustworthy, a good person. She even babysat Alice's grandson! When the cops decided they had no probable cause to hold Alice, they let her go. Alice had just learned what it was like to be arrested, and she had learned why she had been pulled over, cuffed, and stuffed into the back of a police cruiser: her good pal was hiding a dark secret.

In talking with police, Alice learned more about Carolyn's "practical joke." After Carolyn had run out of the bank, which was out of Alice's eyesight, someone had noted the tags on the rented Toyota. The short pursuit ended Carolyn's summer career as a bank robber. Carolyn was also suspected of robbing a few Smyrna restaurants. But serial robbery was only a summer gig. Carolyn Sue Turner had a full-time job that she had enjoyed for 12 years.

Until now, Carolyn had been known as "Coach Turner" to the faculty and students at Smyrna High School, where she taught softball and volleyball and sponsored the school pep squad.

It appeared Carolyn had run into serious money problems, problems that were so overwhelming it seemed there was no legal way out. So she committed a string of robberies as soon as summer vacation began. The robberies began June 7, four days after students burst out of classes, whooping excitedly, escaping the classrooms of Smyrna High School. The 34-year-old teacher became a master of disguises, usually dressing up as a man, and once she even impersonated a cop, complete with a uniform. To the trained eye or anyone looking close it was an obviously fake uniform, but a cashier doesn't have time to scrutinize when quaking in fear and shoving the register's money into a bag.

A bevy of wigs and fake facial hair pieces were found in the rented Toyota, along with a few hats and pieces of clothing. And when the losses were all totaled, Carolyn had taken $11,700 during her crime spree.

School may have been out at Smyrna High School, but that didn't stop the gossip chain. Smyrna High School principal Robert Raikes was forced to make a public statement. "She was very dedicated, hard-working and supportive of the school," Raikes told the media. "This is something you don't imagine could happen. There are just some professions where you just don't think this kind of thing could happen. Teaching is one of them."[4]

Teachers who worked with Carolyn compared notes with one another, sharing their thoughts with reporters. The parents whose children were on Coach Turner's teams were perhaps more shocked and saddened. They all knew her as someone who did not tolerate rule breaking, on the court or in the hallways of Smyrna High. It was one of the reasons that Turner's teams were known for their fiery competitiveness but fairness. You play to win, but you do it by the rules. A fellow coach told the press, "[Turner] wanted her students to do right."[5] Evidently, this did not apply to Coach Turner's life off the field or away from the courts.

Her teams made headlines, but it was the coach who was making front page news now. Carolyn spent the night in jail, and the next day, Wednesday, August 9, she appeared before U.S. Magistrate Kent Sandidge and pled "not guilty" in federal court. Her list of charges were read, and she requested a court-appointed attorney. Bond was denied. If found guilty of the charges, the coach was looking at up to 80 years in prison and up to $1,000,000 in fines. Now the popular coach wore an orange jumpsuit and shackles, and it wasn't a funny prank to play on friends.

At the time of her arrest, Carolyn Turner owed back rent on her house. Her telephone had been shut off. Carolyn's bank account had been closed, and the rental car she was using, the same one used to drive to the Dickson bank robbery, had an outstanding bill of $170.

The list of her suspected robberies was revealed in the court of law:

June 15: Carolyn Turner robbed the Third National Bank at 1200 Gallatin Road in Nashville, getting away with $2,300.
June 27: She robbed the Metropolitan Federal Savings & Loan at 2520 Lebanon Road, also in Nashville, of $1,700.
June 30: Carolyn Turner relieved the Third National Bank at 600 Gallatin Road, Nashville, of $4,500.

Then there was the robbery of the Bank of Dickson for $3,200.

But she wasn't just hitting banks.

The popular coach was a prime suspect in nine armed robberies in Nashville. The businesses included Domino's Pizza, Shoney's, and Cracker Barrel restaurants.

In late August, arrangements were discussed for Carolyn to be released on $50,000 bond into the custody of her parents. Part of the proposal included mandatory psychological counseling sessions or to gain employment. No thanks, Carolyn told the court; I'll stay in lockup. Better to be by yourself behind bars than to be imprisoned in your parents' home, with your family and friends, neighbors and strangers scrutinizing everything you do and say. She did have one familiar visitor: Alice Mitters visited once, bringing her grandchild to say hello to the former babysitter.

But it wasn't just Carolyn's life that was now in shambles. In October, Alice was indicted and appeared before U.S. Magistrate Kent Sandidge on charges of assisting Carolyn in robbing the four banks. Alice posted a $20,000 property bond and left the courthouse in tears. The federal charges would later be dropped.

It all sounded like a movie plot: the bank-robbing teacher. Carolyn had such a great career. She was a dedicated instructor and coach. When did things start going badly?

In 1977, Carolyn Turner's first year of teaching was full of strife. Most teachers will tell you that the first year is the most difficult. In 1978, it appeared, per her teacher evaluations, she had overcome the emotional issues. She received a rating of "Superior" in 1978 and again in 1980. Students were typical students. Some liked her; others felt she was mean, or she had her favorites; some students loved her and admired her. Staff members liked her, admired her drive. Somewhere in her career, money problems started piling up.

In mid–January of 1990, prosecutors requested the federal charges against Alice Mitters be dropped. Their investigation showed state charges were more appropriate, the prosecutors explained. Both Alice and Carolyn were scheduled for trial on January 30; when time came for trial, Carolyn's attorney requested a delay. Then it was announced that Carolyn was going to plead guilty to the four bank robbery charges. On March 12, Carolyn Sue Turner officially pled "guilty" to the federal charges of the four bank robberies. She was scheduled for sentencing, aware that she was facing a maximum penalty of up to 80 years in prison, tagged with a $1,000,000 fine.

On June 6 Carolyn went before U.S. District Judge Thomas A. Wiseman, Jr. It was a sentencing hearing lasting almost three hours, with expert testimony on both sides. Then came the expert witness testimony of one Dr. William Kenner, a Nashville psychiatrist who spoke for the defendant. It might have been one of the strangest excuses for a woman to rob a bank in the history of bank robbery.

Dr. Kenner revealed that Carolyn had been raped twice: an adult cousin had sexually violated her when she was ten years old, and she was again assaulted at knifepoint as a 20-year-old college student. "[Kenner told the judge] the rapes harmed Turner's self-esteem and sexual orientation and—when triggered by a professional setback in the fall of 1988—drove her to robbery 'as an alternative to suicide.'"

The "professional setback" was Smyrna High School's volleyball team being disqualified from competition on a technicality for which the coach blamed herself. "She set out on a course of self-destruction" after this disqualification. Committing robbery, Dr. Kenner had surmised, gave the coach "an overwhelming sense of power … [she could] identify with the aggressor."

Thus, Dr. Kenner surmised, Carolyn became a lesbian because she was raped. She robbed because she unwittingly caused her team to disqualify. Evidently being a lesbian *and* a losing coach led her to bank robbing. Carolyn's attorney requested a lesser sentence due to her history of trauma and the big blow to her ego which triggered her crime spree.

Judge Wiseman agreed, in part, "the things that happened to Ms. Turner are terrible." He then reminded the court that this woman had walked brazenly into four banks and threatened innocent people's lives, demanding cash. "But how much aberrant behavior can our society tolerate," he asked, just because someone suffers childhood trauma?

The judge made his ruling. Carolyn was given credit for the ten months she had served in the county jail and for receiving psychiatric counseling. He ordered her to pay restitution of $8,608 to the victims, meaning, Third National Bank, the Metropolitan Federal Savings & Loan, and the Bank of Dickson. Judge Wiseman then denied the defense attorney's request and sentenced Carolyn Sue Turner to 46 months in prison. The once-proud and revered coach would be trading in her Smyrna purple and gold uniform for a prison-issued khaki shirt and pants.

A few months after Judge Wiseman's ruling, Alice Mitters was arrested and taken to Dickson County, where she posted a $10,000 bond. She appeared in court that September. She was just a part of the collateral damage of her former friend's summer crime spree, she explained: Alice had filed bankruptcy, losing her business due to bad publicity. She started working out of her home, trying to pay bills and struggling to buy necessities. By now, federal charges had been dropped, but she was facing state charges. For this, Alice was going to need a court-appointed attorney. She had no money. She was looking at 8 to 30 years behind bars.

But the saga of the schoolteacher who robbed banks on her summer vacation was far from over. In March 1991, Carolyn Turner received eight more years on a state charge for the Dickson bank robbery.

Carolyn Sue Turner walked out of the federal prison system on July 21, 2002. Like most of the bank robbers in this book, she disappeared from the headlines. The popular teacher with headlining teams now avoided the press, and the shouts and cheers from the stands were echoes in her memory.

42

Hannah Sabata

YouTube's "Chick Bank Robber"

The skinny girl with long, bleached blonde hair was filming herself on YouTube while music by the band "Green Day" played in the background. Sitting on her bedroom floor, she was writing down messages and then holding them up for her audience to read. The problem: the messages were backward because of the camera's mirror image. To aid those watching, she later added captions, one of which read: "I told my mom I'm having the best day of my life."

It was filmed November 27, 2012; the girl's name is Hannah Sabata, and she was telling the story of how she had just stolen a car and robbed a bank. During this YouTube video, she showed off the stack of money, she showed off the car keys, and she explained she was the victim of a corrupt government that had taken her baby, charging her with neglect. The public viewers labeled Hannah "one of the dumbest criminals" for telling her story on YouTube.[1] But was she?

Hannah Sabata was an HIV-positive, 19-year-old divorced mother of one by November 2013 when she was searching through cars in a parking lot located in York, Nebraska. Her son was taken away from her at birth. "[That] pissed me off so bad I wanted to either commit suicide or rob a bank," she writes in a memoir. "I decided I'd do the latter." So, she was searching for a car to steal. A search of one car revealed a stash of marijuana and smoking paraphernalia. Another car search yielded some credit cards. Then Hannah came across a nice Pontiac Grand Am with the keys in it; she slid behind the wheel, and off she drove.

Hannah drove the car to a country road so she could write her bank-robbing note. Then it was home to the nice, neat farmhouse where

November 27, 2012, screenshot of Hannah Sabata's YouTube video as "Chick Bank Robber." She was both heralded and attacked by viewers. She was called one of "the dumbest criminals." Few understood Hannah's personal life and struggles (courtesy Hannah Sabata).

she lived in suburban Stromsburg, Nebraska.

Once home, Hannah gathered up the items she would need for the robbery, the stolen car keys, and off she went. Hannah had everything the well-prepared bank robber needed. Now she just had to find a bank.

She drove to Waco, Nebraska. "I found a tiny Cornerstone bank. I circled it twice because I was super scared. Finally, I parked." Hannah went over her items. "I had my sister's 'Little Bo Peep' pillowcase to hold the money. I had a pellet gun in my pink backpack. I had a black hat to hide my hair in and sunglasses as a disguise." Later, she would ruefully admit, "Not a very good disguise."

Hannah walked into the bank, and a teller asked her, "How may I help you?"

Hannah Sabata did not know she was taking the first step to a long, difficult run. She handed the teller her note: "You are being robbed! No alarms or locks or phones or ink bags! I have a loaded gun. You have two minutes."

Hannah watched the teller read the note, then look at her and hesitate. Thinking the teller was not going to comply, Hannah unzipped the pink backpack for the pellet gun. The teller began to stuff a total of $6,256 into that "Little Bo Peep" pillowcase.

Forty-five seconds later, Hannah walked out of the bank to get into the shiny Pontiac Grand Am and drive away. To send the teller a message, Hannah "flipped her off" as she drove away.

She had stolen the Pontiac in York, but she drove just over 20 miles from the bank to drop it off in a Stromsburg park. Hannah removed the license plates. She unwittingly dropped something else when she was there: Investigators would later find a bracelet with letters spelling out "I love Hannah" near the vehicle.[2]

Hannah went home. She used the credit cards to purchase baby toys for her son. "My uncle came over and asked me if I would smoke a joint with him. After he left, I decided to make a YouTube video so I could remember how courageous I was." The infamous video went into motion.

The video quality is poor, with bad color and slow frames. In the video, Hannah wears the same horizontally striped red and white short-sleeved shirt and blue jeans that she wore when she robbed the bank. She stops to scrawl the notes on paper, holding them up in front of the camera.

Hannah shows off the stolen baggies of marijuana and rolled joints for her audience, a pipe for smoking, and then she gets down to the day's business. She explains how she stole a car ("It was shiny") and dangles the set of keys. Then she tells her audience she robbed a bank. Hannah fans out a handful of cash, moving it towards the camera so that it goes in and out of focus. She is excited, Hannah explains, because she can pay off student loans and go shopping.

Hannah makes a motion as if holding a baby and rocking it. She explains she robbed the bank because the government had taken away her baby.

Later, she added the captions and posted the video as "Chick Bank Robber" on YouTube to add to a few others already under her account, youtube.com/Jellee Beanie. Her other videos included random video of herself with her boyfriend, "Rob." The "Chick Bank Robber" video would garner more than 1,000,000 hits by the time she landed in jail.[3]

York County Sheriff's Office & the Polk County investigators were not laughing. They posted the video of the robbery in social media, asking for tips as to the identity of this scraggly, bold robber. "Common misconceptions are that the reason I got caught was because of the YouTube video," Hannah explains now. The video was not the reason the police came knocking on her door, but the other video—the one of her robbing the bank, released by the police on the evening news—was. "My mother-in-law recognized [me] and turned me in."[4] The day after the robbery, Hannah was arrested.

Hannah's planned shopping spree never transpired because the sheriff's offices surrounded the white frame house where Hannah lived and escorted her out in handcuffs. "I don't know what's going on," she told the cops. Despite a beefy male deputy clasping her handcuffed arms behind her back, Hannah attempted to bolt and twist away, alternately grinning and snarling in anger. She wore that same red and white striped shirt and jeans. As she was being placed in the pickup squad car, she shouted to the media, whom she dubbed "the paparazzi," "[The police] never read me my rights!"[5]

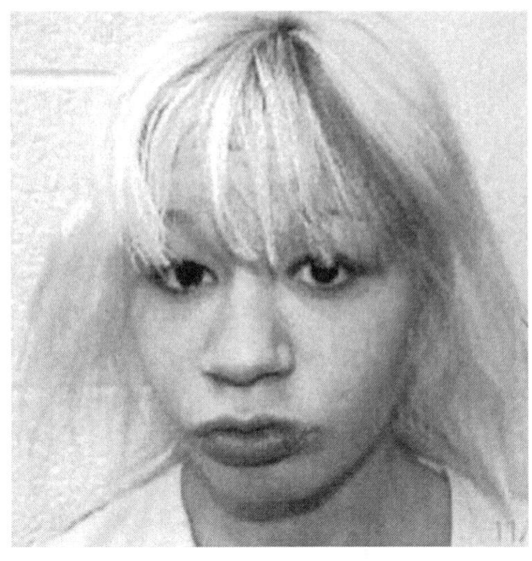

Hannah Sabata robbed the Cornerstone Bank in Waco, Nebraska, of $6,256 on November 27, 2012. Hours later, she garnered millions of YouTube viewers as the "Chick Bank Robber" by making a video boasting of the crimes and showing off the bounty (York County Sheriff's office mug shot).

When interviewed by investigators, she told them she had no intentions of using the gun. She had no intentions of scaring anyone.

Hannah did not expect the infamy garnered by the video. "I was all over TV. Everyone was talking about me. My first court appearance, the room was jam-packed with people and cameras." She also adds, "Not too long later, I was old news and forgotten." She is philosophical about her brush with fame. "That's how the media works."

Initially, Hannah pled not guilty, but in a plea bargain she pled guilty to the bank robbery; the theft of vehicle charge was dropped.

On Monday, June 17, 2013, Hannah Sabata went before Judge Patrick Mullen for sentencing. When asked to make a statement, she explained, "I shouldn't have robbed a bank. It wasn't the best day of my life. I was just manic. I learned that robbing a bank takes you to jail. I'm sorry I scared the teller, I wish I could take it back. I shouldn't have stolen that money, it wasn't mine. I want to be an art teacher and I want to make the world a beautiful place. I'll never rob a bank again."[6]

Judge Mullen was not moved. Hannah was sentenced to 10 to 20 years in prison. She received 203 days of time served in the county jail. Hannah was sentenced to the Nebraska Correctional Center for Women (NCCW).

The story became a laughing stock of the YouTube world and Hannah Sabata a punch line. Judging by the posts on her video, which was copied and sent out numerous times, she became a symbol for what happens when a girl goes wrong, for the mentally ill when problems go unchecked; she became a wet dream for strange men and the "cool chick" for young girls who only dreamed of doing something badass. And she was the dumbass who made an idiot of herself internationally and was now paying the price for it.[7]

On Hannah's Deviant Art webpage, created before she committed the crime, a few people attempt to understand her: "Again, this is what blows my mind, the media, and everyone else is blasting this girl for her recent actions. YET, NONE are willing to explore, learn or understand the F'dup stuff and abuse she has lived through. My heart breaks for such confusion in youth today, life is such an amazing gift and while some of US are dealt a bad hand at birth life is still an amazing gift. Hannah, I am sorry the world has used, abused and spit you out, I hope somehow you will find the strength to rise above and get through all this [*sic*]."[8]

Far more posts are from the haters who posted that she got what she deserved, and they hope with all sincerity she is rotting in hell. On her Facebook page, one such post read: "Horrible worthless cunt whore. Nineteen years old with a CHILD. You are an awful person. I hope your child gets taken away from your sorry cunt ass, and gets a real family that LOVES him/her."[9]

On her YouTube comments: "She is not the sharpest knife in the drawer. She is not even the sharpest spoon in the drawer. I don't think she even is in the drawer. Probably somewhere lost in the dishwasher."[10]

What would cause a 19-year-old girl to commit two felonies and then put it out for the world to see on a popular social media channel?

Hannah Sabata could be the poster child for either ignorance or an incredibly sad life that was spiraling out of control and heading for such a crash. Born in 1992 in what she called "Hicktown, Nebraska, in a small, sinking home surrounded by many tress [*sic*] and broken-down cars," her psychiatric care began when she was nine years old. In her memoirs, she writes there were numerous suicide attempts, beginning at age 16: "I was so intrigued by death. I looked up horrible pictures of corpses who have been drown been shot and that have been run over by a train. I thought it was so cool back then. It made me feel immortal ... like death wasn't a reality." The suicide attempt landed her in group homes, including Boys Town. Hannah ran away from Boys Town, and "while on the run, I lost my virginity to rape. I was 17 years old." She was located and sent home wearing an ankle monitor. She self-reports she was in 16 different hospitals, diagnosed with bipolar disorder. At 17, she lost her virginity to a carnival worker 11 years her senior who gave her HIV.[11]

Hannah met a man and married him in the beginning of 2011; the same month, he went to prison for a crime that occurred prior to their meeting. Hannah admits infidelity. She changed the way she took medication for HIV, increasing the chance of the baby contracting HIV. (Her son was born HIV negative.) Health and Human Services took custody, charging Hannah with child neglect because she changed her medication routine. Her husband was released from prison, and they divorced.

A talented artist, she drew dark and sinister pictures and displayed her work on the webpage deviantart.com. Her life was an open book, and she posted often how she had been a runaway, homeless, and HIV positive. She admits she has hallucinated, including a visit from Satan. She burned a Ouija board because of what it was "telling" her. ("I doused that motherfucker with gasoline and I burned it all to ashes.") There were unexplained panic attacks and grandiose ideations.

Hannah's problems followed her into her incarceration into NCCW. According to a report by the ACLU of Nebraska, Hannah had been diagnosed with schizophrenia. "Throughout her time in prison, she has experienced lapses and delays in receiving prescription medications for her HIV." Thus, Hannah has been placed in isolation several times, each lasting more than a month, totaling more than two years "exacerbat[ing] her psychiatric disability and increased her suicidal ideations."[12] Despite her problems, Hannah earned a paralegal certificate while incarcerated.

"I like to challenge staff," Hannah admits. "I often refuse strip searches."[13]

Hannah Sabata's request for parole was granted in 2017. She had participated and completed pre-release programs and was ordered to complete a one-year program at Living Water Rescue Mission in York, Nebraska. She had been meeting with a representative from the mission while incarcerated and was comfortable with the organization. She was released on parole on November 25.

Freedom did not last. Her parole was revoked, and Hannah was returned to prison where, in November 2020, she received more time for assaulting a prison officer.

"One time, use of force was taken on me and ALL my clothes were cut by staff on video," Hannah complains. At present she calls the mental health unit home, "the 'STAR' unit." She has painted some murals on the prison walls for various projects, including "inspiring quotes." She draws excellent renditions of cartoon characters on her outgoing envelopes and decorates them with bright colors. Hannah is a voracious reader and writer, pounding away on an old-fashioned Epoch typewriter. "I am writing my memoir," she says.[14]

At this writing, Hannah Sabata, YouTube's "Chick Bank Robber," remains incarcerated at the Nebraska Correctional Center for Women (NCCW). She is on the entire staff's radar for being a troublemaker: flooding her cell, destroying prison property, refusal to obey orders. Hannah has a parole hearing slated for August 2021. Her release date is in 2025.

43

Heather "Charli" Johnston and Ashley "Adrienne" Miller

Barbie's Bank Heist Adventure

It all started with an statement everyone mutters at least once in their lives: "I don't want to go to work today." For three friends sitting around an apartment, the trouble started when one of them made the comment. But, like everyone else, the person saying it had to go to work. For this particular trio, there were bills to pay, clothes and shoes and makeup to buy, and drugs to do. A person had to have money.

Well, someone else suggested jokingly, maybe we should rob a bank.

Thus the discussion began of planning the crime. It was either the beginning or the end of one career, if "reality TV celebrityism" can be called a career.

Rewind to the beginning:

Heather Lyn Johnston was preparing for her high school graduation. She had a scholarship, but she also had a boyfriend and a wild streak. Bucking her parents' rules, she ran off to live with the boyfriend. The hot romance fizzled out, and Heather returned home promising to be a good girl. She graduated high school and spent two weeks trying to decide on a career path. She was choosing between swimsuit model or using her scholarship to go to college to become a dental hygienist; she took a job at a nightclub called Shooter Alley until she decided what to do. The money was great—she would make $1,000 a week—and it was easy work. It was just like dancing in front of a mirror, she would later explain, with one exception: at Shooter Alley she was dancing naked under the stage name "Charli."

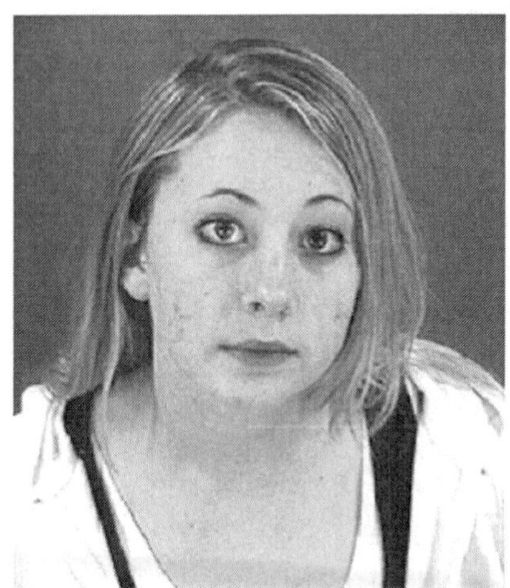

Left: **Heather Lyn Johnston ("Charli") traded pole dancing for bank robbing. It began with someone saying they didn't want to go to work (Cobb County Police Department, Georgia mug shot, February 2007).** ***Right:*** **Ashley Nicole Miller ("Adrienne"), once a high school cheerleader, went from dancing nude to robbing banks in "stunner shades" with her friend Heather Lyn Johnston ("Charli"). Aka "The Barbie Bandits," they robbed the Bank of America in Acworth, Georgia, of $11,000 on February 27, 2007 (Cobb County Police Department, Georgia mug shot).**

When her well-to-do parents discovered what their blonde-haired, sweet-faced daughter was doing, they tossed her out of the house. Heather became friends with 19-year-old Ashley Nicole Miller, also a dancer. Ashley went by the stage name "Adrienne."

Fresh out of high school, Ashley was a former high school cheerleader. Despite her quirkiness and clumsiness, she had a coach, and she showed raw talent. In her high school days, she was a sweetheart who loved doing volunteer work at a nursing home. But after graduation, seeking the attention she had once garnered from the Friday night stadium lights, Ashley drifted into a much faster crowd. She found work in a restaurant that was as popular for their half-naked, hot waitresses as their food. Tips were good. "If I can make this much money with my clothes on," she reportedly told someone, "I could really make some money if just a little more clothes came off." She began working at Shooter Alley, incorporating cheer moves into her dancing.

Ashley ran into legal trouble with a 2006 arrest for driving drunk. She received probation. Alcohol was a staple by now.

Ashley began seeing a regular Shooter Alley customer, a good-looking convicted felon named Michael Darrell Chastang. Soon, Heather and Ashley moved into an apartment together, and it was a great time: drugs, alcohol, parties and, of course, a lot of cash and nice clothes as the result of their grinding work at Shooter Alley. Heather's parents would later blame her troubles on the people she started hanging around with: bad influences, all.

Now comes the day Ashley, Heather, and Michael were at the girls' apartment, and someone bitched that they just did not feel like working that day. Then the bank-robbing suggestion. Michael took the comment further by putting in a call to a friend. Benny Herman Allen III had a good job as a teller at a Bank of America located in a grocery store in Smyrna, Georgia. Benny was handsome, slender, and the type of guy a person could count on to keep his mouth shut. After some discussion, the four hatched a plan.

Benny got on the phone with Heather and gave her instructions on how to rob a bank, using his training as a teller for reference. She grabbed a pen and jotted down instructions on how to write the demand note, including the words "Remember, I will not hesitate to kill you" and "Keep hands where I can see them. Do not pull switch."

Benny gave Heather driving directions to the branch where he worked. It was agreed that in two days Ashley and Heather would drive to the Bank of America in Smyrna, and the girls would walk into the bank, up to Benny's window, and "rob" him.

In the days before the big heist, Ashley and Heather went shopping. One of the things they each purchased was a pair of designer sunglasses. "Our 'stunner' shades," they called them.[1]

On February 27, 2007, Ashley Miller and Heather Johnston dressed in tight jeans and sexy blouses. They pinned their hair up and donned their new designer shades. There was the robbery note, all written out. There was the cute purse, ready for the cash take. The former pole dancers must have decided it is important to look your best when committing a felony.

Once ready, they both got in the car to drive to the bank. On the way they giggled and chattered. Heather would later say they were more excited than nervous. It was more like playing than actually committing a crime. They had "an inside man" after all.

It was a foolproof plan.

They arrived at the bank, checked their lipstick, grabbed their "stunner shades," and waltzed into the Bank of America, suppressing giggles. Both tried to appear casual as they turned to look around for Benny. Strange. He wasn't at any of the tellers' windows. He wasn't in any of the offices. They waited around, but they didn't see him.

Finally, Heather called him on her cell phone. "Where are you?"

Benny sounded incredulous. "I'm at work. Where are *you*?"

Heather told him they were at the Bank of America, where they agreed to meet. After some confusion, Benny told her she was at the wrong bank. Only then did Heather realize they had made a wrong turn when driving.

So now they were back on the road, heading for the correct bank to rob.

They were giggling when they finally entered the Bank of America at a Kroger grocery store in Smyrna, Georgia. Grainy surveillance video footage would show two leggy, white females in oversized sunglasses laughing and leaning on one another to whisper as they approached Benny, the black male teller. Benny begins to empty the till and toss the money at them. They scramble to grab at the money and shovel it all into their bag.

Once outside and away from the building, it was so exciting that they kept touching the money. "We did it!" Heather told Ashley.

"We got the money!" Ashley would squeal.

They drove to their apartment, where they spread the money out on the floor and marveled at how clever and cool they both had been.

The take had to

Heather Johnston and Ashley Miller were recorded robbing the bank wearing their "stunner shades." They used the money to shop and have their hair done (released to the public by Cobb County Police Department, Georgia, February 27, 2007).

be split four ways, with Michael and Benny each getting a cut, so Ashley and Heather began to count the money and stack it by denomination. The take was $11,000. That was $2,750 each. That was what each girl would have made in almost three weeks of dancing at Shooter Alley.

"We'll give some of this money to our parents," one of the girls said loyally. They both agreed.

"What should we do now?"

The answer came easy. They freshened up and drove to the mall, Phipps Plaza, and then Lenox Square.

After some time, bored with shopping, they walked into the pricey Carter-Barnes Hair Artisans salon and sat down to have their locks trimmed and highlighted. Heather would later say it was the most expensive haircut she had ever paid for. At the same time, the television overhead broke with a local news story about two girls in designer sunglasses who had robbed a local bank. No one really paid that much attention. Later, more grainy surveillance video footage, from the salon this time, would show the girls paying for their hairstyles, with one of them lazily stretching. Fingers clasped, she put her hands over her head. She could have been practicing for what was to come only days later.

They also went to Walmart to purchase a television.

On February 28, the day after the robbery, the videotape was released to the media. Someone in the media dubbed the two women "the Barbie Bandits," and it stuck. The story was akin to a Hollywood script: two young, attractive, white females, one blonde and one brunette, stroll into a bank wearing chic designer sunglasses to rob the place in broad daylight. They make no effort at disguise and giggle the entire robbery as a handsome, black male teller shoves money into their bag. Then they just swish their little asses out of sight. Play music, slow-mo camera moves.

"Barbie Bandits!" It went national. So did a hotline number.

Hundreds of prank calls to the hotline number identified the two: "It's Paris Hilton and Nicole Richie!"

Until finally, a real lead came in. "It looks like these two dancers that work at Shooter Alley," said the caller, who was one of the regulars at the club. "Their names are Charli and Adrienne."

Days later, "Charli and Adrienne" were exchanging G-strings for oversized, orange jumpsuits and plastic sandals after they were identified and arrested. Ashley also pled guilty for possession of Ecstasy with intent to distribute. Heather had marijuana and pled guilty to a misdemeanor.

Soon, Michael Chastang and Benny Allen III were being booked in.

"The Barbie Bandits" moniker irked the police but excited the girls. They lived up to their public's expectations, giggling and playing cute. However, in their jailhouse oranges, stripped of beauty supplies, they looked more like tired, old women than cute living dolls. On television, in full, professional makeup and under specialized lighting, wearing tailored clothing, they were the sexy, pretty fantasy girls who brazenly walked into a bank and laughingly stole money. Behind bars, not so much.

In the interrogation room, officers told Heather she could help the cops and herself if she would tell them where the money was.

"Well, I do have some of the money," she said coyly. Reaching into her bra, she pulled out a handful of bills, about $1,000, and laid it on the table, a sly grin playing on her lips.

Heather followed the old advice of "the first person to the window gets the best deal." She pled guilty first and was given probation. She went home to her parents. Heather Lyn Johnston would continue to grant interviews after her celebrity status as the "Barbie Bandit," smiling and joking. She does not appear to be worried that she caused any problems with the robbery, nor does she see it as such. Her parents insist it was "the wrong crowd" that got their daughter in trouble.[2]

Ashley did not get to the window in time and received two years in prison and eight years' probation. She walked into Georgia's Arrandale State Prison in May 2008 as a new inmate and then through the exit door in January of 2011.

On Halloween weekend 2012, Ashley Nicole Miller made the news again when she violated her probation. She and another woman—not her "Barbie Bandit" sidekick—got into fisticuffs in the parking lot of a nightclub with a third female. When the club bouncer made his way outside, Ashley and her buddy had the third woman on the ground, beating her senseless. When Ashley and her friend saw the bouncer, they took off. Both wore "pink costumes" and "had to be 'physically detained' … after being chased for 'about 30 yards.'" Ashley found herself in the

Gwinnett County Jail charged with battery; she pled guilty and received a year's probation. Then she was returned to Cobb County for a 90-day stint for parole violation.[3]

Both "Barbies" have wandered in and out of trouble but never again in and out of additional banks with someone else's money.

44

Wanda Irvin

The One-Armed Bandit

The television news reporter was coming to his audience live from the North Versailles police station in Pittsburgh. He excitedly explained that he was about to interview *a female bank robber*, freshly arrested and off the streets of Pennsylvania. As officers exited the station doors to escort the subject of this big story from the station to the patrol car, the reporter admittedly "peppered" robber Wanda Irvin with questions. Irvin was far from a wild-eyed fugitive with gnashing fangs, straining from chains; rather, she was 52 years old, portly, walking with a limp, and she appeared lost. She answered the reporter's questions in a sotto, breathless voice. There was a uniformed officer on each side, and she wore a leather strap around her waist, one handcuff attached to the strap and the other encircling her right wrist. Wanda Irvin did not have a left arm.

"I don't know why I did it," Wanda told the reporter, the same answer she had given law enforcement officers when they had arrested her only hours earlier. She huffed and puffed to crawl up into the SUV police cruiser, the news microphone still inches from her face. "It's not a good thing," she gasped.[1]

Once the news broke, the jokes about the "one-armed bandit" flowed over social media, popping up in chat rooms and Facebook, Twitter and group discussions. "One arm" jokes were shared along with guffaws and one-ups. Wanda Irvin became the "one-armed woman bank robber" headline literally overnight.

It was a Tuesday evening, October 4, 2017. It was right after 4 p.m., close to closing time at the Key Bank on Fifth Avenue in East

McKeesport, a division of Pittsburgh. A stout woman came through the front doors of the bank and walked up to the teller's window. Her face was flushed, and her brown hair was in a rumpled pageboy cut. She held a knife up at the teller and demanded cash.

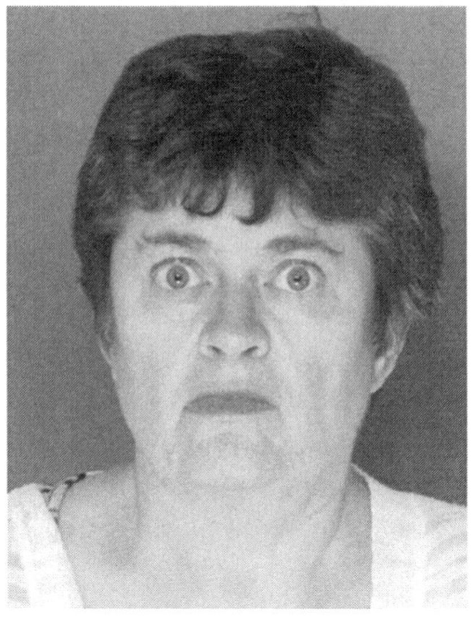

One-armed Wanda Irvin attempted to rob a Key Bank in East McKeesport, Pittsburgh, on October 4, 2017, at knifepoint. When the teller refused to comply, Irvin ran away (Allegheny County Jail, Philadelphia mug shot).

It probably took a moment for the reality to sink in. The teller was being robbed by a grandma with one arm, waving a knife. This is when the teller told the thief "no."

And because most criminals have a set plan, and when someone throws a monkey wrench into that plan there is no Plan B, the one-armed, knife-wielding, limping, stubby grandma ran out of the bank. Employees easily followed her and scribbled down the license plate of the car their would-be bandit queen departed in.

Police arrived soon after at Wanda Irvin's home in East McKeesport. She must have known the jig was up, because she was standing outside with the front door open. The officers knew she had a knife, and they had no idea of the situation they were walking into, so they drew their weapons and ordered her to the ground. She complied. She readily admitted to being the gangster on the run. When they located her purse, the alleged weapon used in the alleged robbery was tucked into the handbag. They had no way to secure her, as her left arm was missing to just above the elbow, so she was led back to a patrol vehicle without restraints. The top of the stocky woman's head didn't come close to the broad shoulders of most of the uniformed officers. She was driven to the North Versailles Township police station, where the reporter jumped her as she was transported for her next ride, to the Allegheny County Jail.

Her bond was set at $50,000. Wanda did not have bond money, so she had to bed down for the duration. She was charged with robbery, possessing an instrument of crime, and simple assault. Now she had to wait for the slow grinding of the wheels of justice to begin their turns.

Wanda Irvin's legal ordeal took two years and multiple visits into the courtroom. This included mental health court reviews and hearings. In April of 2019, she was ready to plead guilty to all three charges: robbery, possessing an instrument of crime and simple assault. She was placed on four years' probation and was to comply with the judge's orders, which included staying far away from Key Bank in East McKeesport. She also agreed to "comply with mental health court prescription medication policy," a telling notation as to why a disabled, 52-year-old woman might walk into a bank and wave a knife at a teller, demanding cash.

Hopefully, Wanda Irvin is now getting the help she needs to lead a happy, law-abiding life. Her crime probably would not have made anything more than a blurb on the back page of the local newspaper had it not been for the fact she had one arm.

45

The Starlet Bandit(s)

A New Kinda Hustle

He wanted to be famous.

Henry McElvane was a young man chasing an old dream of being a big star. So he changed his name to Robert St. John, which he must have thought sounded much more professional. At six feet tall with green eyes against his black skin, he could be an imposing figure. His dream was to go to Hollywood and be a professional stand-up comic and actor, like his idol Eddie Murphy. He did get to Hollywood, but he did not get to the limelight. Instead, he ended up pimping out little girls and slinging dope. He was caught and was sentenced to 11 years in prison. Released on parole, he became a pimp to a coven of bank robbers. It is a real-life story that outshines any fictional movie.

The opening act begins with Henry released on parole in 2007, after he went to prison for pimping girls (average age 13 years old), dealing marijuana, and one count of lewd acts with a child. An electronic bracelet to monitor his movement was strapped to his ankle. A list of rules to follow while on parole was given to him. Henry ignored both.

Henry McElvane bounced back into pimping, using Craigslist escort ads and mass text messaging. He was still trying to be a star, using the social media outlet MySpace for both his "Escort Service" and to showcase his comedy act.[1] He was doing all of this while on parole and wearing the ankle bracelet, which tracked his every movement but not the details of his life.

The money was not coming in fast enough, and he had no real talent. He was no actor, except for his smooth talk on the streets to girls who were too young or too desperate to know better. Talk turned to a new way to make money. Bank robbery was the new way. And Danielle Derosier, one of Henry's prostitutes, said she would give this new gig a try. Hell, it beat prostitution.

On March 25, 2008, Danielle pulled on a baggy gray sweat jacket, a T-shirt, baggy jeans, and swept her hair into a bun. Then she added the piece-de-résistance: a pair of large, dark sunglasses. Danielle checked her cell phone and dialed Henry's number so they would stay in constant contact. Her cell phone cover had glittery fake jewels on it, which would later earn her a moniker. With the cell phone clamped to her left ear, she walked into the Bank of America on Sunset Boulevard in Hollywood and schlepped up to a teller's window.

Without a word and without removing the cell phone from her ear, she set a note down on the counter: "Give me all the money in the register quickly." Rather than comply, the teller opened the drawer and pressed the silent alarm button.

Danielle looked at the teller. The teller looked at Danielle. Well, this was a bust.

Danielle turned and walked calmly away and out the door, talking on her cell phone.

The FBI investigated the video and dubbed the hapless robber "the Starlet Bandit." It was Hollywood, California, and according to witnesses, "she wore movie-star sunglasses." Evidently, those big sunglasses could have been found poolside at some hot-shot producer or filmmaker's home in the hills. And there was the phone with those rhinestones. The moniker stuck.

Four months after the failed attempt, Danielle Derosier, "the Starlet Bandit," walked into the Bank of America on Woodman Avenue in Van Nuys. She again wore those "movie star sunglasses" and the same cell phone clamped to her ear. Evidently the Starlet Bandit had put more thought into the note this time: "Quickly give me all the money in your till. Do not press the alarm. I have a weapon and I would hate to hurt innocent people."

This teller had a different reaction. They took the note, read the note, and then walked over to a supervisor to share the note.

Again not knowing what to do (she didn't have a Plan B) Danielle turned to walk out of the bank.

Henry McElvane and Danielle Derosier decided bank robbing was

Danielle Derosier, one of the "Starlet Bandits" with the ever-present cell phone and "movie star sunglasses." Initially thought to be one person, FBI officers were shocked to discover the truth (released to the public by the FBI, April 29, 2010).

not in their future. She went back to prostitution; he went back to pimping and trying to *be somebody*.

And then Kadara Kilgo arrived on the scene, and that changed things.

Kadara Kilgo was a streetwise, old-school prostitute, which meant she was involved in many a scam, and she had the scars to prove it. She could recount a time when a drug deal went wrong, a box cutter came out, and can show the scar across her back from 23 stitches. Kadara Kilgo was just one of the 58 percent of American prostitutes who had been violently assaulted by "clients."[2] So she called Henry McElvane, who she knew as "Robert St. John." She had been working on her own, but now seemed to be a good time to have the protection of a pimp. She would lose a percentage of her pay, but the investment for her safety seemed worth it.

She was also looking to get out of the prostitution game—it was getting old; she was 19, and there had to be an easier way to make a lot of money fast.

Kadara and Henry decided they would try a robbery, but they would put a layer of safety between them and the danger by introducing a third party. That way, if things went downhill, Henry and Kadara would escape unscathed, and their patsy would do the time. If it was a success; well, they would split the cash. But who would they get to play their puppet?

Enter Mallory Mnichowski to this comedy of errors.

Mallory had been a prostitute in Los Angeles but became pregnant, so she quit the streets and went home to the Midwest. Henry and Kadara started working on getting her back to California. Their sweet talk and promises must have worked, for Mallory came back to the City of Angels.

Henry had doubts about Mallory. She was dim-witted; there was something slow about her thought process. "Mallory's, like, the last person you would send in a bank," he would later say.[3]

On April 21, 2010, the three of them ended up sitting in Henry's car in front of the Bank of America on Woodman Avenue in Van Nuys. It was the same bank that Danielle had tried to rob in July 2008. Kadara scribbled out the demand note on a spiral pad while Mallory kept wondering how she was going to be able to do it. She was only 19 years old. And she was pregnant.

"Here," Kadara tossed the rhinestone-encased cell phone that made Danielle Derosier "the Starlet Bandit," at Mallory. "I'm going to talk you through the whole thing."

Mallory picked up the phone and stared at it.

Kadara tore the sheet of paper off the notebook to thrust it at the teenager.

Mallory read the note out loud. "Don't step away from your drawer or else I will start shooting customers. No dye packs…?"

"I've got your back," Kadara said, holding up her own cell phone. They watched Mallory take a deep breath, shoulder her zebra print purse, and open the car door to slide into the parking lot. She dialed Kadara's number and Kadara answered, then walked her through the process. It was sort of like 1-800-Rob-ABANK.

When Mallory walked out of the bank minutes later, she had $5,685 in her purse. Hours later they would divide it up. Mallory's cut was only $400.

Despite the fact she received so little pay for the biggest risk, Mallory agreed to rob another bank; $400 would buy a lot of Pampers and even a baby bed. Only days later she was walking into the Bank of America in Hollywood. Things did not go well there. So, they moved on to the Chase Bank on North Sepulveda in Mission Hills, and Mallory robbed the bank of $7,000. And she did all of the robberies with the glittery cell phone clamped to her ear, wearing the "movie star sunglasses."

Impressed with Mallory's take, Kadara announced now *she* wanted to exchange working the streets for bank robbery. Donning the glasses and using the cell phone, she robbed the Bank of America in Palmdale. She convinced Henry to return to the Chase Bank in Mission Hills the same day. Despite Mallory having robbed this bank only a few days prior, Kadara boldly went in using the same sunglasses and cell phone. None of the employees noticed she wore the same disguise.

Kadara found her addiction. She went to Las Vegas. Instead of letting the One-Armed Bandits rob her, she robbed a bank on her own. She returned to Los Angeles and talked to Henry. He again drove the getaway car for her to rob two more banks.

Henry must have seen a better profit with little investment. It was much easier to oversee a bevy of bank-robbing babes than a haven of hookers. The money was better. His women were safer. Henry didn't have to break a sweat. Exit the next Eddie Murphy, enter the new John Dillinger.

"The Starlet Bandit" made her public debut when the FBI made a statement on the local news. At this point, investigators believed "the Starlet Bandit" was one woman. Of course, she was always wearing those glasses and talking on that cell phone. She was a white female, and she always had a large purse.

Witnesses did give various descriptions in hair color and height, but witnesses often are confused, particularly in times of high stress. The robber could be wearing a variety of disguises. The camera and the video told it all.

Kadara was excited to see the grainy black-and-white video of herself robbing a bank on television. "I'm a TV star!" she squealed.

"This ain't the same thing" Henry corrected her.[4] This wanna-be actor would know.

Kadara Kilgo, at 19, had seen more of the evil side of life than 90 percent of people have seen in their lifetime. Still, she led a dull life, not a lot of fun stuff went on in her world, nothing she could brag about.

Being on television equated to being a television star in this jumbled-up city of dreams, no matter what role she played. Kadara needed to share her enthusiasm, maybe even brag a little. The only people she knew were people like herself: the flotsam, the addicts, the people who didn't belong or quit trying to belong a long time ago. That's who she talked to. Word travels fast on the street.

So when street hookers showed up at Henry McElvane's door asking to rob a bank, he wondered, since when did pimpin' prostitutes turn into pimpin' bank robbers?

At almost the same time, the FBI was wondering the same thing.

FBI agents who were investigating the string of robberies had glossy black-and-white photos pinned up on the board labeled STARLET BANDIT. Among the photos there were notations and copies of the robber's notes. As the collection of photos grew, investigators noticed the robber was *not* the same woman. There were only similarities. Disguises varied only so much, and the handwriting on the notes was the same, but always the cell phone that had the case with the glittery fake jewels. Perhaps these women knew one another. One of the witnesses had heard the robber say into the phone, "I'm at the counter already," as if giving a play by play of the robbery.[5] The Starlet Bandit had also fled one robbery in a white Toyota Avalon with a male driver. There was at least one male involved.

Thus far there was a list of banks believed to be robbed by the Starlet Bandit:

03/25/2008—Bank of America, 7800 W. Sunset Blvd, Hollywood
07/22/2008—Bank of America, 7255 Woodman Ave, Van Nuys
04/19/2010—Bank of America, 7255 Woodman Ave, Van Nuys
04/21/2010—Bank of America 7800 W. Sunset Blvd, Hollywood
04/21/2010—Chase Bank, 10348 N. Sepulveda, Mission Hills
04/23/2010—Bank of America, 839 E Palmdale, Palmdale
04/23/2010—Chase Bank, 10348 N. Sepulveda, Mission Hills[6]

Investigators also had a map with pins stuck in the bank locations. Looking for a connection to other crimes, agents determined the areas near the banks were known for prostitution.

Every officer understands the inherent danger that goes with prostitution. "The world's oldest profession" has a mortality rate 40 percent higher than the average workplace. AIDS and sexually transmitted diseases run rampant. Drug and alcohol abuse is part of the coping mechanism. Once the average age of a woman entering the profession was 18; today, it is 13.[7] Movies like *Pretty Woman* are just myth. The agents working the Starlet Bandit case asked one another, have Los Angeles hookers found a safer way to make money by bank robbing?

Because of the inherent danger, and because the women and girls are so vulnerable on the street, many worked for pimps. Pimps are cruel, selfish men who are abusers; again, the media's depiction of the pimp as a hip, slick character in furs and diamonds is so off kilter as to be laughable.[8] The FBI agents determined that, just as a pimp was usually behind the LA street prostitute scene, there might be a "pimp" behind the "starlet bandits"—now considered a gang.

The Starlet Bandit "Gang" hit three more banks in April 2010, their busiest month. The public was still believing the bandit to be one woman. On Tuesday, April 27, the Bandit robbed a bank in Granada Hills. The following Thursday, she robbed two banks, both in San Fernando: the Citibank branch in Woodland Hills and a Chase branch in North Hills. That made for a total of eight bank robberies in just 11 days.

It would be a matter of time, the investigators knew, before one of these bandits made a mistake. One thing about bank robbers: they could not stop at one robbery. The first robbery seems so easy. The money seems so plentiful. Soon, it becomes so exciting and so profitable. And they always—always—make a stupid mistake. There had to be a break that would lead to the culprits.

The break came in the form of a hot tip.

On May 8, a new member of the team, Billie Jo Hacker, aka the Starlet Bandit, hit a bank in Granada Hills. FBI investigators arrived and began interviewing tellers and witnesses when these investigators were notified about this possible tip. The real-life movie of the Starlet Bandit saga was about to roll credits.

Agents were told how some woman who spent her time smoking crack and running her mouth in room 317 of the Good Nite Inn in Sylmar knew about the bank robberies. Actually, she knew a lot: she was bragging about doing them.

Another "maybe." The Granada Hills interviews were completed, and the investigators agreed to stop by the Good Nite Inn "just to check it out." And as they pulled into the parking lot, there was a woman who looked just like one of the Starlet Bandits' glossy black-and-white photos pinned up on the office board. She was walking up and down the third floor balcony ... talking on a cell phone.

The woman on the phone was identified as Kadara Kilgo, and she wasn't scared when the handcuffs were slapped on. She was mad. It was her 20th birthday. Now she was going to have "Happy Birthday" sung to her in jail. That's all she would say. She listened to her Miranda rights; then she asked for an attorney.

Mallory's name and number were found in Kadara's cell phone. Another possible player?

While behind bars, Kadara used the jail phone to make repeated calls to a man the investigators could not identify. Both of them talked in code. Kadara never said the man's name.

With Kadara staying in the Bar Hotel, word on the street was still buzzing about Henry McElvane and his bank-robbing women, the easy money, much safer than selling sex on the street corner. The prostitutes were telling one another, but no one was telling the cops.

On May 18, Henry arrived at a house in Lancaster to pick up a young woman named Kayla Canty. It was Kayla who had hit the Granada Hills bank on May 8, the same day as Kadara was arrested. Henry also picked up a girl in Palmdale. The Starlet Bandits continued their mission.

But soon after, the mission was aborted.

A bank in Northridge did not bring forth the funds the robbers expected, so it was discussed, then agreed, to hit another bank. By now bank robbing was so familiar to the group it was akin to discussing where to go eat lunch: McDonalds or Taco Bell?

They parked near Chase Bank in Mission Hills to rob it for the third time. Henry did not really know Kayla, but it was all so old hat by now. What could go wrong?

Henry was aware that Kayla was in the bank longer than usual. But he was not aware that an LAPD plainclothes officer was parked outside the bank, sitting surveillance. The FBI had studied this gang's pattern: they had robbed two banks on the same day on three previous times, so surveillance was set on area banks should the robbers repeat that pattern.

The officer had just settled in to surveil the Chase Bank when an employee came bursting out the front door to race off through a parking lot. The officer jumped out of his car. Now more employees were spilling out the front door, and in the chaos they told the officer they had just been robbed. The officer jumped back into the unmarked car to begin pursuit.

The officer located the employee, who was panting and staring at the rear parking area. He was watching a female, who was running away from the area, cell phone to her ear, screaming into it, "Where are you? They're chasing me! Come and get me!"[9]

The officer gunned it and pulled up alongside of her, but she sprinted. "Police officer!" He screamed at her retreating figure.

She did not stop, arms pumping, head jerking side to side, looking for a place to escape to. She was wearing the "Starlet Bandit" sunglasses.

"I've got a gun on you! Stop!"

This time she skidded to a stop.

Henry had been circling the block looking for her, but the inexperienced Kayla had run the wrong way. He kept looking for her still. When he found her, she was in handcuffs. Henry kept driving. The next time he heard anything about Kayla, it was from her mother, and she was calling Henry demanding he pay her $5,000 bail.

"She's not gonna snitch you out," Kayla's mom promised.

At the same time, Kayla Canty was nervously telling her story to the investigators, answering any and all the questions she could.

"His name is Bob," she told the police. "He gave me the sunglasses and the purse, and he wrote the note."

What about the note?

He wrote it using the roof of his car, she explained. It was a Chevy Malibu, and it was a rental.

It took a few phone calls to trace the rental car to Henry's home in Palmdale. It took a few more phone calls to a parole officer, and reports placed Henry's ankle bracelet at the scene of every bank robbery.

The reports revealed that he sat and waited in certain parking lots, when and where he drove away, and the speed he was driving.

On May 27, 2010, Henry McElvane, aka Robert St. John, aka Bob, aka pimp to the Starlet Bandit(s), was pulled over in his car and placed under arrest. Danielle Derosier was watching from the passenger seat until she was recognized as being one of the bandits. Now Danielle was in handcuffs.

Henry and five of the women were arrested. It was the last act of the Starlet Bandits. Or was it?

Henry McElvane pled guilty and in January was sentenced to eight years with a release date of 2017. He was to pay back $21,000 in restitution. He still harbored dreams of fame.

Although prosecutors attempted to give Kadara Kilgo three and a half years, she received a sentence of 14 months despite being linked to nine bank robberies. She was paroled but violated by catching a drug charge.

The other women received shorter sentences.

Attorneys insisted some of the women were "brainwashed" or threatened into robbing the banks, but the women insisted they were not. The money was easy and plentiful, they explained. And maybe it brought some excitement, some glamour into what was otherwise a sad, scary life. It was, after all, Hollywood, where anyone can be a star, right?

Part X

What the G-Men Know

46

The Current Statistics

Who's Robbing the Banks?

The FBI releases an annual report titled "Bank Crime Statistics." The report counts three types of violations: robberies, burglaries, and larceny. The institutions listed include armored carrier companies.

The most recent report counts 1,788 violations in 2020. This included 1,500 robberies. Most robberies (1,338) were committed in commercial banks.

Most of the robberies occurred on Mondays between 3 p.m. and 6 p.m. in a branch office located in a commercial district. This is practical; it is the end of the day, so more money will be available. There are more roads for the getaway driver to use, more places for the robber to escape to.

A bank is more likely to be robbed if it is located in the city, but there is also a high probability if it is in a small town. And if you are a teller working behind the counter, you are the person who will come in contact with the bank robber.

This FBI 2020 report reveals that of the 1,788 violations, 135 of the known 2,322 perpetrators were women; 46 of these women where white, 69 of these women were black, 15 were Hispanic, 4 were "other," and 8 were listed as "unknown." There was one Asian and 386 were listed as "unknown race/sex. "The use of full disguise makes determination of race and sex impossible"[1] (p. 1).

The reports do not break down the crimes by type of violation for sex; therefore, it is not possible to determine how many of these women were actual bank robbers versus burglars or arrested for theft by larceny. Another glitch in the reporting system: not all bank robberies are reported to the FBI.

In an effort to collect information on wanted and unknown bank robbers, and to enlist the public's assistance in capturing bank robbers, the FBI has both a "Bank Robber" webpage and a mobile app. Anyone can peruse the page and search for robbers by region, city, state, name/nickname, sex, reward, "serial," and if the robber is considered "armed and dangerous." There is an interactive map and color photos of the robbers as taken by surveillance cameras. The website also has downloadable Wanted posters.[2]

47

"Don't Pull from the Clip/ No Dye Packs"

Pat[1] has worked as a bank teller for several years. Pat explains how tellers in most banks are trained in one aspect of security before, and during, a robbery: "There are cameras everywhere—and I mean everywhere. We were taught to pay attention to everyone coming in [the bank]. We are taught to size people up quickly as they come in—to use the objects around them to gauge the person's height, like tables, potted plants, etcetera."[2]

Looking people in the eyes and smiling is not just good customer service; it's also to help remember a face. Smiling can also be used to keep a person calm, to maintain control of both the teller and the robber's anxiety level—for the average person, it's difficult to be angry or abusive to someone smiling at you. Smiling and a quick scan of a customer's body also helps to memorize a face, listen for language and voice, and help identify eye color, scars, tattoos, clothing, and jewelry.

It was in 1965 and in the southern state of Georgia that the term "dye pack" first came into the banking language. A pack of banknotes (in most cases, $10–$20 bills) is hollowed out to create a hidden pouch where the dye pack is secreted. Detection of the dye pack is difficult when handling the stack.[3]

Pat explains how the dye pack and the bills work. "The location of the fake money packet changes all the time. It might be in the back of the till, or in a special clip, but always next to a magnetic plate."

Tellers are told when the fake money packet changes and to where. Each teller has a packet of money with the dye pack in his or her drawer. In case of a robbery, the teller is trained to hand over the dye pack with the rest of the money in the till. When the stack is handed over, bypassing the metal plate, it goes on "armed" status. When this fake packet passes through the bank doorway, it goes on "timer" because it is now triggered via a radio transmitter. About ten seconds after triggering, the dye pack explodes in an aerosol form, painting everything around it a bright red dye (1-methylamino-anthraquinone). Red is the usual color; sometimes the color is a neon green or orange. While the dye releases, it burns at about 400 degrees Fahrenheit (204 degrees Celsius). The dye cannot be removed from the banknotes.

If the dye pack is high tech, it will also release tear gas. About 75 percent of banks use dye packs today. In 2015, close to 2,500 robbers were apprehended and $20,000,000 recovered—all sporting red.

Most recently, banks have turned to placing GPS trackers in the stacks of currency so that the robber(s) may be traced via computer. Or the teller is taught to clandestinely toss a small GPS tracker into the bag while filling it up with cash.

If the cash is recovered, it will be inventoried, then sent to the treasury department and destroyed. The destroyed banknotes will be replaced with newly minted banknotes.

As discussed throughout this book, bank employees also have access to "panic buttons"—alarms that go straight to the closest police station. These are silent alarms. And in larger banks the tellers' windows and vaults are further away from any exits, meaning the thief has further to run out of the bank.

Bank teller Pat says, "Tellers are taught to comply with a bank robber. Nothing is worth your life or the lives of customers. We kept a minimum amount of cash in our tills. We were taught how to draw from the lower to the higher bills."

Banknotes are secured by the FDIC. And money and things can be replaced. A life cannot.[4]

Chapter Notes

Preface

1. Federal Bureau of Investigation (FBI) website (n.d.). "What We Investigate: Bank Crime Statistics." Retrieved May 4, 2018, from https://www.fbi.gov/investigate/violent-crime/bank-robbery/bank-crime-reports.

Introduction

1. U.S. Attorney's Office (March 25, 2015). "Female Bank Robber Faces Federal Charge" (press release). https://www.fbi.gov/contact-us/field-offices/dallas/news/press-releases/female-bank-robber-faces-federal-charge.
2. Name changed for privacy.
3. FBI Bank Crime Statistics 2017 (January 9, 2019). U.S. Department of Justice, Washington, D.C. Retrieved from https://www.fbi.gov/file-repository/bank-crime-statistics-2017.pdf/view.

Chapter 1

1. Peckham, H.H., ed. (1974). *The Toll of Independence: Engagements and Battle Casualties of the American Revolution* (Chicago: University of Chicago Press).
2. A myth exists that Franklin voted for the turkey to be the national symbol. While he did not actually voice this desire, he did write to his daughter he felt the bald eagle was a bird of bad character, and the eagle in the resulting emblem resembled a turkey. Stamp, J. (January 25, 2013). "American Myths: Benjamin Franklin's Turkey and the Presidential Seal." *Smithsonian Magazine*. Retrieved from https://www.smithsonianmag.com/arts-culture/american-myths-benjamin-franklins-turkey-and-the-presidential-seal-6623414/.

Chapter 2

1. *Pittsburgh Weekly Gazette* (August 25, 1798). "American Intelligence: The Health Office of Philadelphia's August 9, 1798," p. 2.
2. Avery, R. (2019). "America's First Bank Robbery." Carpenter's Hall. Retrieved from https://www.carpentershall.org/americas-first-bank-robbery.

Chapter 3

1. Wood, L. (November 17, 2016). "Cora Hubbard: The Second Belle Starr." *Neosho Daily News* (Neosho, Missouri). Retrieved from https://www.neoshodailynews.com/opinion/20161117/larry-wood-cora-hubbard-second-belle-starr.
2. Wood, L. (June 2004). "Cora Hubbard: Female Bank Robber in Missouri." Retrieved from https://www.historynet.com/cora-hubbard-female-bank-robber-in-missouri.htm.
3. *Ibid.*
4. "Bank Robbers Captured" (August 23, 1897). *The Pittsburgh Daily Tribune*, p. 2.
5. *The Inquirer* Sunday Magazine (September 12, 1897). "Bravest and Wickedest Woman Ever Known in America at Last Behind Prison Bars."
6. *Ibid.*
7. *Ibid.*
8. "She Robbed the Bank" (February 18, 1898). *The Atchison Daily Globe*, p. 6.
9. *Ibid.*

10. "Cora Hubbard at Home" (January 5, 1905). *The Pittsburgh Daily Headlight*, p. 8.

Chapter 4

1. Denial, C. (n.d.). "Manifest Destiny: Creating an American Identity." Teaching-History.org. https://www.teachinghistory.org/history-content/ask-a-historian/25502.

2. Alcatraz East Crime Museum display (August 2019). Pigeon Forge, Tennessee.

3. Rogers, Roy (Singer). Unknown (Songwriter). (circa 1800s). RCA Victor. "Pecos Bill [Lyrics]." *Roy Rogers Rip Roaring Adventures of Pecos Bill from Walt Disney's "Melody Time" with Songs by Sons of the Pioneers* (Remastered). Retrieved March 14, 2021, at https://www.elyrics.net/read/r/roy-rogers-lyrics/pecos-bill-lyrics.html.

4. Bommersbach, J. (February 2016). "I Am a Friend to Any Brave and Gallant Outlaw." *True West History of the American Frontier.* Retrieved from https://truewestmagazine.com/article/i-am-a-friend-to-any-brave-and-gallant-outlaw/.

Chapter 5

1. Trimble, M. (July 20, 2015). "Ethel Place." *True West History of the American Frontier.* Retrieved from truewestmagazine.com/ethel-place/.

2. "Place" was Harry's mother's maiden name.

3. Meadows, A. (2003). *Digging Up Butch and Sundance.* Lincoln: University of Nebraska Press, p. x.

4. Ernst, D. (April 1, 2010). *The Sundance Kid: The Life of Harry Alonzo Longabaugh.* Norman: University of Oklahoma Press, p. 95.

5. Hatch, T. (2013). *The Last Outlaws.* New York: Penguin, p. 170.

6. Eckhardt, C. (December 14, 1994). "The Story of the West's Most Notorious Woman." *The Seguin Gazette-Enterprise*, p. 14.

Chapter 6

1. Enumeration District 158, Sheet No. 4, Lines 62–68.

2. *The St. Louis Republic* (November 8, 1901), p. 1.

3. "Woman Train Robber Held" (November 8, 1901). Special to the *New York Times*, p. 2.

Chapter 7

1. Bergreen, Laurence (1996). *Capone: The Man and the Era.* New York: Simon & Schuster, pp. 365–366.

2. Pells, R.H., and C.D. Romer (n.d.). "Great Depression." Retrieved from www.britannica.com/event/Great-Depression/Popular-culture.

Chapter 8

1. Fortune, J. (1968). *The True Story of Bonnie & Clyde*, 1st ed. New York: Signet, p. 49.

2. *Ibid.*, pp. 50–60.

3. An excellent reference for the list of banks can be found in Appendix 4 of James R. Knight's *Bonnie & Clyde: A Twenty-First Century Update* (2003).

Chapter 9

1. "Ma Barker (The Leader of a Gang of Thugs)" (n.d.). Retrieved March 16, 2021, from https://persona.rin.ru/eng/view/f/0/36614/ma-barker.

2. *Ibid.*

3. Stewart, T. (2018). *Ma Barker in Ocklawaha.* Bloomington: Tony Stewart, p. 13.

4. Maccabee, P. *John Dillinger Slept Here: A Crook's Tour of Crime and Corruption in St. Paul, 1920–1936.* Minnesota Historical Society, 1995, p. 105.

5. Karpis, A., with B. Trent (1971). *The Alvin Karpis Story.* New York: Coward, McCann, & Geoghegan.

Chapter 10

1. Cecil, M. (2016). *The Ballad of Ben and Stella Mae: Great Plains Outlaws Who Became FBI Public Enemies Nos. 1 and 2.* Lawrence: University Press of Kansas, p. 15.

2. *Ibid.*, p. 65.

3. *Ibid.*, p. 85.

4. Griffith, T. (2008). *Outlaw Tales of South Dakota: True Stories of the Mount Rushmore State's Most Infamous Crooks,*

Culprits, and Cutthroats. New York: Two Dot, p. 96.

5. Kirby, J., and J. Simon (November 1947). *Stella Mae Dickson ... the Bobby Sox Bandit Queen* (comic book). Headline #27, Prize Comics.

Chapter 11

1. Pearl Harbor Warbirds (December 27, 2017). "Pearl Harbor Nurses: The Women Who Cared for the Wounded." https://pearlharborwarbirds.com/pearl-harbor-nurses/.

2. "The Unexpected Heroines of Pearl Harbor" (n.d.). Pearl Harbor Visitors Bureau Online. https://visitpearlharbor.org/unexpected-heroines-pearl-harbor/.

3. Green, A.B. (Fall 1989). "Private Bosanko Goes to Basic: A Minnesota Woman in World War II." *Minnesota History* 51, no. 7: 246–258.

4. McEuen, M. (June 2016). "Women, Gender, & WWII." *Oxford Research Encyclopedia of American History*.

5. Pizarro, J., R.C. Silver, and J. Prause. (2006). "Physical and Mental Health Costs of Traumatic War Experiences Among Civil War Veterans." *Archives of General Psychiatry* 63, no. 2: 193–200. doi:10.1001/archpsyc.63.2.193.

6. Madigan, T. (September 11, 2015). "Their War Ended 70 Years Ago. Their Trauma Didn't." *The Washington Post*. Retrieved from https://www.washingtonpost.com/opinions/the-greatest-generations-forgotten-trauma/2015/09/11/8978d3b0-46b0-11e5-8ab4-c73967a143d3_story.html.

Chapter 12

1. *The Des Moines Register* (January 25, 1947), p. 1.

2. *The Des Moines Register* (January 23, 1947), p.1.

3. *The Des Moines Register* (January 25, 1947), p. 1.

4. "Cool Bank Bandit Awaits Penalty" (January 22, 1947). *Des Moines Tribune*, p. 1.

5. *Ibid.*, p. 3.

6. "Dixon Says Wife Told of First Holdup" (January 24, 1947). *Des Moines Register*, p. 1.

7. McLaughlin, L. (January 23, 1947). *Des Moines Tribune*, p. 1.

8. *Ibid.*, p. 2.

9. "Life Threatened by Her Husband" (February 18, 1947). *Council Bluffs Nonpareil*, p. 2.

10. "Mrs. Dixon to Be Recalled" (February 18, 1947). *Iowa City Press-Citizen*, p. 2.

11. "Opal Dixon in Hospital for Hysteria" (July 29, 1947). *Des Moines Register*, p. 3.

12. "Prison magazine calls Opal Dixon model inmate" (November 29, 1953). *Des Moines Register*, p. 25.

Chapter 13

1. "Mother, Daughter Among Those Held" (October 23, 1951). *Green Bay Press-Gazette*, p. 1.

2. "Articles Recovered in Mother's Home" (October 24, 1951). *Green Bay Press Gazette*, p. 1.

3. "Theft Suspect Takes Own Life" (October 26, 1951). *Green Bay Press-Gazette*, p. 1.

Chapter 14

1. "'Despondent' Gun-Girl Held for Bank Robbery" (January 27, 1953). *Windsor Daily Star*, p. 1.

2. "Girl, 24, Tries Bank Stickup" (January 27, 1953). *Salt Lake Tribune*, p. 2.

3. "Police Put Obstacles in Way of Miami Trip" (January 27, 1953). *The Evening Telegram* (Herkimer, New York), p. 6.

4. "Girl, 24, Tries Bank Stickup" (January 27, 1953). *Salt Lake Tribune*, p. 2.

5. "Brunette Nabbed as Bank Robber" (January 28, 1953). *Panama City News*, p. 1.

6. "Thrilling Chase" (January 27, 1953). *Alton Evening Telegraph* (Alton, Illinois), p. 1.

7. Wynn, M. (January 29, 1953). "Girl Bandit Seeks New Life." *Buffalo Courier Express*, pp. 1–2.

Chapter 15

1. O'Malley, M. (January 12, 2019). "Cleveland Bank Robbery Was First to Be Captured on Film: Greater Cleveland Innovations (gallery)." *The Plain Dealer*. https://www.cleveland.com/metro/2012/08/cleveland_bank_robbery_was_fir.html.

2. *Ibid.*
3. *Ibid.*
4. *Ibid.*
5. *Ibid.*

Chapter 16

1. "Bride of 11 Days Charged in Gary Bank Holdup" (February 1, 1963). *The Indianapolis Star*, p. 17.

Chapter 17

1. Botwright, K.O. (December 22, 1968). "Double Murder Motive Baffles Boston Police." *Boston Globe*, p. 49.
2. The names of the Parker children have been changed.

Chapter 18

1. This group is defunct at this writing.

Chapter 19

1. Brooks, W., and J. McGuire (March 28, 1975). "City Cop Arrests Top FBI Fugitive." *Philadelphia Daily News.*
2. "Susan Saxe Admits Role in Bank Robbery" (January 18, 1977). *New York Times*, p. 12.
3. A nationwide clearinghouse for student protests.
4. "Power to the people" was the slogan of the Black Panther Party for Self Defense, and other leftist organizations took it up as a statement for everyman—particularly minorities—to take control of their lives and their destinies, particularly the government. It became a call to action to rise up and create change.
5. Kantrowitz, B. (September 26, 1993). "The Fugitive." *Newsweek*. Retrieved from https://www.newsweek.com/fugitive-193128.
6. A Molotov cocktail is a weapon used to ignite; it is any flammable liquid in a glass bottle with some sort of wick for a stopper. The origin of the name comes from the Finns *polttopullo* or *Molotovin koktaili* to mock Soviet prime minister Vyacheslav Molotov.
7. "Girl Holding Bomb Aids Holdup of S&L" (September 2, 1970). *The Philadelphia Inquirer*, p. 9.
8. Gilday would claim innocence of shooting the officer until his deathbed confession in 2011; even then, he stated it was an accidental shot that "ricocheted off a brick wall" to strike the officer. See Abel, D. (September 16, 2011). "Apologetic in the End, William Gilday Dies." *Boston Globe*, pp. 1–2.
9. Gelin, D. (January 18, 1977). "Susan Saxe Pleads Guilty; Receives 10–12 Year Sentence." *The Harvard Crimson*. Retrieved from www.thecrimson.com/article/1977/1/18/susan-saxe-pleads-guilty-receives-10-12/.
10. On January 6, 1982, Susan Saxe, numerous inmates, and several civilians were charged with evading state taxes on profits made from the inmate-run business Con'Puter Systems Programming. There were also questions of running a gambling ring and drug violations related to this company. She pled innocent. She was released on personal recognizance for the charge, while paroled for the charges stemming from the bank robbery. All charges against her were dropped in 1983.
11. Carlson, Margaret (September 27, 1993). "The Return of the Fugitive." *Time*.
12. *Ibid.*

Chapter 20

1. Toobin, J. (2016). *American Heiress: The Wild Saga of the Kidnapping, Crimes, and Trial of Patricia Hearst*. Doubleday: New York, p. 15.
2. Documents, studies, and historical references about the SLA have confirmed. DeFreeze, according to Patricia Hearst, mispronounced these words on a regular basis, as he did on "communiqués" (audiotapes) sent to radio stations to be played in public.
3. When Pat Soltysik's brother Fred went searching for Pat after she joined the SLA, the Soltysik family was just as concerned for Camilla Hall. Soltysik, F. (1976). *In Search of a Sister*. Bantam: New York.
4. Patricia Hearst details Emily "Yolanda" Harris' salty language and political rants numerous times in her 1988 memoir *Patty Hearst* (with A. Moscow, London: Corgi).

5. Stone, R., N. Fraser, M. Samels, D. Kleszy, and G. Lionelli (writers) (2005). *Guerrilla: The Taking of Patty Hearst* (motion picture on DVD). New York: Docurama.

6. Pat Soltysik's letters and poetry examples can be found in Soltysik, F. (1976). *In Search of a Sister*. Bantam: New York.

7. As discussed in Hearst, P., and A. Moscow (1988). *Patty Hearst*. London: Corgi.

8. In *The Mind of the Political Terrorist* (1991) R. Pearlstein notes, "political terrorism offers its practitioners certain distinct and powerfully alluring psychic benefits or 'rewards'" (p. 8).

9. Testimony of Eden Shea, *United States v. Patricia Campbell Hearst* (February 4, 1976). Retrieved from https://famous-trials.com/pattyhearst/2214-sheatestimony.

10. CAMC Collection 13, Box 2, Folder 4: Personal Correspondence and Poems of Camilla Hall, found in her knapsack following her death (1974). Hall Family Archives, Gustavus Adolphus College.

Chapter 21

1. Haga, C. (March 21, 2008). "June 27, 1999: The Life and Times of Sara Jane Olson." *Star Tribune*. Retrieved from http://www.startribune.com/june-27-1999-the-life-and-times-of-sara-jane-olson/16894551/.

2. Toobin, p. 186.

3. Soliah's interest in politics began while she attended the University of California at Santa Barbara. As she grew older, the more radical her ideas became. Author S. Darby Henry (2011) details Soliah's transformation in *Soliah: The Sara Jane Olson Story* (Brule, WI: Cable).

4. As depicted in *Patty Hearst* (1988).

5. In her autobiography *Patty Hearst: Her Own Story* (1982), Hearst describes the altercations between Emily and Bill Harris and Jim Kilgore regarding the preparations for this robbery and the use of this shotgun. (New York: Avon, pp. 357–258).

6. In her autobiography *Patty Hearst: Her Own Story* (1982), Hearst recalls the argument. Bill Harris' notes were used to document such exchanges in J. Toobin's 2016 book *American Heiress: The Wild Saga of the Kidnapping, Crimes, and Trial of Patricia Hearst*.

7. Toobin, p. 231.

8. *Ibid.*

9. *Ibid.*

10. Name changed for victim's privacy.

11. In her autobiography *Patty Hearst: Her Own Story* (1982), Hearst describes the bank robbers as screaming at one another, arguing who was most incompetent. The only worry over victims was who was to blame for Myrna's death, and not for her safety or welfare (pp. 361–363).

12. Toobin, p. 233.

Chapter 22

1. Decker, T. (August 5, 2001). "Unbroken." Retrieved from https://www.latimes.com/archives/la-xpm-2001-aug-05-tm-30695-story.html.

2. Declamecy, D. (November 1, 2001). "Angry Judge Orders Hearing on Olson Plea Deal." Retrieved October 1, 2019, from http://www.cnn.com/2001/LAW/11/01/olson.plea/index.html.

3. Sternberg, B. (March 21, 2008). "Feb. 15, 2003: Olson Sentenced in Deadly Bank Robbery." *Star Tribune* (Minneapolis). Retrieved December 7, 2020, from https://www.startribune.com/feb-15-2003-olson-sentenced-in-deadly-bank-robbery/16894571/.

Chapter 23

1. Bright, C., M. Johnson-Reid, and P. Kohl (2014). "Females in the Juvenile Justice System: Who Are They and How Do They Fare?" *Crime & Delinquency* 60, no. 1.

2. Ehrmann, S., J. Hyland and C. Puzzanchera (April 2019)." Juvenile Justice Statistics National Reports Series Bulletin." U.S. Department of Justice Office of Justice Programs. Ojjdp.gov.

3. Fernández, C., J.C. Pascual, J. Soler, M. Elices, M.J. Portella, and E. Fernández-Abascal (2012). "Physiological Responses Induced by Emotion-Eliciting Films." *Applied Psychophysiology and Biofeedback* 37, no. 2: 73–79.

4. Deng, Y., L. Chang, M. Yang, M. Huo, and R. Zhou (2016). "Gender Differences in Emotional Response: Inconsistency Between Experience and Expressivity."

PLOS One, June 30. https://doi.org/10.1371/journal.pone.0158666.

5. Klein, S. (January 5, 2012). "Girls in the Juvenile Justice System: The Case for Girls' Courts." Retrieved December 7, 2019, from https://www.americanbar.org/groups/litigation/committees/childrens-rights/articles/2012/girls-juvenile-justice-system-case-for-girls-courts/.

6. Harp, C. (December 19, 2017). "Adolescent Brain Science: Proceed with Caution." Juvenile Justice Information Exchange. Retrieved April 1, 2019, from https://jjie.org/2017/05/08/adolescent-brain-science-proceed-with-caution/.

Chapter 24

1. Venezia, T. (September 25, 2003). "Twin-sis Crooks—Teens Robbed Bank to Save Their Home." *New York Post*. Retrieved December 7, 2020, from https://nypost.com/2003/09/25/twin-sis-crooks-teens-robbed-bank-to-save-their-home/.

2. Name changed for privacy.

3. McCarthy, S. (October 2003). "The Perils of Gambling with Stolen Loot." *The Globe and Mail*. Retrieved January 22, 2020, from https://www.theglobeandmail.com/news/world/the-perils-of-gambling-with-stolen-loot/article1046549/.

4. Curran, J. (September 25, 2003). "Twin Girls, 15: Why We Robbed a Bank." CBSNews.com. Retrieved January 21, 2020, from https://www.cbsnews.com/news/twin-girls-15-why-we-robbed-bank/.

5. *Seventeen Magazine* (June 1, 2007). *Seventeen Real Girls, Real-Life Stories: True Crime*. New York: Hearst, p. 59.

6. *Ibid.*, p. 60.

7. *Ibid.*, pp. 62–63.

8. McCarthy, S. (October 2003).

9. Venezia, T. (September 25, 2003).

10. Aftermath Services (August 26, 2020). U.S. Suicide Statistics. Retrieved January 5, 2021, from https://www.aftermath.com/content/us-suicide-statistics/.

Chapter 25

1. At this time the bank was operating under the Promistar name.

2. "The Youngest Bank Robber? Girl, 13, Robs Pennsylvania Bank" (December 8, 2005). https://www.securityinfowatch.com/retail/news/10592555/the-youngest-bank-robber-girl-13-robs-pennsylvania-bank.

Chapter 26

1. WLWT (October 8, 2017). "Police: Teenage Girls Rob Symmes Twp. Bank." https://www.wlwt.com/article/police-teenage-girls-rob-symmes-twp-bank/3504264.

2. Dykes, T. (July 17, 2018). "Baby-Faced Bank Robbers Still Eluding Investigators Nearly a Decade Later." https://www.wlwt.com/article/baby-faced-bank-robbers-still-eluding-investigators-nearly-a-decade-later/22213619.

3. For an interesting case of tracking bait money, read about the 1932 kidnapping of aviator Charles Lindbergh's baby: https://lindberghbabykidnapping.wikispaces.com/Ransom+Money.

4. Goldman, R. (January 7, 2010). "Dragnet for Girls, 12 and 14, Who Pulled Ohio Bank Heist." ABC News. https://abcnews.go.com/US/girls-12-14-suspected-ohio-bank-robbery/story?id=9502425.

5. Dykes, T. (July 17, 2018).

6. *Ibid.*

Chapter 27

1. Petracco, B. (May 22, 2014). "Teen Takes Plea Deal, Pleads Guilty to Oakley Bank Robbery." WLWT5 News. https://www.wlwt.com/article/teen-takes-plea-deal-pleads-guilty-to-oakley-bank-robbery/3543101.

Chapter 28

1. Gavin, C. (February 22, 2019). "Two Teen Girls Robbed a Bank in Fall River, Police Say." https://www.boston.com/news/crime/2019/02/22/teen-girls-robbed-bank-fall-river-police-say.

2. Burke, A. February 21, 2019). "Pair of Teenage Girls Charged in Fall River Bank Heist." *Fall River Herald News*. https://www.heraldnews.com/news/20190221/pair-of-teenage-girls-charged-in-fall-river-bank-heist.

Chapter 29

1. Name changed because subject is a juvenile.

2. Name changed because subject is a juvenile.

3. This "friend" would later be identified as Tia Woods.

4. Schenk, M. (March 19, 2015). "Bank Robbery an Alleged Family Affair." *News-Gazette* (Champaign, IL). https://www.news-gazette.com/news/bank-robbery-an-alleged-family-affair/article_8a29ee7f-db57-5bfe-ab80-ce6d1f9c196a.html.

5. Schenk, M. (May 6, 2015). "16 Year-old Girl Sent to Juvenile Prison for Bank Robbery." *News-Gazette* (Champaign, IL). https://www.news-gazette.com/news/year-old-girl-sent-to-juvenile-prison-for-bank-robbery/article_d51d290a-6a26-5c32-b38b-a2fba2f3c405.html.

6. Schenk, M. (April 2, 2015). "Fourth Suspect in Heartland Bank Arrested." *News-Gazette* (Champaign, IL). https://www.news-gazette.com/news/fourth-suspect-in-heartland-bank-robberies-arrested/article_8ab3f22c-15e0-5879-8e42-c8be3038e61c.html.

7. Schenk, M. (September 14, 2015). "Driver in Bank Robbery Sentenced to Probation." *News-Gazette* (Champaign, IL). https://www.news-gazette.com/news/driver-in-bank-robbery-sentenced-to-probation/article_9b53b2a3-6124-544a-a8e0-308230d37dad.html.

8. Schenk, M. (August 17, 2015). "Woman Sentenced to 5 Years for Role in Bank Robbery." *News-Gazette* (Champaign, IL). https://www.news-gazette.com/news/woman-sentenced-to-years-for-role-in-bank-robbery/article_3e3b719c-169a-5c6b-ab7c-40071316aeea.html.

Chapter 30

1. Cited in Piccardo, R. (July 25, 2016). "Women Take Lead Role in Bank Robberies as Need for Weapons, Accomplices Wanes." Retrieved January 06, 2021, from https://www.sun-sentinel.com/local/broward/fl-female-bank-robbers-20160722-story.html.

2. Mutchler, Jan E., Yang Li, and Ping Xu (2016). "Living Below the Line: Economic Insecurity and Older Americans Insecurity in the States 2016." Center for Social and Demographic Research on Aging Publications. Paper 13. http://scholarworks.umb.edu/demographyofaging/13.

3. Creamer, J., M. Kollar, J. Semega, and E.A. Shrider (2019). "Income and Poverty in the United States: 2019" (Report Number P60-270). United States Census Bureau.

4. Semega, J. (September 10, 2019). "Payday, Poverty, and Women." Retrieved January 6, 2021, from https://www.census.gov/library/stories/2019/09/payday-poverty-and-women.html. United States Census Bureau Results: Income & Poverty.

5. Bank Crime Statistics 2018 (March 28, 2019). Retrieved from https://www.fbi.gov/file-repository/bank-crime-statistics-2018.pdf/view.

Chapter 31

1. Heflin, L.P.P. (executive producer). *America's Most Wanted*. 2004-05-22 (TV series). 20th Century Fox Television, Walsh Productions, Michael Linder Productions, Fox Television Stations Productions.

2. Heflin, L.P.P. (executive producer). *America's Most Wanted*. 2004-06-19 (TV series). 20th Century Fox Television, Walsh Productions, Michael Linder Productions, Fox Television Stations Productions.

3. *Ibid.*

4. Address changed for family privacy.

5. Name changed for family privacy.

6. *Standard Democrat* (April 12, 2008). "Fugitive Featured on TV Caught." https://standard-democrat.com/story/1342520.html.

Chapter 32

1. McMahon, P. (September 30, 2015). "Female Suspect in Broward Bank Heist Was on Probation for Palm Beach County Robberies." https://www.sun-sentinel.com/news/crime/fl-bank-robbery-broward-palm-20150930-story.html.

2. Piccardo, R. (July 15, 2016). "Women Take Lead Role in Bank Robberies as Need for Weapons, Accomplices Wanes." *South Florida Sun-Sentinel.*

3. Clarkson, B. (June 3, 2014). "Arrested: Female Serial Bank Robber Who Wore Lil' Bow Wow T-shirt, Agents Say." *South Florida Sun-Sentinel*. https://www.sun-sentinel.

com/news/fl-xpm-2014-06-03-fl-palm-female-bank-robbery-arrest-20140603-story.html.

4. Personal correspondence (Fall 2018).

5. Personal correspondence (various dates, 2018).

6. McMahon, P. (September 30, 2015).

7. Personal correspondence (various dates, 2019).

Chapter 33

1. Horning, S., and S. McMahon (Fall 2014). "Living Below the Line: Economic Insecurity & America's Families." Wider Opportunities for Women. http://www.ncdsv.org/images/WOW_Living-Below-the-Line-Economic-Insecurity-and-America%27s-Families_Fall-2013.pdf.

2. Name changed for safety.

3. Personal correspondence (Fall 2018).

4. Eaton, J. (June 2017). "The New Opioid Dealers." Special Report: The Opioid Epidemic. https://www.aarp.org/health/drugs-supplements/info-2017/selling-prescription-medications-opioids.html.

5. *Ibid.*

6. Hegstrom, C., B.F. Kingshott, and M.J. Palmiotto (2013). "Older Criminals and the Crimes They Commit." Conference: ACJS. https://www.researchgate.net/publication/283291818_Older_Criminals_and_the_Crimes_they_Commit.

7. Feinberg, G. (1984). "White Haired Criminals: An Emergent Social Problem," in *Elderly Criminals*, edited by W. Wilbanks and P. Kim. Lanham, MD: University Press of America, pp. 83–108.

8. Juergens, J. (November 24, 2020). "Addiction in the Elderly Population" (1122332640 847114638 T. Parisi, Clinical Reviewer). Retrieved February 1, 2018, from https://www.addictioncenter.com/addiction/elderly/.

Chapter 34

1. "Woman Shoots Self on Chicago street" (June 6, 1987). *Southern Illinoisan*, State section, 2.

2. *Ibid.*

3. MacKittrick, D., and D. MacVea (2002). *Making Sense of the Troubles: The Story of the Conflict in Northern Ireland* (Chicago: New Amsterdam).

4. "Woman's Pressures May Have Led to Robbery" (June 8, 1987). *The Pantagraph*, p. 6.

5. O'Connor, M. (September 25, 1980). "Woman Gets 8 Years in Robbery." *Chicago Tribune*. https://www.chicagotribune.com/news/ct-xpm-1990-09-25-9003200169-story.html.

Chapter 35

1. Personal correspondence.

2. Personal communication.

Chapter 36

1. WPVI (May 18, 2016). "Police: Green Purse Ties Woman to Multiple NJ Bank Robberies." Retrieved 2017 from https://6abc.com/news/police-green-purse-ties-woman-to-multiple-nj-bank-robberies/1344626/.

2. Name changed for privacy.

Chapter 37

1. In June of 2016, a settlement was reached, determining Rios had been underpaid at least $2,076,093 for his work.

2. Name changed for privacy.

Chapter 39

1. Personal interview, September 22–23, 2018, name withheld by request.

2. Page, D. (November 6, 2017). "The Science Behind Why We Can't Look Away from Tragedy." Retrieved December 11, 2020, from https://www.nbcnews.com/better/health/science-behind-why-we-can-t-look-away-disasters-ncna804966.

3. Vaish, A., T. Grossmann, and A. Woodward (2008). "Not All Emotions Are Created Equal: The Negativity Bias in Social-Emotional Development." *Psychological Bulletin* 134, no. 3: 383–403. https://doi.org/10.1037/0033-2909.134.3.383.

Chapter 40

1. Kirchner, L.R. (2003). *Robbing Banks: An American History, 1831–1999* (Edison, NJ: Castle Books).

Chapter 41

1. Name changed for privacy.
2. "Dixon Bandit Linked to Bank Heist String" (August 10, 1989). *The Leaf-Chronicle* (Clarksville, TN), p. 1.
3. Comment upi.com/4922864. (August 9, 1989). "High School Teacher a Suspect in Four Mid-State Bank Robberies." Retrieved June 5, 2019, from https://www.upi.com/Archives/1989/08/09/High-school-teacher-a-suspect-in-four-Mid-state-bank-robberies/1553618638400/.
4. *Ibid.*
5. Dahnke, E., and J. East (August 13, 1989). "Rules Important to Holdup Suspect." *The Tennessean*, p. 1.

Chapter 42

1. Sabata, H. [Jellee Beanie] (December 4, 2012). *Chick Bank Robber* (video). YouTube. https://www.youtube.com/watch?v=lAZoo5KRMZ4&has_verified=1.
2. Wikinson, M. (November 29, 2012). "UPDATE: Bank Robbery Suspect Arrested." https://yorknewstimes.com/news/update-bank-robbery-suspect-arrested/article_7efde8aa-3987-11e2-be8c-001a4bcf887a.html.
3. "Hannah Sabata Bank Robbery (ORIGINAL VIDEO)."
4. Personal communication (April 2021).
5. Wikinson, M. (November 29, 2012).
6. Wilkinson, M. (June 17, 2013). "Woman Who Bragged About Bank Robbery in YouTube Video Gets 10–20 Years." https://omaha.com/news/woman-who-bragged-about-bank-robbery-in-youtube-video-gets-10-20-years/article_1ee410e2-db2e-5fab-af1b-1c41f24f0678.html."
7. "Hannah Sabata Bank Robbery (ORIGINAL VIDEO)."
8. Hannah Sabata, artist. "angelgabriel989." DeviantArt.com. https://www.deviantart.com/angel-gabriel989.
9. Shortly after this writing, the Facebook page was deleted.
10. "Hannah Sabata Bank Robbery (ORIGINAL VIDEO)."
11. Hannah Sabata, artist. "angel-gabriel 989."
12. "Let Down and Locked Up: Nebraska Women in Prison" (December 6, 2017). Retrieved December 12, 2020, from https://www.aclunebraska.org/en/publications/let-down-and-locked-nebraska-women-prison.
13. Personal communication (April 2021).
14. *Ibid.*

Chapter 43

1. Lopez, R. (April 29, 2010). "'Starlet Bandit' Wanted in String of L.A.-Area Bank Robberies." *Los Angeles Times*. Retrieved December 16, 2020, from https://latimesblogs.latimes.com/lanow/2010/04/starlet-bandit.html.
2. Faber, C. (director) (2012). "Barbie Bandits" (television series episode). *Pretty Bad Girls*. Investigation Discovery.
3. Stevens, A. (August 11, 2012). "'Barbie Bandit' Back in Jail Following Brawl Outside Gwinnett Club." *Atlanta Journal Constitution*. https://www.ajc.com/news/local/barbie-bandit-back-jail-following-brawl-outside-gwinnett-club/KaXMdID5Lped2DY4XtWxFJ/.

Chapter 44

1. Seiger, Theresa, and Brianna Chambers (October 4, 2017). "One-Armed Woman Arrested After Attempted Bank Robbery, Police Say." Retrieved December 12, 2020, from https://www.wpxi.com/news/top-stories/one-armed-woman-arrested-after-attempted-bank-robbery-police-say/619093427.

Chapter 45

1. At this writing, the MySpace page no longer exists.
2. "The Prostitution Statistics You Have to Know" (n.d.). Retrieved December 16, 2020, from http://sex-crimes.islaws.com/prostitution/prostitution-statistics.
3. Maddaus, G. (May 22, 2019). "The Case of the Bank-Robbing Prostitutes: How a Team of L.A. Hookers Became the 'Starlet Bandits.'" *LA Weekly*. Retrieved December 16, 2020, from https://www.laweekly.com/the-case-of-the-bank-robbing-prostitutes-how-a-team-of-l-a-hookers-became-the-starlet-bandits/.
4. *Ibid.*

5. Lopez, R. (April 29, 2010). "'Starlet Bandit' Wanted in String of L.A.-Area Bank Robberies." Retrieved December 16, 2020, from https://latimesblogs.latimes.com/lanow/2010/04/starlet-bandit.html.

6. Eimiller, L. (June 1, 2011). "'Starlet Bandit' Hits Two Banks Today, Five in the Week, Now Suspected in Seven Bank Robberies Since 2008." Retrieved December 16, 2020, from https://archives.fbi.gov/archives/losangeles/press-releases/2010/la042310.htm.

7. Numerous personal communications and volunteers work with activist Clemmie Greenlee, "Peacemakers," Nashville, TN.

8. *Ibid.*

9. Maddaus, G. (May 22, 2019).

Chapter 46

1. U.S. Department of Justice, Federal Bureau of Investigations (n.d.). Bank Crime Statistics—2020. Washington, D.C.

2. Bank Robbers Nationwide (February 21, 2012). Retrieved January 7, 2021, from https://bankrobbers.fbi.gov/#grid.

Chapter 47

1. Name changed for privacy.

2. Personal interview (July 3, 2018).

3. US5485143A Security dye pack having flexible heat-resistant chemical pouch (n.d.). Retrieved December 16, 2020, from https://patents.google.com/patent/US5485143A/en.

4. Before the reader exclaims, "this book just taught people how to rob a bank!" keep in mind that bank robbers know all of this information and more. And there are many more systems in place not listed here for banking institutions to keep their employees and customers safe.

Bibliography

Abel, D. (September 16, 2011). "Apologetic in the end, William Gilday dies." *Boston Globe*, pp. 1–2.

Aftermath Services (August 26, 2020). U.S. Suicide Statistics. Retrieved January 5, 2021, from https://www.aftermath.com/content/us-suicide-statistics/.

Alcatraz East Crime Museum display (August 2019). Pigeon Forge, Tennessee.

"Articles Recovered in Mother's Home" (October 24, 1951) *Green Bay Press Gazette*, p. 1.

Avery, R. (2019). "America's First Bank Robbery." Carpenter's Hall. Retrieved from https://www.carpentershall.org/americas-first-bank-robbery.

Bank Crime Statistics 2020 (January 12, 2022). Retrieved from https://www.fbi.gov/file-repository/bank-crime-statistics-2018.pdf/view.

"Bank Robbers Capture" (August 23, 1897). *The Pittsburgh Daily Tribune*, p. 2.

Bank Robbers Nationwide (February 21, 2012). Retrieved January 7, 2021, from https://bankrobbers.fbi.gov/#grid.

Bergreen, Laurence (1996). *Capone: The Man and the Era*. New York: Simon & Schuster.

Bommersbach, J. (February 2016). "I Am a Friend to Any Brave and Gallant Outlaw." *True West History of the American Frontier*. Retrieved from https://truewestmagazine.com/article/i-am-a-friend-to-any-brave-and-gallant-outlaw/.

Botwright, K.O. (December 22, 1968). "Double Murder Motive Baffles Boston Police." *Boston Globe*, p. 49.

"Bride of 11 days Charged in Gary Bank Holdup" (February 1, 1963). *The Indianapolis Star*, p. 17.

Bright, C., M. Johnson-Reid, and P. Kohl (2014). "Females in the Juvenile Justice System: Who Are They and How Do They Fare?" *Crime & Delinquency* 60, no. 1.

Brooks, W., and J. McGuire (March 28, 1975). "City Cop Arrests Top FBI Fugitive." *Philadelphia Daily News*.

"Brunette Nabbed as Bank Robber" (January 28, 1953). *Panama City News*,. p. 1.

Burke, A. (February 21, 2019). "Pair of Teenage Girls Charged in Fall River Bank Heist." *Fall River Herald News*. https://www.heraldnews.com/news/20190221/pair-of-teenage-girls-charged-in-fall-river-bank-heist.

CAMC Collection 13, Box 2, Folder 4: Personal Correspondence and Poems of Camilla Hall, found in her knapsack following her death (1974). Hall Family Archives, Gustavus Adolphus College.

Carlson, Margaret (September 27, 1993). "The Return of the Fugitive." *Time*.

Carrington, Ashley (2018–2019). Interviews by email with the author.

Cecil, M. (2016). *The Ballad of Ben and Stella Mae: Great Plains Outlaws Who Became FBI Public Enemies Nos. 1 and 2*. Topeka: University Press of Kansas, p. 15.

Clarkson, B. (June 3, 2014). "Arrested: Female Serial Bank Robber Who Wore Lil' Bow Wow T-shirt, Agents Say." *South Florida Sun-Sentinel*. https://www.sun-sentinel.com/news/fl-xpm-2014-06-03-fl-palm-female-bank-robbery-arrest-20140603-story.html.

Comment upi.com/4922864 (August 9, 1989). "High School Teacher a Suspect in Four Mid-State Bank Robberies." Retrieved June 5, 2019, from https://www.upi.com/Archives/1989/08/09/High-school-teacher-a-suspect-in-four-Mid-state-bank-robberies/1553618638400/.

"Cool Bank Bandit Awaits Penalty" (January 22, 1947) *Des Moines Tribune*, p. 1.

"Cora Hubbard at Home" (January 5, 1905). *The Pittsburgh Daily Headlight*, p. 8.

Creamer, J., M. Kollar, J. Semega, and E.A. Shrider (2019). "Income and Poverty in the United States: 2019" (Report Number P60-270). United States Census Bureau.

Curran, J. (September 25, 2003). "Twin Girls, 15: Why We Robbed a Bank." CBSNews.com. Retrieved January 21, 2020, from https://www.cbsnews.com/news/twin-girls-15-why-we-robbed-a-bank/.

Dahnke, E., and J. East (August 13, 1989). "Rules Important to Holdup Suspect." *The Tennessean*, p. 1.

"Daisy" (Fall 2018). Interviews with the author.

Decker, T. (August 5, 2001). "Unbroken." Retrieved December 7, 2020, from https://www.latimes.com/archives/la-xpm-2001-aug-05-tm-30695-story.html.

Declamecy, D. (November 1, 2001). "Angry judge orders hearing on Olson plea deal." Retrieved October 1, 2019, from http://www.cnn.com/2001/LAW/11/01/olson.plea/index.html.

Deng, Y., L. Chang, M. Yang, M. Huo, and R. Zhou (2016). "Gender Differences in Emotional Response: Inconsistency Between Experience and Expressivity." *PLOS One*, June 30. https://doi.org/10.1371/journal.pone.0158666.

Denial, C. (n.d.). "Manifest Destiny: Creating an American Identity." TeachingHistory.org. https://www.teachinghistory.org/history-content/ask-a-historian/25502.

The Des Moines Register (January 23, 1947), p.1.

The Des Moines Register (January 25, 1947), p.1.

"'Despondent' Gun-Girl Held for Bank Robbery" (January 27, 1953). *Windsor Daily Star*, p. 1.

"Dixon Bandit Linked to Bank Heist String" (August 10, 1989). *The Leaf-Chronicle* (Clarksville, TN), p. 1.

"Dixon Says Wife Told of First Holdup" (January 24, 1947). *Des Moines Register*, p. 1.

Dykes, T. (July 17, 2018). "Baby-Faced Bank Robbers Still Eluding Investigators Nearly a Decade Later." https://www.wlwt.com/article/baby-faced-bank-robbers-still-eluding-investigators-nearly-a-decade-later/22213619.

Eaton, J. (June 2017). "The New Opioid Dealers." Special Report: The Opioid Epidemic. https://www.aarp.org/health/drugs-supplements/info-2017/selling-prescription-medications-opioids.html.

Eckhardt, C. (December 14, 1994). "The Story of the West's Most Notorious Woman." *The Seguin Gazette-Enterprise* (Seguin, Texas), p. 14.

Ehrmann, S., N. Hyland, and C. Puzzancher (April 2019). "Juvenile Justice Statistics National Reports Series Bulletin." U.S. Department of Justice Office of Justice Programs. Ojjdp.gov.

Eimiller, L. (June 1, 2011). "'Starlet Bandit" Hits Two Banks Today, Five in the Week, Now Suspected in Seven Bank Robberies Since 2008." Retrieved December 16, 2020, from https://archives.fbi.gov/archives/losangeles/press-releases/2010/la042310.htm.

Enumeration District 158, Sheet No. 4, Lines 62–68.

Ernst, D. (April 1, 2010). *The Sundance Kid: The Life of Harry Alonzo Longabaugh*. Norman: University of Oklahoma Press, p. 95.

Faber, C. (Director) (2012). "Barbie Bandits" (television series episode). *Pretty Bad Girls*. Investigation Discovery.

FBI Bank Crime Statistics 2017 (January 9, 2019). U.S. Department of Justice, Washington, D.C., retrieved from https://www.fbi.gov/file-repository/bank-crime-statistics-2017.pdf/view.

Federal Bureau of Investigations (FBI) website. "What We Investigate: Bank Crime Statistics." Retrieved May 4, 2018, from https://www.fbi.gov/investigate/violent-crime/bank-robbery/bank-crime-reports.

Feinberg, G. (1984). "White Haired Criminals: An Emergent Social Problem," in *Elderly Criminals*, edited by W. Wilbanks and P. Kim. Lanham, MD: University Press of America, pp. 83–108.

Fernández, C., J.C. Pascual, J. Soler, M. Elices, M.J. Portella, and E. Fernández-Abascal (2012). "Physiological Responses Induced by Emotion-Eliciting Films." *Applied Psychophysiology and Biofeedback* 37, no. 2: 73–79.

Fortune, J. (1968). *The True Story of Bonnie & Clyde*, 1st ed. New York: Signet.
Gavin, C. (2019, February 22). "Two teen girls robbed a bank in Fall River, police say." https://www.boston.com/news/crime/2019/02/22/teen-girls-robbed-bank-fall-river-police-say.
Gelin, D. (January 18, 1977). "Susan Saxe Pleads Guilty; Receives 10–12 Year Sentence." *The Harvard Crimson*. Retrieved from www.thecrimson.com/article/1977/1/18/susan-saxe-pleads-guilty-receives-10-12/.
"Girl Holding Bomb Aids Holdup of S&L" (September 2, 1970). *The Philadelphia Inquirer*, p. 9.
"Girl, 24, Tries Bank Stickup" (1953, January 27). *Salt Lake Tribune*, p. 2.
Goldman, R. (2010, January 7). "Dragnet for Girls, 12 and 14, Who Pulled Ohio Bank Heist." ABC News. https://abcnews.go.com/US/girls-12-14-suspected-ohio-bank-robbery/story?id=9502425.
Green, A.B. (Fall 1989). "Private Bosanko Goes to Basic: A Minnesota Woman in World War II." *Minnesota History* 51, no. 7: 246–258.
Griffith, T. (2008) *Outlaw Tales of South Dakota: True Stories of the Mount Rushmore State's Most Infamous Crooks, Culprits, and Cutthroats*. New York: TwoDot.
Haga, C. (2008, March 21)." June 27, 1999: The Life and Times of Sara Jane Olson." *Star Tribune*. doi: http://www.startribune.com/june-27-1999-the-life-and-times-of-sara-jane-olson/16894551/.
Hannah Sabata, artist (n.d.). "angel-gabriel989." DeviantArt.com. https://www.deviantart.com/angel-gabriel989.
Harp, C. (2017, December 19). "Adolescent Brain Science: Proceed with Caution." Retrieved April 1, 2019, from https://jjie.org/2017/05/08/adolescent-brain-science-proceed-with-caution/.
Hatch, T. (2013). *The Last Outlaws*. New York: Penguin.
Hearst, P. (1982). *Patty Hearst: Her Own Story*. New York: Avon Books.
Hearst, P., and A. Moscow (1988). *Patty Hearst*. London: Corgi.
Heflin, L.P.P. (executive producer). *America's Most Wanted*. 2004-06-19 (TV series). 20th Century Fox Television, Walsh Productions, Michael Linder Productions, Fox Television Stations Productions.
Heflin, L.P.P. (executive producer). *America's Most Wanted*. 2004-05-22 (TV series). 20th Century Fox Television, Walsh Productions, Michael Linder Productions, Fox Television Stations Productions.
Hegstrom, C., B.F. Kingshott, and M.J. Palmiotto (2013). "Older Criminals and the Crimes They Commit." Conference: ACJS. https://www.researchgate.net/publication/283291818_Older_Criminals_and_the_Crimes_they_Commit.
Hendry, S. (2011). *Soliah: The Sara Jane Olson Story*. Brule, WI: Cable.
Horning, S., and S. McMahon (Fall 2014). "Living Below the Line: Economic Insecurity & America's Families." Wider Opportunities for Women. http://www.ncdsv.org/images/WOW_Living-Below-the-Line-Economic-Insecurity-and-America%27s-Families_Fall-2013.pdf.
The Inquirer Sunday Magazine (September 12, 1897). "Bravest and Wickedest Woman Ever Known in America at Last Behind Prison Bars."
Investigators, Gail Cooke bank robbery case (various dates, 2019). Interviews by phone and in-person with the author, Wilson County, Tennessee.
Juergens, J. (November 24, 2020). "Addiction in the Elderly Population" (1122332640 847114638 T. Parisi, Clinical Reviewer). Retrieved February 1, 2018, from https://www.addictioncenter.com/addiction/elderly/.
Kantrowitz, B. (September 26, 1993). "The Fugitive." *Newsweek*. https://www.newsweek.com/fugitive-193128.
Karpis, A., with B. Trent (1971). *The Alvin Karpis Story*. New York: Coward, McCann, & Geoghegan.
Kirby, J., and J. Simon (November 1947). *Stella Mae Dickson ... the Bobby Sox Bandit Queen* (comic book). Headline #27, Prize Comics.
Kirchner, L.R. (2003). *Robbing Banks: An American History, 1831–1999*. Edison, NJ: Castle.
Klein, S. (January 5, 2012). "Girls in the Juvenile Justice System: The Case for Girls' Courts."

Retrieved December 7, 2019, from https://www.americanbar.org/groups/litigation/committees/childrens-rights/articles/2012/girls-juvenile-justice-system-case-for-girls-courts/.

Knight, J.R., and J. Davis (2003). *Bonnie & Clyde: A Twenty-First Century Update*. Fort Worth: Eakin Press.

"Let Down and Locked Up: Nebraska Women in Prison" (December 6, 2017). Retrieved December 12, 2020, from https://www.aclunebraska.org/en/publications/let-down-and-locked-nebraska-women-prison.

"Life Threatened by Her Husband" (February 18, 1947). *Council Bluffs Nonpareil* (Council Bluffs, Iowa), p. 2.

Lopez, R. (April 29, 2010). "'Starlet Bandit' wanted in string of L.A.-area bank robberies." *Los Angeles Times*. Retrieved December 16, 2020, from https://latimesblogs.latimes.com/lanow/2010/04/starlet-bandit.html.

Ma Barker (The Leader of a Gang of Thugs) (n.d.). Retrieved March 16, 2021, from https://persona.rin.ru/eng/view/f/0/36614/ma-barker.

Maccabee, P. (August 15, 1995). "John Dillinger Slept Here: A Crooks' Tour of Crime and Corruption in St. Paul, 1920–1936." Minnesota Historical Society.

MacKittrick, D., and D. MacVea (2002). *Making Sense of the Troubles: The Story of the Conflict in Northern Ireland*. Chicago: New Amsterdam.

Maddaus, G. (2019, May 22). "The Case of the Bank-Robbing Prostitutes: How a Team of L.A. Hookers Became the 'Starlet Bandits.'" *LA Weekly*. Retrieved December 16, 2020, from https://www.laweekly.com/the-case-of-the-bank-robbing-prostitutes-how-a-team-of-l-a-hookers-became-the-starlet-bandits/.

Madigan, T. (September 11, 2015). "Their War Ended 70 Years Ago. Their Trauma Didn't." *The Washington Post*. Retrieved from https://www.washingtonpost.com/opinions/the-greatest-generations-forgotten-trauma/2015/09/11/8978d3b0-46b0-11e5-8ab4-c73967a143d3_story.html.

McCarthy, S. (October 2003). "The Perils of Gambling with Stolen Loot." *The Globe and Mail*. Retrieved January 22, 2020, from https://www.theglobeandmail.com/news/world/the-perils-of-gambling-with-stolen-loot/article1046549/.

McEuen, M. (June 2016). *Women, Gender, & WWII*. Oxford Research Encyclopedia of American History.

McLaughlin, L. (January 23, 1947). *The Des Moines Tribune*, p. 1.

McMahon, P. (2015, September 30). "Female Suspect in Broward Bank Heist Was on Probation for Palm Beach County Robberies." *South Florida Sun-Sentinel*. https://www.sun-sentinel.com/news/crime/fl-bank-robbery-broward-palm-20150930-story.html.

Meadows, A. (2003). *Digging Up Butch and Sundance*. Lincoln: University of Nebraska Press.

"Mother, Daughter Among Those Held" (October 23, 1951). *Green Bay Press-Gazette*, p. 1.

"Mrs. Dixon to be recalled" (February 18, 1947) *Iowa City Press-Citizen*, p. 2.

Mutchler, Jan E., Yang Li, and Ping Xu (2016). "Living Below the Line: Economic Insecurity and Older Americans Insecurity in the States 2016." Center for Social and Demographic Research on Aging Publications. Paper 13. http://scholarworks.umb.edu/demographyofaging/13.

O'Connor, M. (September 25, 1980). "Woman Gets 8 Years in Robbery." *Chicago Tribune*. https://www.chicagotribune.com/news/ct-xpm-1990-09-25-9003200169-story.html.

O'Malley, M. (January 12, 2019). "Cleveland Bank Robbery Was First to Be Captured on Film: Greater Cleveland Innovations (gallery)." *The Plain Dealer*. https://www.cleveland.com/metro/2012/08/cleveland_bank_robbery_was_fir.html.

"Opal Dixon in Hospital for Hysteria" (July 29, 1947). *Des Moines Register*, p. 3.

Page, D. (November 6, 2017). "The Science Behind Why We Can't Look Away from Tragedy." NBC News. Retrieved December 11, 2020, from https://www.nbcnews.com/better/health/science-behind-why-we-can-t-look-away-disasters-ncna804966.

"Pat," bank teller (July 3, 2018). Interview in-person with the author.

Pearl Harbor Warbirds (December 27, 2017). "Pearl Harbor Nurses: The Women Who Cared for the Wounded." https://pearlharborwarbirds.com/pearl-harbor-nurses/.

Pearlstein, R. (1991). *The Mind of the Political Terrorist*. Lanham, MD: Rowman & Littlefield.

Peckham, H.H., ed. (1974). *The Toll of Independence: Engagements and Battle Casualties of the American Revolution*. Chicago: University of Chicago Press.
Pells, R.H., and C.D. Romer. "Great Depression." Britannica. Recovered from www.britannica.com/event/Great-Depression/Popular-culture.
Petracco, B. (May 22, 2014). "Teen Takes Plea Deal, Pleads Guilty to Oakley Bank Robbery." WLWT5 News. https://www.wlwt.com/article/teen-takes-plea-deal-pleads-guilty-to-oakley-bank-robbery/3543101.
Piccardo, R. (July 25, 2016). "Women Take Lead Role in Bank Robberies as Need for Weapons, Accomplices Wanes." *South Florida Sun-Sentinel*. Retrieved January 6, 2021, from https://www.sun-sentinel.com/local/broward/fl-female-bank-robbers-20160722-story.html.
Pittsburgh Weekly Gazette (August 25, 1798). "American Intelligence: "The Health Office of Philadelphia's August 9, 1798," p. 2.
Pizarro, J., R.C. Silver, and J. Prause. (2006). "Physical and Mental Health Costs of Traumatic War Experiences Among Civil War Veterans." *Archives of General Psychiatry* 63, no. 2: 193–200. doi:10.1001/archpsyc.63.2.193.
"Police Put Obstacles in Way of Miami Trip" (January 27, 1953). *The Evening Telegram* (Herkimer, New York), p. 6.
"Prison Magazine Calls Opal Dixon Model Inmate" (November 29, 1953) *Des Moines Register*, p. 25.
"The Prostitution Statistics You Have to Know" (n.d.). Retrieved December 16, 2020, from http://sex-crimes.islaws.com/prostitution/prostitution-statistics.
Rogers, Roy (Singer). Unknown (songwriter). (circa 1800s). RCA Victor. "Pecos Bill [Lyrics]." *Roy Rogers Rip Roaring Adventures of Pecos Bill from Walt Disney's "Melody Time" with Songs by Sons of the Pioneers* (Remastered). Retrieved March 14, 2021, at https://www.elyrics.net/read/r/roy-rogers-lyrics/pecos-bill-lyrics.html.
Sabata, H. [Jellee Beanie] (December 4, 2012). *Chick Bank Robber* (video). YouTube. https://www.youtube.com/watch?v=lAZoo5KRMZ4&has_verified=1.
Sabata, Hannah (April 2021). Interviews by mail with the author.
The St. Louis Republic (November 8, 1901), p. 1.
Schenk, M. (March 19, 2015). "Bank Robbery an Alleged Family Affair." *News-Gazette* (Champaign, IL). https://www.news-gazette.com/news/bank-robbery-an-alleged-family-affair/article_8a29ee7f-db57-5bfe-ab80-ce6d1f9c196a.html.
Schenk, M. (April 2, 2015). "Fourth Suspect in Heartland Bank Arrested." *News-Gazette* (Champaign, IL). https://www.news-gazette.com/news/fourth-suspect-in-heartland-bank-robberies-arrested/article_8ab3f22c-15e0-5879-8e42-c8be3038e61c.html.
Schenk, M. (May 6, 2015). "16-Year-old Girl Sent to Juvenile Prison for Bank Robbery." *News-Gazette* (Champaign, IL). https://www.news-gazette.com/news/year-old-girl-sent-to-juvenile-prison-for-bank-robbery/article_d51d290a-6a26-5c32-b38b-a2fba2f3c405.html.
Schenk, M. (August 17, 2015). "Woman Sentenced to 5 Years for Role in Bank Robbery." *News-Gazette* (Champaign, IL). https://www.news-gazette.com/news/woman-sentenced-to-years-for-role-in-bank-robbery/article_3e3b719c-169a-5c6b-ab7c-40071316aeea.html.
Schenk, M. (September 14, 2015). "Driver in Bank Robbery Sentenced to Probation." *News-Gazette* (Champaign, IL). https://www.news-gazette.com/news/driver-in-bank-robbery-sentenced-to-probation/article_9b53b2a3-6124-544a-a8e0-308230d37dad.html.
Seiger, Theresa, and Brianna Chambers (October 4, 2017). "One-Armed Woman Arrested After Attempted Bank Robbery, Police say." Retrieved December 12, 2020, from https://www.wpxi.com/news/top-stories/one-armed-woman-arrested-after-attempted-bank-robbery-police-say/619093427.
Semega, J. (September 10, 2019). "Payday, Poverty, and Women." Retrieved January 6, 2021, from https://www.census.gov/library/stories/2019/09/payday-poverty-and-women.html. United States Census Bureau Results: Income & Poverty.
Seventeen Magazine (June 1, 2007). *Seventeen Real Girls, Real-Life Stories: True Crime*. New York: Hearst.
"She Robbed the Bank" (February 18, 1898). *The Atchison Daily Globe*, p. 6.

Soltysik, F. (1976). *In Search of a Sister*. New York: Bantam.
Stamp, J. (January 25, 2013). "American Myths: Benjamin Franklin's Turkey and the Presidential Seal." *Smithsonian Magazine*. Retrieved from https://www.smithsonianmag.com/arts-culture/american-myths-benjamin-franklins-turkey-and-the-presidential-seal-6623414/.
Standard Democrat (April 12, 2008). "Fugitive Featured on TV Caught." https://standard-democrat.com/story/1342520.html.
Sternberg, B. (March 21, 2008). "Feb. 15, 2003: Olson Sentenced in Deadly Bank Robbery." *Star Tribune* (Minneapolis). Retrieved December 7, 2020, from https://www.startribune.com/feb-15-2003-olson-sentenced-in-deadly-bank-robbery/16894571/.
Stevens, A. (August 11, 2012). "'Barbie Bandit' Back in Jail Following Brawl Outside Gwinnett Club." *Atlanta Journal Constitution*. https://www.ajc.com/news/local/barbie-bandit-back-jail-following-brawl-outside-gwinnett-club/KaXMdID5Lped2DY4XtWxFJ/.
Stewart, T. (2018). *Ma Barker in Ocklawaha*. Bloomington: Tony Stewart.
Stone, R., N. Fraser, M. Samels, D. Kleszy, and G. Lionelli (writers) (2005). *Guerrilla: The Taking of Patty Hearst* (motion picture on DVD). New York: Docurama.
"Susan Saxe Admits Role in Bank Robbery" (January 18, 1977). *New York Times*, p. 12.
Television Producer, "Anonymous" (2018). Interview in-person with the author.
"Theft Suspect Takes Own Life" (October 26, 1951). *Green Bay Press-Gazette*, p. 1.
"Thrilling Chase" (January 27, 1953). *Alton Evening Telegraph* (Alton, Illinois), p. 1.
Toobin, J. (2016). *American Heiress: The Wild Saga of the Kidnapping, Crimes, and Trial of Patricia Hearst*. New York: Doubleday.
Trimble, M. (July 20, 2015). "Ethel Place." *True West History of the American Frontier*. Retrieved from truewestmagazine.com/ethel-place/.
"The Unexpected Heroines of Pearl Harbor" (n.d.). Pearl Harbor Visitors Bureau Online. https://visitpearlharbor.org/unexpected-heroines-pearl-harbor/.
United States v. Patricia Campbell Hearst (February 4, 1976). https://famous-trials.com/pattyhearst/2214-sheatestimony.
U.S. Attorney's Office (March 25, 2015). "Female Bank Robber Faces Federal Charge" (press release). https://www.fbi.gov/contact-us/field-offices/dallas/news/press-releases/female-bank-robber-faces-federal-charge.
US5485143A Security dye pack having flexible heat-resistant chemical pouch (n.d.). Retrieved December 16, 2020, from https://patents.google.com/patent/US5485143A/en.
Vaish, A., T. Grossmann, and A. Woodward (2008). "Not All Emotions Are Created Equal: The Negativity Bias in Social-Emotional Development." *Psychological Bulletin* 134, no. 3: 383–403. https://doi.org/10.1037/0033-2909.134.3.383.
Venezia, T. (September 25, 2003). "Twin-sis Crooks—Teens Robbed Bank to Save Their Home." *New York Post*. Retrieved December 7, 2020, from https://nypost.com/2003/09/25/twin-sis-crooks-teens-robbed-bank-to-save-their-home/.
Wikinson, M. (November 29, 2012). "UPDATE: Bank Robbery Suspect Arrested." *York News-Times* (York, Nebraska). https://yorknewstimes.com/news/update-bank-robbery-suspect-arrested/article_7efde8aa-3987-11e2-be8c-001a4bcf887a.html.
Wikinson, M. (November 30, 2012). "Sheriff: 'We Found All but $30.'" *York News-Times* (York, Nebraska). https://yorknewstimes.com/news/sheriff-we-found-all-but-30/article_ba2a3028-3a31-11e2-b5d8-0019bb2963f4.html.
Wilkinson, M. (June 17, 2013). "Woman Who Bragged About Bank Robbery in YouTube Video Gets 10–20 Years." https://omaha.com/news/woman-who-bragged-about-bank-robbery-in-youtube-video-gets-10-20-years/article_1ee410e2-db2e-5fab-af1b-1c41f24f0678.html.
WLWT (October 8, 2017). "Police: Teenage Girls Rob Symmes Twp. Bank." https://www.wlwt.com/article/police-teenage-girls-rob-symmes-twp-bank/3504264.
"Woman Shoots Self on Chicago Street" (June 6, 1987). *Southern Illinoisan*, State section, p. 2.
"Woman Train Robber Held" (November 8, 1901). Special to *The New York Times*, p. 2.
"Woman's Pressures May Have Led to Robbery" (June 8, 1987). *The Pantagraph*, p. 6.
Wood, L. (November 17, 2016). "Cora Hubbard: The Second Belle Starr." *Neosho Daily News* (Neosho, Missouri). https://www.neoshodailynews.com/opinion/20161117/larry-wood-cora-hubbard-second-belle-starr.

Wood, L. (June 2004). "Cora Hubbard: Female Bank Robber in Missouri." Retrieved from https://www.historynet.com/cora-hubbard-female-bank-robber-in-missouri.htm.

WPVI (May 18, 2016). "Police: Green Purse Ties Woman to Multiple NJ Bank Robberies." Retrieved 2017 from https://6abc.com/news/police-green-purse-ties-woman-to-multiple-nj-bank-robberies/1344626/

Wynn, M. (January 29, 1953). "Girl Bandit Seeks New Life. *Buffalo Courier Express*, pp. 1–2.

"The Youngest Bank Robber? Girl, 13, Robs Pennsylvania Bank" (December 8, 2005). https://www.securityinfowatch.com/retail/news/10592555/the-youngest-bank-robber-girl-13-robs-pennsylvania-bank.

Index

Numbers in ***bold italics*** indicate pages with illustrations